Course Booklet

Connecting Networks

ciscopress.com

Cisco | Networking Academy
Mind Wide Open

Connecting Networks Course Booklet

Published by:
Cisco Press
800 East 96th Street
Indianapolis, IN 46240 USA

Printed in the United States of America

First Printing   December 2013

Library of Congress data is on file.

ISBN-13: 978-1-58713-330-5

ISBN-10: 1-58713-330-X

Warning and Disclaimer

This book is designed to provide information about Cisco Networking Academy Connecting Networks course. Every effort has been made to make this book as complete and as accurate as possible, but no warranty or fitness is implied.

The information is provided on an "as is" basis. The authors, Cisco Press, and Cisco Systems, Inc. shall have neither liability nor responsibility to any person or entity with respect to any loss or damages arising from the information contained in this book or from the use of the discs or programs that may accompany it.

The opinions expressed in this book belong to the author and are not necessarily those of Cisco Systems, Inc.

Publisher
Paul Boger

Associate Publisher
Dave Dusthimer

Business Operations Manager, Cisco Press
Jan Cornelssen

Executive Editor
Mary Beth Ray

Managing Editor
Sandra Schroeder

Project Editor
Seth Kerney

Editorial Assistant
Vanessa Evans

Cover Designer
Louisa Adair

Interior Designer
Mark Shirar

Composition
Bronkella Publishing, LLC

CISCO.

Trademark Acknowledgments

All terms mentioned in this book that are known to be trademarks or service marks have been appropriately capitalized. Cisco Press or Cisco Systems, Inc., cannot attest to the accuracy of this information. Use of a term in this book should not be regarded as affecting the validity of any trademark or service mark.

Feedback Information

At Cisco Press, our goal is to create in-depth technical books of the highest quality and value. Each book is crafted with care and precision, undergoing rigorous development that involves the unique expertise of members from the professional technical community.

Readers' feedback is a natural continuation of this process. If you have any comments regarding how we could improve the quality of this book, or otherwise alter it to better suit your needs, you can contact us through email at feedback@ciscopress.com. Please make sure to include the book title and ISBN in your message.

We greatly appreciate your assistance.

CISCO

Americas Headquarters
Cisco Systems, Inc.
San Jose, CA

Asia Pacific Headquarters
Cisco Systems (USA) Pte. Ltd.
Singapore

Europe Headquarters
Cisco Systems International BV
Amsterdam, The Netherlands

Cisco has more than 200 offices worldwide. Addresses, phone numbers, and fax numbers are listed on the Cisco Website at www.cisco.com/go/offices.

CCDE, CCENT, Cisco Eos, Cisco HealthPresence, the Cisco logo, Cisco Lumin, Cisco Nexus, Cisco StadiumVision, Cisco TelePresence, Cisco WebEx, DCE, and Welcome to the Human Network are trademarks; Changing the Way We Work, Live, Play, and Learn and Cisco Store are service marks; and Access Registrar, Aironet, AsyncOS, Bringing the Meeting To You, Catalyst, CCDA, CCDP, CCIE, CCIP, CCNA, CCNP, CCSP, CCVP, Cisco, the Cisco Certified Internetwork Expert logo, Cisco IOS, Cisco Press, Cisco Systems, Cisco Systems Capital, the Cisco Systems logo, Cisco Unity, Collaboration Without Limitation, EtherFast, EtherSwitch, Event Center, Fast Step, Follow Me Browsing, FormShare, GigaDrive, HomeLink, Internet Quotient, IOS, iPhone, iQuick Study, IronPort, the IronPort logo, LightStream, Linksys, MediaTone, MeetingPlace, MeetingPlace Chime Sound, MGX, Networkers, Networking Academy, Network Registrar, PCNow, PIX, PowerPanels, ProConnect, ScriptShare, SenderBase, SMARTnet, Spectrum Expert, StackWise, The Fastest Way to Increase Your Internet Quotient, TransPath, WebEx, and the WebEx logo are registered trademarks of Cisco Systems, Inc. and/or its affiliates in the United States and certain other countries.

All other trademarks mentioned in this document or website are the property of their respective owners. The use of the word partner does not imply a partnership relationship between Cisco and any other company. (0812R)

Contents at a Glance

Contents

Command Syntax Conventions

The conventions used to present command syntax in this book are the same conventions used in the IOS Command Reference. The Command Reference describes these conventions as follows:

- **Boldface** indicates commands and keywords that are entered literally as shown. In actual configuration examples and output (not general command syntax), boldface indicates commands that are manually input by the user (such as a **show** command).

- *Italic* indicates arguments for which you supply actual values.

- Vertical bars (|) separate alternative, mutually exclusive elements.

- Square brackets ([ ]) indicate an optional element.

- Braces ({ }) indicate a required choice.

- Braces within brackets ([{ }]) indicate a required choice within an optional element.

About This Course Booklet

Your Cisco Networking Academy Course Booklet is designed as a study resource you can easily read, highlight, and review on the go, wherever the Internet is not available or practical:

- The text is extracted directly, word-for-word, from the online course so you can highlight important points and take notes in the "Your Chapter Notes" section.

- Headings with the exact page correlations provide a quick reference to the online course for your classroom discussions and exam preparation.

- An icon system directs you to the online curriculum to take full advantage of the images imbedded within the Networking Academy online course interface and reminds you to perform the labs, Class activities, Interactive activities, Packet Tracer activities, and chapter quizzes and exams.

The *Course Booklet* is a basic, economical paper-based resource to help you succeed with the Cisco Networking Academy online course.

Companion Guide

Looking for more than the online curriculum? The Companion Guide is fully aligned to Networking Academy's online course chapters and offers additional book-based pedagogy to reinforce key concepts, enhance student comprehension, and promote retention. Using this full-fledged textbook, students can focus scarce study time, organize review for quizzes and exams, and get the day-to-day reference answers they're looking for.

The Companion Guide also offers instructors additional opportunities to assign take-home reading or vocabulary homework, helping students prepare more for in-class lab work and discussions.

Available in print and all major eBook formats (Book: 9781587133329   eBook: 9780133476521)

Introduction to Course

0.0 Connecting Networks

0.0.1 Message to the Student

0.0.1.1 Welcome

Welcome to the CCNA R&S Connecting Networks course. The goal of this course is to introduce you to fundamental networking concepts and technologies. These online course materials will assist you in developing the skills necessary to plan and implement small networks across a range of applications. The specific skills covered in each chapter are described at the start of each chapter.

You can use your smart phone, tablet, laptop, or desktop to access your course, participate in discussions with your instructor, view your grades, read or review text, and practice using interactive media. However, some media are complex and must be viewed on a PC, as well as Packet Tracer activities, quizzes, and exams.

Refer to
Online Course
for Illustration

0.0.1.2 A Global Community

When you participate in the Networking Academy, you are joining a global community linked by common goals and technologies. Schools, colleges, universities, and other entities in over 160 countries participate in the program. A visualization of the global Networking Academy community is available at http://www.academynetspace.com.

Look for the Cisco Networking Academy official site on Facebook© and LinkedIn©. The Facebook site is where you can meet and engage with other Networking Academy students from around the world. The Cisco Networking Academy LinkedIn site connects you with job postings, and you can see how others are effectively communicating their skills.

Refer to
Online Course
for Illustration

0.0.1.3 More Than Just Information

The NetSpace learning environment is an important part of the overall course experience for students and instructors in the Networking Academy. These online course materials include course text and related interactive media, Packet Tracer simulation activities, real equipment labs, remote access labs, and many different types of quizzes. All of these materials provide important feedback to help you assess your progress throughout the course.

The material in this course encompasses a broad range of technologies that facilitate how people work, live, play, and learn by communicating with voice, video, and other data. Networking and the internet affect people differently in different parts of the world. Although we have worked with instructors from around the world to create these materials, it is important that you work with your instructor and fellow students to make the material in this course applicable to your local situation.

Refer to
Online Course
for Illustration

0.0.1.4   How We Teach

E-doing is a design philosophy that applies the principle that people learn best by doing. The curriculum includes embedded, highly interactive e-doing activities to help stimulate learning, increase knowledge retention, and make the whole learning experience much richer – and that makes understanding the content much easier.

Refer to
Online Course
for Illustration

0.0.1.5   Practice Leads to Mastery

In a typical lesson, after learning about a topic for the first time, you will check your understanding with some interactive media items. If there are new commands to learn, you will practice them with the Syntax Checker before using the commands to configure or troubleshoot a network in Packet Tracer, the Networking Academy network simulation tool. Next, you will do practice activities on real equipment in your classroom or accessed remotely over the internet.

Packet Tracer can also provide additional practice any time by creating your own activities or you may want to competitively test your skills with classmates in multi-user games. Packet Tracer skills assessments and skills integration labs give you rich feedback on the skills you are able to demonstrate and are great practice for chapter, checkpoint, and final exams.

Refer to
Online Course
for Illustration

0.0.1.6   Mind Wide Open

An important goal in education is to enrich you, the student, by expanding what you know and can do. It is important to realize, however, that the instructional materials and the instructor can only facilitate the process. You must make the commitment yourself to learn new skills. The following pages share a few suggestions to help you learn and prepare for transitioning your new skills to the workplace.

Refer to
Online Course
for Illustration

0.0.1.7   Engineering Journals

Professionals in the networking field often keep Engineering Journals in which they write down the things they observe and learn such as how to use protocols and commands. Keeping an Engineering Journal creates a reference you can use at work in your ICT job. Writing is one way to reinforce your learning – along with Reading, Seeing, and Practicing.

A sample entry for implementing a technology could include the necessary software commands, the purpose of the commands, command variables, and a topology diagram indicating the context for using the commands to configure the technology.

Refer to
Online Course
for Illustration

0.0.1.8   Explore the World of Networking

Packet Tracer is a networking learning tool that supports a wide range of physical and logical simulations. It also provides visualization tools to help you understand the internal workings of a network.

The pre-made Packet Tracer activities consist of network simulations, games, activities, and challenges that provide a broad range of learning experiences. These tools will help you develop an understanding of how data flows in a network.

Refer to
Online Course
for Illustration

0.0.1.9   Create Your Own Worlds

You can also use Packet Tracer to create your own experiments and networking scenarios. We hope that, over time, you consider using Packet Tracer - not only for experiencing the pre-built activities, but also to become an author, explorer, and experimenter.

The online course materials have embedded Packet Tracer activities that will launch on computers running Windows® operating systems, if Packet Tracer is installed. This integration may also work on other operating systems using Windows emulation.

Refer to
Online Course
for Illustration

0.0.1.10   How Packet Tracer Helps Master Concepts

Educational Games

Packet Tracer Multi-User games enable you or a team to compete with other students to see who can accurately complete a series of networking tasks the fastest. It is an excellent way to practice the skills you are learning in Packet Tracer activities and hands-on labs.

Cisco Aspire is a single-player, standalone strategic simulation game. Players test their networking skills by completing contracts in a virtual city. The Networking Academy Edition is specifically designed to help you prepare for the CCENT certification exam. It also incorporates business and communication skills ICT employers seek in job candidates.

Performance-Based Assessments

The Networking Academy performance-based assessments have you do Packet Tracer activities like you have been doing all along, only now integrated with an online assessment engine that will automatically score your results and provide you with immediate feedback. This feedback helps you to more accurately identify the knowledge and skills you have mastered and where you need more practice. There are also questions on chapter quizzes and exams that use Packet Tracer activities to give you additional feedback on your progress.

Refer to
Online Course
for Illustration

0.0.1.11   Course Overview

As the course title states, the focus of this course is on the WAN technologies and network services required by converged applications in a complex network. In this course, you will learn the selection criteria of network devices and WAN technologies to meet network requirements. You will do the following:

- Describe different WAN technologies and their benefits
- Describe the operations and benefits of virtual private networks (VPNs) and tunneling
- Configure and troubleshoot serial connections
- Configure and troubleshoot broadband connections
- Configure and troubleshoot IPsec tunneling operations
- Monitor and troubleshoot network operations using syslog, SNMP, and NetFlow
- Describe network architectures

By the end of this course, you will be able to configure and troubleshoot network devices and resolve common issues with data link protocols. Students will also develop the knowledge and skills needed to implement IPsec and virtual private network (VPN) operations in a complex network.

Refer to
Interactive Graphic
in online course.

0.1.1.1   Course GUI Tutorial

Go to the online course to take the quiz and exam.

Chapter 0 Quiz

This quiz is designed to provide an additional opportunity to practice the skills and knowledge presented in the chapter and to prepare for the chapter exam. You will be allowed multiple attempts and the grade does not appear in the gradebook.

Chapter 0 Exam

The chapter exam assesses your knowledge of the chapter content.

Your Chapter Notes

Hierarchical Network Design

1.0   Hierarchical Network Design

1.0.1.1   Introduction

Networks must meet the current needs of organizations and be able to support emerging technologies as new technologies are adopted. Network design principles and models can help a network engineer design and build a network that is flexible, resilient, and manageable.

This chapter introduces network design concepts, principles, models, and architectures. It covers the benefits that are obtained by using a systematic design approach. Emerging technology trends that will affect network evolution are also discussed.

Refer to **Lab Activity** for this chapter

1.0.1.2   Class Activity - Design Hierarchy

Design Hierarchy

A network administrator is tasked with designing an expanded network for the company.

After speaking with network administrators in other branches of the company, it was decided to use the Cisco three-layer hierarchical network design model to influence the expansion. This model was chosen for its simple influence upon network planning.

The three layers of the expanded network design include:

- Access
- Distribution
- Core

Refer to **Interactive Graphic** in online course.

1.1   Hierarchical Network Design Overview

1.1.1   Enterprise Network Campus Design

1.1.1.1   Network Requirements

When discussing network design, it is useful to categorize networks based on the number of devices serviced:

- **Small network**- Provides services for up to 200 devices.
- **Medium-sized network**- Provides services for 200 to 1000 devices.
- **Large network**- Provides services for 1000+ devices.

Network designs vary depending on the size and requirements of the organizations. For example, the networking infrastructure needs of a small organization with fewer devices will be less complex than the infrastructure of a large organization with a significant number of devices and connections.

There are many variables to consider when designing a network. For instance, consider the example in the figure. The sample high-level topology diagram is for a large enterprise network that consists of a main campus site connecting small, medium, and large sites.

Network design is an expanding area and requires a great deal of knowledge and experience. The intent of this section is to introduce commonly accepted network design concepts.

Note   The Cisco Certified Design Associate (CCDA®) is an industry-recognized certification for network design engineers, technicians, and support engineers, who demonstrate the skills required to design basic campus, data center, security, voice, and wireless networks.

Refer to
Online Course
for Illustration

1.1.1.2   Structured Engineering Principles

Regardless of network size or requirements, a critical factor for the successful implementation of any network design is to follow good structured engineering principles. These principles include:

- **Hierarchy**- A hierarchical network model is a useful high-level tool for designing a reliable network infrastructure. It breaks the complex problem of network design into smaller and more manageable areas.

- **Modularity**- By separating the various functions that exist on a network into modules, the network is easier to design. Cisco has identified several modules, including the enterprise campus, services block, data center, and Internet edge.

- **Resiliency**- The network must remain available for use under both normal and abnormal conditions. Normal conditions include normal or expected traffic flows and traffic patterns, as well as scheduled events such as maintenance windows. Abnormal conditions include hardware or software failures, extreme traffic loads, unusual traffic patterns, Denial-of-Service (DoS) events, whether intentional or unintentional, and other unplanned events.

- **Flexibility**- The ability to modify portions of the network, add new services, or increase capacity without going through a major fork-lift upgrade (i.e., replacing major hardware devices).

To meet these fundamental design goals, a network must be built on a hierarchical network architecture that allows for both flexibility and growth.

Refer to
Online Course
for Illustration

1.1.2   Hierarchical Network Design

1.1.2.1   Network Hierarchy

In networking, a hierarchical design involves dividing the network into discrete layers. Each layer, or tier, in the hierarchy provides specific functions that define its role within the overall network. This helps the network designer and architect to optimize and select the right network hardware, software, and features to perform specific roles for that network layer. Hierarchical models apply to both LAN and WAN design.

A typical enterprise hierarchical LAN campus network design includes the following three layers:

- **Access layer**- Provides workgroup/user access to the network.
- **Distribution layer**- Provides policy-based connectivity and controls the boundary between the access and core layers.
- **Core layer**- Provides fast transport between distribution switches within the enterprise campus.

The benefit of dividing a flat network into smaller, more manageable blocks is that local traffic remains local. Only traffic that is destined for other networks is moved to a higher layer.

Layer 2 devices in a flat network provide little opportunity to control broadcasts or to filter undesirable traffic. As more devices and applications are added to a flat network, response times degrade until the network becomes unusable.

Click play in Figure 1 to view a transition of a flat network to a hierarchical network design.

Another sample three-layer hierarchical network design is displayed in Figure 2. Notice that each building is using the same hierarchical network model that includes the access, distribution, and core layers.

Note There are no absolute rules for the way a campus network is physically built. While it is true that many campus networks are constructed using three physical tiers of switches, this is not a strict requirement. In a smaller campus, the network might have two tiers of switches in which the core and distribution elements are combined in one physical switch. This is referred to as a collapsed core design.

Refer to
Online Course
for Illustration

1.1.2.2 The Access Layer

In a LAN environment, the access layer grants end devices access to the network. In the WAN environment, it may provide teleworkers or remote sites access to the corporate network across WAN connections.

As shown in the figure, the access layer for a small business network generally incorporates Layer 2 switches and access points providing connectivity between workstations and servers.

The access layer serves a number of functions including:

- Layer 2 switching
- High availability
- Port security
- QoS classification and marking and trust boundaries
- Address Resolution Protocol (ARP) inspection

- Virtual Access Control Lists (VACLs)

- Spanning tree

- Power over Ethernet (PoE) and auxiliary VLANs for VoIP

Refer to
Online Course
for Illustration

1.1.2.3   The Distribution Layer

The distribution layer aggregates the data received from the access layer switches before it is transmitted to the core layer for routing to its final destination. In the figure, the distribution layer is the boundary between the Layer 2 domains and the Layer 3 routed network.

The distribution layer device is the focal point in the wiring closets. Either a router or a multilayer switch is used to segment workgroups and isolate network problems in a campus environment.

A distribution layer switch may provide upstream services for many access layer switches.

The distribution layer can provide:

- Aggregation of LAN or WAN links

- Policy-based security in the form of access control lists (ACLs) and filtering

- Routing services between LANs and VLANs and between routing domains (e.g., EIGRP to OSPF)

- Redundancy and load balancing

- A boundary for route aggregation and summarization configured on interfaces toward the core layer

- Broadcast domain control, because routers or multilayer switches do not forward broadcasts. The device acts as the demarcation point between broadcast domains

Refer to
Online Course
for Illustration

1.1.2.4   The Core Layer

The core layer is also referred to as the network backbone. The core layer consists of high-speed network devices such as the Cisco Catalyst 6500 or 6800. These are designed to switch packets as fast as possible and interconnect multiple campus components, such as distribution modules, service modules, the data center, and the WAN edge.

As shown in the figure, the core layer is critical for interconnectivity between distribution layer devices; for example, interconnecting the distribution block to the WAN and Internet edge. The core should be highly available and redundant. The core aggregates the traffic from all the distribution layer devices, so it must be capable of forwarding large amounts of data quickly.

Considerations at the core later include:

- Providing high-speed switching (i.e., fast transport)

- Providing reliability and fault tolerance

- Scaling by using faster, and not more, equipment

- Avoiding CPU-intensive packet manipulation caused by security, inspection, quality of service (QoS) classification, or other processes

Refer to
Online Course
for Illustration

1.1.2.5 Two-Tier Collapsed Core Design

The three-tier hierarchical design maximizes performance, network availability, and the ability to scale the network design.

However, many small enterprise networks do not grow significantly larger over time. Therefore, a two-tier hierarchical design where the core and distribution layers are collapsed into one layer is often more practical. A "collapsed core" is when the distribution layer and core layer functions are implemented by a single device. The primary motivation for the collapsed core design is reducing network cost, while maintaining most of the benefits of the three-tier hierarchical model.

The example in the figure has collapsed the distribution layer and core layer functionality into multilayer switch devices.

The hierarchical network model provides a modular framework that allows flexibility in network design and facilitates ease of implementation and troubleshooting.

Refer to
Interactive Graphic
in online course.

1.1.2.6 Activity - Identify Hierarchical Network Characteristics

Refer to
Online Course
for Illustration

1.2 Cisco Enterprise Architecture

1.2.1 Modular Network Design

1.2.1.1 Modular Design

While the hierarchical network design works well within the campus infrastructure, networks have expanded beyond these borders. As shown in the figure, networks have become more sophisticated and complex, with some requiring connections to dedicated data centers, often off-site. Branch sites often require connectivity to the campus backbones, and employees wanted to be able to work from home offices or other remote locations. As the complexity of the network increased to meet these demands, it became necessary to adjust the network design to one that uses a more modular approach.

A modular network design separates the network into various functional network modules, each targeting a specific place or purpose in the network. The modules represent areas that have different physical or logical connectivity. They designate where different functions occur in the network. Using a modular approach has several benefits, including:

- Failures that occur within a module can be isolated from the remainder of the network, providing for simpler problem detection and higher overall system availability.

- Network changes, upgrades, or the introduction of new services can be made in a controlled and staged fashion, allowing greater flexibility in the maintenance and operation of the campus network.

- When a specific module no longer has sufficient capacity or is missing a new function or service, it can be updated or replaced by another module that has the same structural role in the overall hierarchical design.

- Security can be implemented on a modular basis allowing for more granular security control.

The use of modules in network design enables flexibility and facilitates implementation and troubleshooting.

Refer to
Online Course
for Illustration

1.2.1.2 Modules in the Enterprise Architecture

A modular approach to network design further divides the three-layer hierarchical design, by pulling out specific blocks or modular areas. These basic modules are connected together via the core of the network.

Basic network modules include:

- **Access-distribution**- Also called the distribution block, this is the most familiar element and fundamental component of a campus design. (Figure 1).

- **Services**- This is a generic block used to identify services such as centralized Lightweight Access Point Protocol (LWAPP) wireless controllers, unified communications services, policy gateways, and more. (Figure 2).

- **Data center**- Originally called the server farm. This block is responsible for managing and maintaining many data systems that are vital to modern business operations. Employees, partners, and customers rely on data and resources in the data center to effectively create, collaborate, and interact. (Figure 3).

- **Enterprise Edge**- Consists of the Internet Edge and the WAN Edge. These blocks offer connectivity to voice, video, and data services outside the enterprise. (Figure 4).

Refer to
Interactive Graphic
in online course.

1.2.1.3 Activity - Identify Modules in a Network Design

Refer to
Online Course
for Illustration

1.2.2 Cisco Enterprise Architecture Model

1.2.2.1 Cisco Enterprise Architecture Model

To accommodate the need for modularity in network design, Cisco developed the Cisco Enterprise Architecture model. This model provides all the benefits of the hierarchical network design on the campus infrastructure, and facilitates the design of larger, more scalable networks.

The Cisco Enterprise Architecture model separates the enterprise network into functional areas that are referred to as modules. The modularity that is built into the architecture allows flexibility in network design and facilitates implementation and troubleshooting.

As shown in the figure, the following are the primary Cisco Enterprise Architecture modules:

- Enterprise Campus
- Enterprise Edge
- Service Provider Edge

Connected to the Service Provider Edge are additional modules including:

- Enterprise Data Center
- Enterprise Branch
- Enterprise Teleworker

Refer to
Online Course
for Illustration

1.2.2.2   Cisco Enterprise Campus

A campus network is a building or group of buildings connected into one enterprise network that consists of many LANs. A campus is generally limited to a fixed geographic area, but it can span several neighboring buildings, for example, an industrial complex or business park environment. Regional offices, SOHOs, and mobile workers may need to connect to the central campus for data and information.

The enterprise campus module describes the recommended methods to create a scalable network, while addressing the needs of campus-style business operations. The architecture is modular and can easily expand to include additional campus buildings or floors as the enterprise grows.

The enterprise campus module consists of the following submodules:

- Building access
- Building distribution
- Campus core
- Data center

Together these submodules:

- Provide high availability through a resilient hierarchical network design.
- Integrate IP communications, mobility, and advanced security.
- Utilize multicast traffic and QoS to optimize network traffic.
- Provide increased security and flexibility using access management, VLANs and IPSec VPNs.

The enterprise campus module architecture provides the enterprise with high availability through a resilient multilayer design, redundant hardware and software features, and automatic procedures for reconfiguring network paths when failures occur. Integrated security protects against and mitigates the impact of worms, viruses, and other attacks on the network, even at the switch port level.

A high-capacity, centralized data center module can provide internal server resources to users. The data center module typically also supports network management services for the enterprise, including monitoring, logging, troubleshooting, and other common management features from end to end. The data center submodule typically contains internal email and corporate servers that provide application, file, print, email, and Domain Name System (DNS) services to internal users.

Click the enterprise campus module in the figure for more information.

Refer to
Online Course
for Illustration

1.2.2.3   Cisco Enterprise Edge

The enterprise edge module provides connectivity for voice, video, and data services outside the enterprise. This module often functions as a liaison between the enterprise campus module and the other modules.

The enterprise edge module consists of the following submodules:

- **E-commerce networks and servers**- The e-commerce submodule enables enterprises to support e-commerce applications through the Internet. It uses the high availability designs of the data center module. Devices located in the e-commerce submodule include web, application, and database servers, firewall and firewall routers, and network intrusion prevention systems (IPS).

- **Internet connectivity and demilitarized zone (DMZ)**- The Internet submodule of the enterprise edge provides internal users with secure connectivity to Internet services such as public servers, email, and DNS. Connectivity to one or several Internet Service Providers (ISP) is also provided. Components of this submodule include firewall and firewall routers, Internet edge routers, FTP and HTTP servers, SMTP relay servers, and DNS servers.

- **Remote Access and VPN**- The VPN/remote access submodule of the enterprise edge provides remote-access termination services, including authentication for remote users and sites. Components of this submodule include firewalls, dial-in access concentrators, Cisco Adaptive Security Appliances (ASA), and network Intrusion Prevention System (IPS) appliances.

- **WAN**- The WAN submodule uses various WAN technologies for routing traffic between remote sites and the central site. Enterprise WAN links include technologies such as Multiprotocol Label Switching (MPLS), Metro Ethernet, leased lines, Synchronous Optical Network (SONET) and Synchronous Digital Hierarchy (SDH), PPP, Frame Relay, ATM, cable, digital subscriber line (DSL), and wireless.

Click the Enterprise Edge module in the figure for more information.

Refer to
Online Course
for Illustration

1.2.2.4   Service Provider Edge

Enterprises use Service Providers (SPs) to link to other sites. As shown in Figure 1, the SP edge module can include:

- Internet Service Providers (ISPs)

- WAN services such as Frame Relay, ATM, and MAN

- Public Switched Telephone Network (PSTN) services

The SP edge provides connectivity between the enterprise campus module to the remote enterprise data center, enterprise branch, and enterprise teleworker modules.

The SP edge module:

- Spans across large geographic areas in a cost effective manner

- Converges voice, video, and data services over a single IP communications network

- Supports QoS and service level agreements

- Supports security using VPNs (IPsec / MPLS) over Layer 2 and Layer 3 WANs

Click the Service Provider Edge in Figure 1 for more information.

When acquiring Internet services from an ISP, redundancy or failover should be considered. As shown in Figure 2, redundant connections to a single ISP can include:

- **Single-homed**- A single connection to an ISP

- **Dual-homed**- Two or more connections to a single ISP

Alternatively, it is possible to set up redundancy using multiple ISPs, as shown in Figure 3. Options for connecting to multiple ISPs include:

- **Multihomed**- Connections to two or more ISPs

- **Dual-multihomed**- Multiple connections to two or more ISPs

Refer to
Online Course
for Illustration

1.2.2.5   Remote Functional Area

The remote functional area is responsible for remote connectivity options and includes several modules:

Enterprise Branch

The enterprise branch module includes remote branches that allow employees to work at non-campus locations. These locations are typically responsible for providing security, telephony, and mobility options to employees, as well as general connectivity into the campus network and the different components located inside the enterprise campus. The enterprise branch module allows enterprises to extend head-office applications and services, such as security, Cisco Unified Communications, and advanced application performance, to the remote branches. The edge device connecting the remote site to the central site varies depending on the needs and size of the site. Large remote sites may use high-end Cisco Catalyst switches, while smaller sites may use an ISR G2 router. These remote sites rely on the SP edge to provide services and applications from the main site. In the figure the enterprise branch module connects to the enterprise campus site primarily using a WAN link; however, it also has an Internet link as a backup. The Internet link uses site-to-site IPsec VPN technology to encrypt corporate data.

Enterprise Teleworker

The enterprise teleworker module is responsible for providing connectivity for workers who operate out of different geographically dispersed locations, including home offices, hotels or customer/client sites. The teleworker module recommends that mobile users connect to the Internet using the services of a local ISP, such as cable modem or DSL. VPN services can then be used to secure communications between the mobile worker and central campus. Integrated security- and identity-based networking services enable the enterprise to extend campus security policies to the teleworker. Staff can securely log into the network over the VPN and gain access to authorized applications and services from a single cost-effective platform.

Enterprise Data Center

The enterprise data center module is a data center with all of the same functional options as a campus data center, but exists at a remote location. This provides an added layer of security as the offsite data center can provide disaster recovery and business continuance services for the enterprise. High-end switches such as the Cisco Nexus series switch use fast WAN services such as Metro Ethernet (MetroE) to connect the enterprise campus to the remote enterprise data center. Redundant data centers provide backup using synchronous and asynchronous data and application replication. Additionally, the network and devices offer server and application load balancing to maximize performance. This solution allows the enterprise to scale without major changes to the infrastructure.

> Refer to
> **Interactive Graphic**
> in online course.

1.2.2.6   Activity - Identify Modules of the Cisco Enterprise Architecture

> Refer to
> **Online Course**
> for Illustration

1.3   Evolving Network Architectures

1.3.1   Cisco Enterprise Architectures

1.3.1.1   IT Challenges

As businesses have grown more dependent on networks for success, network architectures have evolved over the years. Traditionally, users, data, and applications were housed on premise. Users could only access network resources with company-owned computers. The network had distinct borders and access requirements. Maintaining security, productivity, and services was simpler. Today, the network border has shifted, creating new challenges for IT departments. Networks are transforming from a data-only transportation system of connected LAN devices, to a system that enables the connections of people, devices, and information in a media rich, converged network environment.

As new technologies and end user devices come to market, businesses and consumers must continue to adjust to this ever-changing environment. There are several new networking trends that continue to effect organizations and consumers. Some of the top trends include:

- Bring Your Own Device (BYOD)
- Online collaboration
- Video communication
- Cloud computing

These trends, while allowing for more advanced services than ever before, also introduce new security risks that IT must address.

1.3.1.2   Emerging Enterprise Architectures

The speed of change in market and business environments is requiring IT to be more strategic than ever before. Evolving business models are creating complex technology challenges that IT must address.

To address these emerging network trends, new business network architectures are necessary. These architectures must account for the network design principles established in the Cisco Enterprise Architecture, as well as the overlaying policies and technologies that allow organizations to support emerging trends in a safe and manageable way.

To meet this need, Cisco has introduced the following three network architectures, as shown in the figure:

■ Cisco Borderless Network Architecture

■ Collaboration Architecture

■ Data Center/Virtualization Architecture

Note   Network architectures continually evolve. The intent of this section is to provide an introduction and overview of emerging architecture trends.

Refer to **Online Course** for Illustration

1.3.2   Emerging Network Architectures

1.3.2.1   Cisco Borderless Networks

The Cisco Borderless Network Architecture is a network solution that allows organizations and individuals to connect securely, reliably, and seamlessly to the corporate network in a BYOD environment. It is based on wired, wireless, routing, switching, security, and application optimization devices working in harmony to help IT balance demanding business challenges and changing business models.

It is not a static solution, but an evolving solution to help IT evolve its infrastructure to deliver secure, reliable, and seamless user experiences in a world with many new and shifting borders.

It enables an IT department to architect and deploy its systems and policies efficiently to all end user devices that require connection to the network. In doing this, it provides secure, reliable, and seamless access to resources from multiple locations, from multiple devices, and to applications that can be located anywhere.

Specifically, the Cisco Borderless network architecture delivers two primary sets of services:

■ **Borderless end-point/user services**- As shown in Figure 1, Borderless end-point / user services connect the various devices to provide access to network services. Devices that can connect to the borderless network can range from PCs, to tablets and smart phones. It removes the location and device borders, providing unified access to wired and wireless devices. Endpoint / user services define the user experience and enable the attributes of secure, reliable, and seamless performance on a broad range of devices and environments, as shown in the figure. For example, most smart phones and tablets can download and use the Cisco AnyConnect software. It enables the device to establish a secure, persistent, policy-based connection for a seamless user experience.

■ **Borderless network services**- As shown in Figure 2, Borderless network services unify the approach to securely delivering applications to users in a highly distributed environment. It securely connects internal users and remote users and provides access to network resources. The crucial element to scaling secure access is a policy-based architecture that allows IT to implement centralized access controls.

The borderless network architecture supports a highly secure, high-performing network that is accessible to a wide range of devices. It needs to be flexible enough to scale in its support for future growth in terms of business expansion, including BYOD, mobility and cloud computing and must be able to support the growing requirements for online voice and video.

Refer to
Online Course
for Illustration

1.3.2.2 Collaboration Architecture

Working in a collaborative environment helps increase productivity. Collaboration and other types of groupware are used to bring people together for one reason or another: such as to socialize, to work together, to cooperate and contribute to the production of something, and to innovate.

The Cisco Collaboration Architecture comprises a portfolio of products, applications, software development kits (SDKs), and APIs. The individual components work together to provide a comprehensive solution.

As shown in the figure, Cisco's collaboration architecture is composed of three layers:

- **Application and Devices**- This layer contains unified communications and conference applications such as Cisco WebEx Meetings, WebEx Social, Cisco Jabber, and TelePresence. The applications within this layer help users stay connected and productive. These applications include voice, video, web conferencing, messaging, mobile applications, and enterprise social software.

- **Collaboration Services**- This layer supports collaboration applications including the following services: presence, location, session management, contact management, client frameworks, tagging, and policy and security management.

- **Network and Computer Infrastructure**- This layer is responsible for allowing collaboration anytime, from anywhere, on any device. It includes virtual machines, the network, and storage.

Refer to
Online Course
for Illustration

1.3.2.3 Data Center and Virtualization

The Cisco Data Center/Virtualization architecture is built upon Cisco Data Center 3.0. It comprises a comprehensive set of virtualization technologies and services that bring the network, computing, storage, and virtualization platforms together.

The data center architecture consists of three components, as shown in Figure 1:

- **Cisco Unified Management Solutions**- Management solutions simplify and automate the process of deploying IT infrastructure and services with speed and enterprise reliability. Solutions operate transparently across physical and virtual resources in cloud environments.

- **Unified Fabric Solutions**- Flexible network solutions deliver network services to servers, storage, and applications, providing transparent convergence, scalability, and sophisticated intelligence. Solutions include Cisco Nexus switches, Catalyst switches, Cisco Fabric Manager, and Cisco NX-OS software.

- **Unified Computing Solutions**- Cisco's next-generation data center system unites computing, network, storage access, and virtualization into a cohesive system designed to reduce total cost of ownership (TCO) and increase business agility. The Cisco Unified

Computing System (Cisco UCS) is built with blade servers, rack-mount servers, fabric interconnects, and virtual interface cards (VICs).

Click Play in Figure 2 to see a short video on the Cisco Unified Fabric.

Refer to
Online Course
for Illustration

1.3.2.4   Expanding the Network

These three architectures are built on an infrastructure of scalable and resilient hardware and software. Components of the architecture come together to build network systems that span an organization from network access to the cloud, and provide organizations with the services they need.

Building off the basic network infrastructure, organizations can use these network architectures to grow their network over time, adding features and functionality in an integrated solution.

One of the first steps in growing the network is expanding from the campus infrastructure to a network that connects remote sites through the Internet and through the WAN.

Click Play in the figure to view the evolution of a network to a WAN infrastructure.

Refer to
Interactive Graphic
in online course.

1.3.2.5   Activity - Identify Evolving Network Architecture Terminology

Refer to
Online Course
for Illustration

1.4   Summary

Refer to
Lab Activity
for this chapter

1.4.1.1   Class Activity - Borderless Innovations - Everywhere

Borderless Innovations - Everywhere

You are the network administrator for your small- to medium-sized business. Borderless network services interest you as you plan your network's future.

While planning for network policies and services, you realize that your wired and wireless networks need manageability and deployment design.

Therefore, this leads you to consider the following Cisco borderless services as possible options for your business:

- Security - TrustSec

- Mobility - Motion

- Application Performance - App Velocity

- Multimedia Performance - Medianet

- Energy Management - EnergyWise

Refer to **Packet Tracer Activity** for this chapter

1.4.1.2   Packet Tracer - Skills Integration Challenge - OSPF

This Packet Tracer activity provides an opportunity to review skills from previous course-work.

Background/Scenario

Your business has just expanded into a different town and needs to expand its presence across the Internet. You are tasked with completing the upgrades to the enterprise network which includes dual-stacked IPv4 and IPv6 as well as a variety of addressing and routing technologies.

Refer to **Packet Tracer Activity** for this chapter

1.4.1.3   Packet Tracer - Skills Integration Challenge - EIGRP

This Packet Tracer activity provides an opportunity to review skills from previous course-work.

Background/Scenario

You are a network technician new to a company that has lost its last technician in the middle of a system upgrade. You are tasked with completing upgrades to the network infrastructure that has two locations. Half of the enterprise network uses IPv4 addressing and the other half uses IPv6 addressing. The requirements also include a variety of routing and switching technologies.

Refer to **Online Course** for Illustration

1.4.1.4   Summary

The structured engineering principles of good network design include hierarchy, modularity, resiliency, and flexibility.

A typical enterprise hierarchical LAN campus network design includes the access layer, distribution layer, and the core layer. In smaller enterprise networks, a "collapsed core" hierarchy, where the distribution layer and core layer functions are implemented in a single device, can be more practical. The benefits of a hierarchical network include scalability, redundancy, performance, and maintainability.

A modular design that separates the functions of a network enables flexibility and facilitates implementation and management. The basic module blocks that are connected by the core include the access distribution block, the services block, the data center, and the enterprise edge. The Cisco Enterprise Architecture modules are used to facilitate the design of large, scalable networks. The primary modules include the Enterprise Campus, Enterprise Edge, Service Provider Edge, Enterprise Data Center, Enterprise Branch, and Enterprise Teleworker.

Go to the online course to take the quiz and exam.

Chapter 1 Quiz

This quiz is designed to provide an additional opportunity to practice the skills and knowledge presented in the chapter and to prepare for the chapter exam. You will be allowed multiple attempts and the grade does not appear in the gradebook.

Chapter 1 Exam

The chapter exam assesses your knowledge of the chapter content.

Your Chapter Notes

Connecting to the WAN

2.0 Connecting to the WAN

2.0.1.1 Introduction

Businesses must connect LANs together to provide communications between them, even when these LANs are far apart. Wide-area networks (WANs) are used to connect remote LANs together. A WAN may cover a city, country, or global region. A WAN is owned by a service provider, and a business pays a fee to use the provider's WAN network services.

Different technologies are used for WANs than for LANs. This chapter introduces WAN standards, technologies, and purposes. It covers selecting the appropriate WAN technologies, services, and devices to meet the changing business requirements of an evolving enterprise.

Refer to
Lab Activity
for this chapter

2.0.1.2 Class Activity - Branching Out

Branching Out

Your medium-sized company is opening a new branch office to serve a wider, client-based network. This branch will focus on regular, day-to-day network operations, but will also provide TelePresence, web conferencing, IP telephony, video on demand, and wireless services.

Although you know that an ISP can provide WAN routers and switches to accommodate the branch office connectivity for the network, you prefer to use your own customer premises equipment (CPE). To ensure interoperability, Cisco devices have been used in all other branch-office WANs.

As the branch-office network administrator, it is your responsibility to research possible network devices for purchase and use over the WAN.

Refer to
Interactive Graphic
in online course.

2.1 WAN Technologies Overview

2.1.1 Purpose of WANs

2.1.1.1 Why a WAN?

A WAN operates beyond the geographic scope of a LAN. As shown in the figure, WANs are used to interconnect the enterprise LAN to remote LANs in branch sites and telecommuter sites.

A WAN is owned by a service provider. An organization must pay a fee to use the provider's network services to connect remote sites. WAN service providers include carriers, such as a telephone network, cable company, or satellite service. Service providers provide links to interconnect remote sites for the purpose of transporting data, voice, and video.

In contrast, LANs are typically owned by the organization and used to connect local computers, peripherals, and other devices within a single building or other small geographic area.

Refer to
Online Course
for Illustration

2.1.1.2   Are WANs Necessary?

Without WANs, LANs would be a series of isolated networks. LANs provide both speed and cost-efficiency for transmitting data over relatively small geographic areas. However, as organizations expand, businesses require communication among geographically separated sites. The following are some examples:

- Regional or branch offices of an organization need to be able to communicate and share data with the central site.

- Organizations need to share information with other customer organizations. For example, software manufacturers routinely communicate product and promotional information to distributors that sell their products to end users.

- Employees who travel on company business frequently need to access information that resides on their corporate networks.

Home computer users also need to send and receive data across increasingly larger distances. Here are some examples:

- Consumers now commonly communicate over the Internet with banks, stores, and a variety of providers of goods and services.

- Students do research for classes by accessing library indexes and publications located in other parts of their country and in other parts of the world.

It is not feasible to connect computers across a country, or around the world, with physical cables. Therefore, different technologies have evolved to support this communication requirement. Increasingly, the Internet is being used as an inexpensive alternative to enterprise WANs. New technologies are available to businesses to provide security and privacy for their Internet communications and transactions. WANs used by themselves, or in concert with the Internet, allow organizations and individuals to meet their wide-area communication needs.

Refer to
Online Course
for Illustration

2.1.1.3   Evolving Networks

Every business is unique and how an organization grows depends on many factors. These factors include the type of products or service the business sells, the management philosophy of the owners, and the economic climate of the country in which the business operates.

In slow economic times, many businesses focus on increasing their profitability by improving the efficiency of their existing operations, increasing employee productivity, and lowering operating costs. Establishing and managing networks can represent significant installation and operating expenses. To justify such a large expense, companies expect their networks to perform optimally and to be able to deliver an ever increasing array of services and applications to support productivity and profitability.

The example used in this chapter is of a fictitious company called SPAN Engineering. Watch how its network requirements change as the company grows from a small local business into a global enterprise.

Refer to
Online Course
for Illustration

2.1.1.4   Small Office

SPAN Engineering, an environmental consulting firm, has developed a special process for converting household waste into electricity and is developing a small pilot project for a municipal government in its local area. The company, which has been in business for four years, has grown to include 15 employees: six engineers, four computer-aided drawing (CAD) designers, a receptionist, two senior partners, and two office assistants.

SPAN Engineering's management is working to win full-scale contracts after the pilot project successfully demonstrates the feasibility of their process. Until then, the company must manage its costs carefully.

For their small office, SPAN Engineering uses a single LAN to share information between computers, and to share peripherals, such as a printer, a large-scale plotter (to print engineering drawings), and fax equipment. They have recently upgraded their LAN to provide inexpensive Voice over IP (VoIP) service to save on the costs of separate phone lines for their employees.

Connection to the Internet is through a common broadband service called DSL, which is supplied by their local telephone service provider. With so few employees, bandwidth is not a significant problem.

The company cannot afford in-house IT support staff, and uses support services purchased from the DSL provider. The company also uses a hosting service rather than purchasing and operating its own FTP and email servers.

The figure shows an example of a small office and its network.

Refer to
Online Course
for Illustration

2.1.1.5   Campus Network

Five years later, SPAN Engineering has grown rapidly. The company was contracted to design and implement a full-sized waste conversion facility soon after the successful implementation of their first pilot plant. Since then, SPAN has won other projects in neighboring municipalities, and in other parts of the country.

To handle the additional workload, the business has hired more staff and leased more office space. It is now a small- to medium-sized business with several hundred employees. Many projects are being developed at the same time, and each requires a project manager and support staff. The company has organized itself into functional departments, with each department having its own organizational team. To meet its growing needs, the company has moved into several floors of a larger office building.

As the business has expanded, the network has also grown. Instead of a single small LAN, the network now consists of several subnetworks, each devoted to a different department. For example, all the engineering staff is on one LAN, while the marketing staff is on another LAN. These multiple LANs are joined to create a company-wide network, or campus, which spans several floors of the building.

The business now has in-house IT staff to support and maintain the network. The network includes dedicated servers for email, data transfer, and file storage, and web-based productivity tools and applications. There is also a company intranet to provide in-house documents and information to employees. An extranet provides project information to designated customers.

The figure shows an example of SPAN's campus network.

Refer to **Online Course** for Illustration

2.1.1.6   Branch Networks

Another six years later, SPAN Engineering has been so successful with its patented process that demand for its services has skyrocketed. New projects are underway in multiple cities. To manage those projects, the company has opened small branch offices closer to the project sites.

This situation presents new challenges to the IT team. To manage the delivery of information and services throughout the company, SPAN Engineering now has a data center, which houses the various databases and servers of the company. To ensure that all parts of the business are able to access the same services and applications regardless of where the offices are located, the company must now implement a WAN.

For its branch offices that are in nearby cities, the company decides to use private dedicated lines through their local service provider. However, for those offices that are located in other countries, the Internet is an attractive WAN connection option. Although connecting offices through the Internet is economical, it introduces security and privacy issues that the IT team must address.

Refer to **Online Course** for Illustration

2.1.1.7   Distributed Network

SPAN Engineering has now been in business for 20 years and has grown to thousands of employees distributed in offices worldwide, as shown in Figure 1. The cost of the network and its related services is a significant expense. The company is looking to provide its employees with the best network services at the lowest cost. Optimized network services would allow each employee to work at a high rate of efficiency.

To increase profitability, SPAN Engineering must reduce its operating expenses. It has relocated some of its office facilities to less expensive areas. The company is also encouraging teleworking and virtual teams. Web-based applications, including web-conferencing, e-learning, and online collaboration tools, are being used to increase productivity and reduce costs. Site-to-site and remote access Virtual Private Networks (VPNs) enable the company to use the Internet to connect easily and securely with employees and facilities around the world. To meet these requirements, the network must provide the necessary converged services and secure Internet WAN connectivity to remote offices and individuals, as shown in Figure 2.

As seen in this example, network requirements of a company can change dramatically as the company grows over time. Distributing employees saves costs in many ways, but it puts increased demands on the network. Not only must a network meet the day-to-day operational needs of the business, but it must be able to adapt and grow as the company changes. Network designers and administrators meet these challenges by carefully choosing network technologies, protocols, and service providers, and by optimizing their networks using many of the network design techniques and architectures described in this course.

Refer to **Interactive Graphic** in online course.

2.1.1.8   Activity - Identify WAN Topologies

Refer to
Online Course
for Illustration

2.1.2   WAN Operations

2.1.2.1   WANs in the OSI Model

WAN operations focus primarily on the physical layer (OSI Layer 1) and the data link layer (OSI Layer 2). WAN access standards typically describe both physical layer delivery methods and data link layer requirements, including physical addressing, flow control, and encapsulation.

WAN access standards are defined and managed by a number of recognized authorities, including the:

- Telecommunication Industry Association and the Electronic Industries Alliance (TIA/EIA)

- International Organization for Standardization (ISO)

- Institute of Electrical and Electronics Engineers (IEEE)

Layer 1 protocols describe how to provide electrical, mechanical, operational, and functional connections to the services of a communications service provider.

Layer 2 protocols define how data is encapsulated for transmission toward a remote location, and the mechanisms for transferring the resulting frames. A variety of different technologies are used, such as the Point-to-Point Protocol (PPP), Frame Relay, and ATM. Some of these protocols use the same basic framing or a subset of the High-Level Data Link Control (HDLC) mechanism.

Most WAN links are point-to-point. For this reason, the address field in the Layer 2 frame is usually not used.

Refer to
Online Course
for Illustration

2.1.2.2   Common WAN Terminology

One primary difference between a WAN and a LAN is that a company or organization must subscribe to an outside WAN service provider to use WAN carrier network services. A WAN uses data links provided by carrier services to access the Internet and connect different locations of an organization to each other, to locations of other organizations, to external services, and to remote users.

The physical layer of a WAN describes the physical connections between the company network and the service provider network. The figure illustrates the terminology commonly used to describe WAN connections, including:

- **Customer Premises Equipment (CPE)**- The devices and inside wiring located on the enterprise edge connecting to a carrier link. The subscriber either owns the CPE or leases the CPE from the service provider. A subscriber, in this context, is a company that arranges for WAN services from a service provider.

- **Data Communications Equipment (DCE)**- Also called data circuit-terminating equipment, the DCE consists of devices that put data on the local loop. The DCE primarily provides an interface to connect subscribers to a communication link on the WAN cloud.

- **Data Terminal Equipment (DTE)**- The customer devices that pass the data from a customer network or host computer for transmission over the WAN. The DTE connects to the local loop through the DCE.

- **Demarcation Point**- A point established in a building or complex to separate customer equipment from service provider equipment. Physically, the demarcation point is the cabling junction box, located on the customer premises, that connects the CPE wiring to the local loop. It is usually placed for easy access by a technician. The demarcation point is the place where the responsibility for the connection changes from the user to the service provider. When problems arise, it is necessary to determine whether the user or the service provider is responsible for troubleshooting or repair.

- **Local Loop**- The actual copper or fiber cable that connects the CPE to the CO of the service provider. The local loop is also sometimes called the "last-mile".

- **Central Office (CO)**- The CO is the local service provider facility or building that connects the CPE to the provider network.

- **Toll network**- This consists of the long-haul, all-digital, fiber-optic communications lines, switches, routers, and other equipment inside the WAN provider network.

2.1.2.3   WAN Devices

There are many types of devices that are specific to WAN environments, including:

- **Dialup modem**- Considered to be a legacy WAN technology, a voiceband modem converts (i.e., modulates) the digital signals produced by a computer into voice frequencies that can be transmitted over the analog lines of the public telephone network. On the other side of the connection, another modem converts the sounds back into a digital signal (i.e., demodulates) for input to a computer or network connection.

- **Access server**- Concentrates dialup modem, dial-in and dial-out user communications. Considered to be a legacy technology, an access server may have a mixture of analog and digital interfaces and support hundreds of simultaneous users.

- **Broadband modem**- A type of digital modem used with high-speed DSL or cable Internet service. Both operate in a similar manner to the voiceband modem, but use higher broadband frequencies and transmission speeds.

- **CSU/DSU**- Digital-leased lines require a CSU and a DSU. A CSU/DSU can be a separate device like a modem or it can be an interface on a router. The CSU provides termination for the digital signal and ensures connection integrity through error correction and line monitoring. The DSU converts the line frames into frames that the LAN can interpret and vice versa.

- **WAN switch**- A multiport internetworking device used in service provider networks. These devices typically switch traffic, such as Frame Relay or ATM and operate at Layer 2.

- **Router**- Provides internetworking and WAN access interface ports that are used to connect to the service provider network. These interfaces may be serial connections, Ethernet, or other WAN interfaces. With some types of WAN interfaces, an external device, such as a DSU/CSU or modem (analog, cable, or DSL), is required to connect the router to the local service provider.

- **Core router/Multilayer switch**- A router or multilayer switch that resides within the middle or backbone of the WAN, rather than at its periphery. To fulfill this role, a router or multilayer switch must be able to support multiple telecommunications interfaces of the highest speed used in the WAN core. It must also be able to forward IP packets at full speed on all of those interfaces. The router or multilayer switch must also support the routing protocols being used in the core.

Note   The preceding list is not exhaustive and other devices may be required, depending on the WAN access technology chosen.

WAN technologies are either circuit-switched or packet-switched. The type of devices used depends on the WAN technology implemented.

2.1.2.4   Circuit Switching

A circuit-switched network is one that establishes a dedicated circuit (or channel) between nodes and terminals before the users may communicate. Specifically, circuit switching dynamically establishes a dedicated virtual connection for voice or data between a sender and a receiver. Before communication can start, it is necessary to establish the connection through the network of the service provider.

As an example, when a subscriber makes a telephone call, the dialed number is used to set switches in the exchanges along the route of the call so that there is a continuous circuit from the caller to the called party. Because of the switching operation used to establish the circuit, the telephone system is called a circuit-switched network. If the telephones are replaced with modems, then the switched circuit is able to carry computer data.

If the circuit carries computer data, the usage of this fixed capacity may not be efficient. For example, if the circuit is used to access the Internet, there is a burst of activity on the circuit while a web page is transferred. This could be followed by no activity while the user reads the page, and then another burst of activity while the next page is transferred. This variation in usage between none and maximum is typical of computer network traffic. Because the subscriber has sole use of the fixed capacity allocation, switched circuits are generally an expensive way of moving data.

The two most common types of circuit-switched WAN technologies are the public switched telephone network (PSTN) and the Integrated Services Digital Network (ISDN).

Click the Play button in the figure to see how circuit switching works.

2.1.2.5   Packet Switching

Refer to **Online Course** for Illustration

In contrast to circuit switching, packet switching splits traffic data into packets that are routed over a shared network. Packet-switching networks do not require a circuit to be established, and they allow many pairs of nodes to communicate over the same channel.

The switches in a packet-switched network (PSN) determine the links that packets must be sent over based on the addressing information in each packet. The following are two approaches to this link determination:

- **Connectionless systems**- Full addressing information must be carried in each packet. Each switch must evaluate the address to determine where to send the packet. An example of a connectionless system is the Internet.

- **Connection-oriented systems**- The network predetermines the route for a packet, and each packet only has to carry an identifier. The switch determines the onward route by looking up the identifier in tables held in memory. The set of entries in the tables identifies a particular route or circuit through the system. When the circuit is estab-lished temporarily while a packet is traveling through it, and then breaks down again, it is called a virtual circuit (VC). An example of a connection-oriented system is Frame Relay. In the case of Frame Relay, the identifiers used are called data-link connection identifiers (DLCIs).

Because the internal links between the switches are shared between many users, the cost of packet switching is lower than that of circuit-switching. However, delays (latency) and variability of delay (jitter) are greater in packet-switched networks than in circuit-switched networks. This is because the links are shared, and packets must be entirely received at one switch before moving to the next. Despite the latency and jitter inherent in shared networks, modern technology allows satisfactory transport of voice and video communica-tions on these networks.

Click the Play button in the figure to see a packet-switching example. In the animation, SRV1 is sending data to SRV2. As the packet traverses the provider network, it arrives at the second provider switch. The packet is added to the queue and forwarded after the other packets in the queue have been forwarded. Eventually, the packet reaches SRV2.

Refer to
Interactive Graphic
in online course.

2.1.2.6   Activity - Identify WAN Terminology

Refer to
Online Course
for Illustration

2.2   Selecting a WAN Technology

2.2.1   WAN Services

2.2.1.1   WAN Link Connection Options

There are several WAN access connection options that ISPs can use to connect the local loop to the enterprise edge. These WAN access options differ in technology, speed, and cost. Each has distinct advantages and disadvantages. Familiarity with these technologies is an important part of network design.

As shown in Figure 1, an enterprise can get WAN access over a:

■ **Private WAN infrastructure**- Service providers may offer dedicated point-to-point leased lines, circuit-switched links, such as PSTN or ISDN, and packet-switched links, such as Ethernet WAN, ATM, or Frame Relay.

■ **Public WAN infrastructure**- Service provider may offer broadband Internet access using digital subscriber line (DSL), cable, and satellite access. Broadband connection options are typically used to connect small offices and telecommuting employees to a corporate site over the Internet. Data travelling between corporate sites over the public WAN infrastructure should be protected using VPNs.

The topology in Figure 2 illustrates some of these WAN access technologies.

Refer to
Online Course
for Illustration

2.2.1.2   Service Provider Network Infrastructure

When a WAN service provider receives data from a client at a site, it must forward the data to the remote site for final delivery to the recipient. In some cases, the remote site may be connected to the same service provider as the originating site. In other cases, the remote site may be connected to a different ISP, and the originating ISP must pass the data to the connecting ISP.

Long-range communications are usually those connections between ISPs, or between branch offices in very large companies.

Service provider networks are complex. They consist mostly of high-bandwidth fiber optic media, using either the Synchronous Optical Networking (SONET) or Synchronous Digital Hierarchy (SDH) standard. These standards define how to transfer multiple data, voice, and video traffic over optical fiber using lasers or light-emitting diodes (LEDs) over great distances.

Note   SONET is an American-based ANSI standard, while SDH is a European-based ETSI and ITU standard. Both are essentially the same and, therefore, often listed as SONET/SDH.

A newer fiber optic media development for long-range communications is called dense wavelength division multiplexing (DWDM). DWDM multiplies the amount of bandwidth that a single strand of fiber can support, as shown in Figure 1.

Specifically, DWDM:

■ Enables bidirectional communications over one strand of fiber.

■ Can multiplex more than 80 different channels of data (i.e., wavelengths) onto a single fiber.

■ Each channel is capable of carrying a 10 Gb/s multiplexed signal.

■ Assigns incoming optical signals to specific wavelengths of light (i.e., frequencies).

■ Can amplify these wavelengths to boost the signal strength.

■ Supports SONET and SDH standards.

DWDM circuits are used in all modern submarine communications cable systems and other long-haul circuits, as shown in Figure 2.

Refer to
Interactive Graphic
in online course.

2.2.1.3   Activity - Classify WAN Access Options

Refer to
Online Course
for Illustration

2.2.2   Private WAN Infrastructures

2.2.2.1   Leased Lines

When permanent dedicated connections are required, a point-to-point link is used to provide a pre-established WAN communications path from the customer premises to the provider network. Point-to-point lines are usually leased from a service provider and are called leased lines.

Leased lines have existed since the early 1950s and for this reason, are referred to by different names such as leased circuits, serial link, serial line, point-to-point link, and T1/E1 or T3/E3 lines. The term leased line refers to the fact that the organization pays a monthly lease fee to a service provider to use the line. Leased lines are available in different capacities and are generally priced based on the bandwidth required and the distance between the two connected points.

In North America, service providers use the T-carrier system to define the digital transmission capability of a serial copper media link, while Europe uses the E-carrier system, as shown in the figure. For instance, a T1 link supports 1.544 Mb/s, an E1 supports 2.048 Mb/s, a T3 supports 43.7 Mb/s, and an E3 connection supports 34.368 Mb/s. Optical Carrier (OC) transmission rates are used to define the digital transmitting capacity of a fiber optic network.

The advantages of leased lines include:

- **Simplicity**- Point-to-point communication links require minimal expertise to install and maintain.

- **Quality**- Point-to-point communication links usually offer high service quality, if they have adequate bandwidth. The dedicated capacity removes latency or jitter between the endpoints.

- **Availability**- Constant availability is essential for some applications, such as e-commerce. Point-to-point communication links provide permanent, dedicated capacity which is required for VoIP or Video over IP.

The disadvantages of leased lines include:

- **Cost**- Point-to-point links are generally the most expensive type of WAN access. The cost of leased line solutions can become significant when they are used to connect many sites over increasing distances. In addition, each endpoint requires an interface on the router, which increases equipment costs.

- **Limited flexibility**- WAN traffic is often variable, and leased lines have a fixed capacity, so that the bandwidth of the line seldom matches the need exactly. Any change to the leased line generally requires a site visit by ISP personnel to adjust capacity.

The Layer 2 protocol is usually HDLC or PPP.

Refer to
Online Course
for Illustration

2.2.2.2   Dialup

Dialup WAN access may be required when no other WAN technology is available. For example, a remote location could use a modem and analog dialed telephone lines to provide low capacity and dedicated switched connections. Dialup access is suitable when intermittent, low-volume data transfers are needed.

Traditional telephony uses a copper cable, called the local loop, to connect the telephone handset in the subscriber premises to the CO. The signal on the local loop during a call is a continuously varying electronic signal that is a translation of the subscriber voice into an analog signal.

Traditional local loops can transport binary computer data through the voice telephone network using a modem. The modem modulates the binary data into an analog signal at the source and demodulates the analog signal to binary data at the destination. The physical characteristics of the local loop and its connection to the PSTN limit the rate of the signal to less than 56 kb/s.

For small businesses, these relatively low-speed dialup connections are adequate for the exchange of sales figures, prices, routine reports, and email. Using automatic dialup at night or on weekends for large file transfers and data backup can take advantage of lower off-peak tariffs (toll charges). Tariffs are based on the distance between the endpoints, time of day, and the duration of the call.

The advantages of modem and analog lines are simplicity, availability, and low implementation cost. The disadvantages are the low data rates and a relatively long connection time. The dedicated circuit has little delay or jitter for point-to-point traffic, but voice or video traffic does not operate adequately at these low bit rates.

Note   Although very few enterprises support dialup access, it is still a viable solution for remote areas with limited WAN access options.

Refer to
Online Course
for Illustration

2.2.2.3   ISDN

Integrated Services Digital Network (ISDN) is a circuit-switching technology that enables the local loop of a PSTN to carry digital signals, resulting in higher capacity switched connections.

ISDN changes the internal connections of the PSTN from carrying analog signals to time-division multiplexed (TDM) digital signals. TDM allows two or more signals, or bit streams, to be transferred as subchannels in one communication channel. The signals appear to transfer simultaneously; but physically, the signals are taking turns on the channel.

Figure 1 displays a sample ISDN topology. The ISDN connection may require a terminal adapter (TA) which is a device used to connect ISDN Basic Rate Interface (BRI) connections to a router.

ISDN turns the local loop into a TDM digital connection. This change enables the local loop to carry digital signals that result in higher capacity switched connections. The connection uses 64 kb/s bearer channels (B) for carrying voice or data and a signaling, delta channel (D) for call setup and other purposes.

There are two types of ISDN interfaces:

■ **Basic Rate Interface (BRI)**- ISDN BRI is intended for the home and small enterprise and provides two 64 kb/s B channels and a 16 kb/s D channel. The BRI D channel is designed for control and often underused, because it has only two B channels to control (Figure 2).

■ **Primary Rate Interface (PRI)**– ISDN is also available for larger installations. In North America, PRI delivers 23 B channels with 64 kb/s and one D channel with 64 kb/s for a total bit rate of up to 1.544 Mb/s. This includes some additional overhead for synchronization. In Europe, Australia, and other parts of the world, ISDN PRI provides 30 B channels and one D channel, for a total bit rate of up to 2.048 Mb/s, including synchronization overhead (Figure 3).

BRI has a call setup time that is less than a second, and the 64 kb/s B channel provides greater capacity than an analog modem link. If greater capacity is required, a second B channel can be activated to provide a total of 128 kb/s. Although inadequate for video, this permits several simultaneous voice conversations in addition to data traffic.

Another common application of ISDN is to provide additional capacity as needed on a leased line connection. The leased line is sized to carry average traffic loads while ISDN is added during peak demand periods. ISDN is also used as a backup if the leased line fails. ISDN tariffs are based on a per-B channel basis and are similar to those of analog voice connections.

With PRI ISDN, multiple B channels can be connected between two endpoints. This allows for videoconferencing and high-bandwidth data connections with no latency or jitter. However, multiple connections can be very expensive over long distances.

Note   Although ISDN is still an important technology for telephone service provider networks, it is declining in popularity as an Internet connection option with the introduction of high-speed DSL and other broadband services.

Refer to
Online Course
for Illustration

2.2.2.4   Frame Relay

Frame Relay is a simple Layer 2 non-broadcast multiaccess (NBMA) WAN technology used to interconnect enterprise LANs. A single router interface can be used to connect to multiple sites using PVCs. PVCs are used to carry both voice and data traffic between a source and destination, and support data rates up to 4 Mb/s, with some providers offering even higher rates.

An edge router only requires a single interface, even when multiple virtual circuits (VCs) are used. The short-leased line to the Frame Relay network edge allows cost-effective connections between widely scattered LANs.

Frame Relay creates PVCs which are uniquely identified by a data-link connection identifier (DLCI). The PVCs and DLCIs ensure bidirectional communication from one DTE device to another.

For instance, in the figure, R1 will use DLCI 102 to reach R2 while R2 will use DLCI 201 to reach R1.

Refer to
Online Course
for Illustration

2.2.2.5   ATM

Asynchronous Transfer Mode (ATM) technology is capable of transferring voice, video, and data through private and public networks. It is built on a cell-based architecture rather than on a frame-based architecture. ATM cells are always a fixed length of 53 bytes. The ATM cell contains a 5-byte ATM header followed by 48 bytes of ATM payload. Small, fixed-length cells are well-suited for carrying voice and video traffic because this traffic is intolerant of delay. Video and voice traffic do not have to wait for larger data packets to be transmitted.

The 53-byte ATM cell is less efficient than the bigger frames and packets of Frame Relay. Furthermore, the ATM cell has at least 5 bytes of overhead for each 48-byte payload. When the cell is carrying segmented network layer packets, the overhead is higher because the ATM switch must be able to reassemble the packets at the destination. A typical ATM line needs almost 20 percent greater bandwidth than Frame Relay to carry the same volume of network layer data.

ATM was designed to be extremely scalable and to support link speeds of T1/E1 to OC-12 (622 Mb/s) and faster.

ATM offers both PVCs and SVCs, although PVCs are more common with WANs. As with other shared technologies, ATM allows multiple VCs on a single leased-line connection to the network edge.

2.2.2.6   Ethernet WAN

Refer to **Online Course** for Illustration

Ethernet was originally developed to be a LAN access technology. At that time however, it really was not suitable as a WAN access technology because the maximum cable length supported was only up to a kilometer. However, newer Ethernet standards using fiber optic cables have made Ethernet a reasonable WAN access option. For instance, the IEEE 1000BASE-LX standard supports fiber optic cable lengths of 5 km, while the IEEE 1000BASE-ZX standard supports up to 70 km cable lengths.

Service providers now offer Ethernet WAN service using fiber optic cabling. The Ethernet WAN service can go by many names, including Metropolitan Ethernet (MetroE), Ethernet over MPLS (EoMPLS), and Virtual Private LAN Service (VPLS).

Benefits of Ethernet WAN include:

- **Reduced expenses and administration**- Ethernet WAN provides a switched, high-bandwidth Layer 2 network capable of managing data, voice, and video all on the same infrastructure. This characteristic increases bandwidth and eliminates expensive conversions to other WAN technologies. The technology enables businesses to inexpensively connect numerous sites, in a metropolitan area, to each other and to the Internet.

- **Easy integration with existing networks**- Ethernet WAN connects easily to existing Ethernet LANs, reducing installation costs and time.

- **Enhanced business productivity**- Ethernet WAN enables businesses to take advantage of productivity-enhancing IP applications that are difficult to implement on TDM or Frame Relay networks, such as hosted IP communications, VoIP, and streaming and broadcast video.

Note   Ethernet WANs have gained in popularity and are now commonly being used to replace the traditional Frame Relay and ATM WAN links.

2.2.2.7   MPLS

Refer to **Online Course** for Illustration

Multiprotocol Label Switching (MPLS) is a multiprotocol high-performance WAN technology that directs data from one router to the next, based on short path labels rather than IP network addresses.

MPLS has several defining characteristics. It is multiprotocol, meaning it has the ability to carry any payload including IPv4, IPv6, Ethernet, ATM, DSL, and Frame Relay traffic. It uses labels which tell a router what to do with a packet. The labels identify paths between distant routers rather than endpoints, and while MPLS actually routes IPv4 and IPv6 packets, everything else is switched.

MPLS is a service provider technology. Leased lines deliver bits between sites, and Frame Relay and Ethernet WAN deliver frames between sites. However, MPLS can deliver any type of packet between sites. MPLS can encapsulate packets of various network protocols. It supports a wide range of WAN technologies including T-carrier / E-carrier links, Carrier Ethernet, ATM, Frame Relay, and DSL.

The sample topology in the figure illustrates how MPLS is used. Notice that the different sites can connect to the MPLS cloud using different access technologies. In the figure, CE refers to the customer edge, PE is the provider edge router which adds and removes labels, while P is an internal provider router which switches MPLS labeled packets.

Note   MPLS is primarily a service provider WAN technology.

Refer to
Online Course
for Illustration

2.2.2.8   VSAT

All private WAN technologies discussed so far used either copper or fiber optics media. What if an organization needed connectivity in a remote location where there are no service providers that offer WAN service?

Very small aperture terminal (VSAT) is a solution that creates a private WAN using satellite communications. A VSAT is a small satellite dish similar to those used for home Internet and TV. VSATs create a private WAN while providing connectivity to remote locations.

Specifically, a router connects to a satellite dish which is pointed to a service provider's satellite in a geosynchronous orbit in space. The signals must travel approximately 35,786 kilometers (22,236 miles) to the satellite and back.

The example in the figure displays a VSAT dish on the roofs of the buildings communicating with a satellite dish thousands of kilometers away in space.

Refer to
Interactive Graphic
in online course.

2.2.2.9   Activity - Identify Private WAN Infrastructure Terminology

Refer to
Online Course
for Illustration

2.2.3   Public WAN Infrastructure

2.2.3.1   DSL

DSL technology is an always-on connection technology that uses existing twisted-pair telephone lines to transport high-bandwidth data, and provides IP services to subscribers. A DSL modem converts an Ethernet signal from the user device to a DSL signal, which is transmitted to the central office.

Multiple DSL subscriber lines are multiplexed into a single, high-capacity link using a DSL access multiplexer (DSLAM) at the provider location. DSLAMs incorporate TDM technology to aggregate many subscriber lines into a single medium, generally a T3 (DS3) connection. Current DSL technologies use sophisticated coding and modulation techniques to achieve fast data rates.

There is a wide variety of DSL types, standards, and emerging standards. DSL is now a popular choice for enterprise IT departments to support home workers. Generally, a subscriber cannot choose to connect to an enterprise network directly, but must first connect to an ISP, and then an IP connection is made through the Internet to the enterprise. Security risks are incurred in this process, but can be mediated with security measures.

The topology in the figure displays a sample DSL WAN connection.

Refer to
Online Course
for Illustration

2.2.3.2 Cable

Coaxial cable is widely used in urban areas to distribute television signals. Network access is available from many cable television providers. This allows for greater bandwidth than the conventional telephone local loop.

Cable modems provide an always-on connection and a simple installation. A subscriber connects a computer or LAN router to the cable modem, which translates the digital signals into the broadband frequencies used for transmitting on a cable television network. The local cable TV office, which is called the cable headend, contains the computer system and databases needed to provide Internet access. The most important component located at the headend is the cable modem termination system (CMTS), which sends and receives digital cable modem signals on a cable network and is necessary for providing Internet services to cable subscribers.

Cable modem subscribers must use the ISP associated with the service provider. All the local subscribers share the same cable bandwidth. As more users join the service, available bandwidth may be below the expected rate.

The topology in the figure displays a sample cable WAN connection.

Refer to
Online Course
for Illustration

2.2.3.3 Wireless

Wireless technology uses the unlicensed radio spectrum to send and receive data. The unlicensed spectrum is accessible to anyone who has a wireless router and wireless technology in the device they are using.

Until recently, one limitation of wireless access has been the need to be within the local transmission range (typically less than 100 feet) of a wireless router or a wireless modem that has a wired connection to the Internet. The following new developments in broadband wireless technology are changing this situation:

■ **Municipal Wi-Fi**- Many cities have begun setting up municipal wireless networks. Some of these networks provide high-speed Internet access for free or for substantially less than the price of other broadband services. Others are for city use only, allowing police and fire departments and other city employees to do certain aspects of their jobs remotely. To connect to a municipal Wi-Fi, a subscriber typically needs a wireless modem, which provides a stronger radio and directional antenna than conventional wireless adapters. Most service providers provide the necessary equipment for free or for a fee, much like they do with DSL or cable modems.

■ **WiMAX**- Worldwide Interoperability for Microwave Access (WiMAX) is a new technology that is just beginning to come into use. It is described in the IEEE standard 802.16. WiMAX provides high-speed broadband service with wireless access and provides broad coverage like a cell phone network rather than through small Wi-Fi hotspots. WiMAX operates in a similar way to Wi-Fi, but at higher speeds, over greater distances, and for a greater number of users. It uses a network of WiMAX towers that are similar to cell phone towers. To access a WiMAX network, subscribers must subscribe to an ISP with a WiMAX tower within 30 miles of their location. They also need some type of WiMAX receiver and a special encryption code to get access to the base station.

■ **Satellite Internet**- Typically used by rural users where cable and DSL are not available. A VSAT provides two-way (upload and download) data communications. The upload speed is about one-tenth of the 500 kb/s download speed. Cable and DSL have higher download speeds, but satellite systems are about 10 times faster than an analog modem. To access satellite Internet services, subscribers need a satellite dish, two modems (uplink and downlink), and coaxial cables between the dish and the modem.

The figure displays an example of a WiMAX network.

Refer to **Online Course** for Illustration

2.2.3.4   3G/4G Cellular

Increasingly, cellular service is another wireless WAN technology being used to connect users and remote locations where no other WAN access technology is available. Many users with smart phones and tablets can use cellular data to email, surf the web, download apps, and watch videos.

Phones, tablet computers, laptops, and even some routers can communicate through to the Internet using cellular technology. These devices use radio waves to communicate through a nearby mobile phone tower. The device has a small radio antenna, and the provider has a much larger antenna sitting at the top of a tower somewhere within miles of the phone.

Common cellular industry terms include:

■ **3G/4G Wireless**- Abbreviation for 3rd generation and 4th generation cellular access. These technologies support wireless Internet access.

■ **Long-Term Evolution (LTE)**- Refers to a newer and faster technology and is considered to be part of fourth generation (4G) technology.

Refer to **Online Course** for Illustration

2.2.3.5   VPN Technology

Security risks are incurred when a teleworker or a remote office worker uses broadband services to access the corporate WAN over the Internet. To address security concerns, broadband services provide capabilities for using VPN connections to a VPN server, which is typically located at the corporate site.

A VPN is an encrypted connection between private networks over a public network, such as the Internet. Instead of using a dedicated Layer 2 connection, such as a leased line, a VPN uses virtual connections called VPN tunnels, which are routed through the Internet from the private network of the company to the remote site or employee host.

Benefits of VPN include the following:

■ **Cost savings**- VPNs enable organizations to use the global Internet to connect remote offices and remote users to the main corporate site, thus eliminating expensive, dedicated WAN links and modem banks.

■ **Security**- VPNs provide the highest level of security by using advanced encryption and authentication protocols that protect data from unauthorized access.

- **Scalability**- Because VPNs use the Internet infrastructure within ISPs and devices, it is easy to add new users. Corporations are able to add large amounts of capacity without adding significant infrastructure.

- **Compatibility with broadband technology**- VPN technology is supported by broadband service providers such as DSL and cable, so mobile workers and telecommuters can take advantage of their home high-speed Internet service to access their corporate networks. Business-grade, high-speed broadband connections can also provide a cost-effective solution for connecting remote offices.

There are two types of VPN access:

- **Site-to-site VPNs**- Site-to-site VPNs connect entire networks to each other; for example, they can connect a branch office network to a company headquarters network, as shown in Figure 1. Each site is equipped with a VPN gateway, such as a router, firewall, VPN concentrator, or security appliance. In the figure, a remote branch office uses a site-to-site-VPN to connect with the corporate head office.

- **Remote-access VPNs**- Remote-access VPNs enable individual hosts, such as telecommuters, mobile users, and extranet consumers, to access a company network securely over the Internet. Each host (Teleworker 1 and Teleworker 2) typically has VPN client software loaded or uses a web-based client, as shown in Figure 2.

Refer to
Interactive Graphic
in online course.

2.2.3.6   Activity - Identify Public WAN Infrastructure Terminology

Refer to
Online Course
for Illustration

2.2.4   Selecting WAN Services

2.2.4.1   Choosing a WAN Link Connection

There are many important factors to consider when choosing an appropriate WAN connection. For a network administrator to decide which WAN technology best meets the requirements of their specific business, they must answer the following questions:

What is the purpose of the WAN?

Considerations include:

- Will the enterprise connect local branches in the same city area, connect remote branches, or connect to a single branch?

- Will the WAN be used to connect internal employees, or external business partners and customers, or all three?

- Will the enterprise connect to customers, connect to business partners, connect to employees, or some combination of these?

- Will the WAN provide authorized users limited or full access to the company intranet?

What is the geographic scope?

Considerations include:

- Is the WAN local, regional, or global?
- Is the WAN one-to-one (single branch), one-to-many branches, or many-to-many (distributed)?

What are the traffic requirements?

Considerations include:

- What type of traffic must be supported (data only, VoIP, video, large files, streaming files)? This determines the quality and performance requirements.
- What volume of traffic type (voice, video, or data) must be supported for each destination? This determines the bandwidth capacity required for the WAN connection to the ISP.
- What Quality of Service is required? This may limit the choices. If the traffic is highly sensitive to latency and jitter, eliminate any WAN connection options that cannot provide the required quality.
- What are the security requirements (data integrity, confidentiality, and security)? These are important factors if the traffic is of a highly confidential nature, or if it provides essential services, such as emergency response.

Refer to
Online Course
for Illustration

2.2.4.2   Choosing a WAN Link Connection, cont.

In addition to gathering information about the scope of the WAN, the administrator must also determine:

- **Should the WAN use a private or public infrastructure?**- A private infrastructure offers the best security and confidentiality, whereas the public Internet infrastructure offers the most flexibility and lowest ongoing expense. The choice depends on the purpose of the WAN, the types of traffic it carries, and available operating budget. For example, if the purpose is to provide a nearby branch with high-speed secure services, a private dedicated or switched connection may be best. If the purpose is to connect many remote offices, a public WAN using the Internet may be the best choice. For distributed operations, a combination of options may be the solution.

- **For a private WAN, should it be dedicated or switched?**- Real-time, high-volume transactions have special requirements that could favor a dedicated line, such as traffic flowing between the data center and the corporate head office. If the enterprise is connecting to a local single branch, a dedicated leased line could be used. However, that option would become very expensive for a WAN connecting multiple offices. In that case, a switched connection might be better.

- **For a public WAN, what type of VPN access is required?**- If the purpose of the WAN is to connect a remote office, a site-to-site VPN may be the best choice. To connect teleworkers or customers, remote-access VPNs are a better option. If the WAN is serving a mixture of remote offices, teleworkers, and authorized customers, such as a global company with distributed operations, a combination of VPN options may be required.

- **Which connection options are available locally?**- In some areas, not all WAN connection options are available. In this case, the selection process is simplified, although the resulting WAN may provide less than optimal performance. For example, in a rural or remote area, the only option may be VSAT or cellular access.

- **What is the cost of the available connection options?**- Depending on the option chosen, the WAN can be a significant ongoing expense. The cost of a particular option must be weighed against how well it meets the other requirements. For example, a dedicated leased line is the most expensive option, but the expense may be justified if it is critical to ensure secure transmission of high volumes of real-time data. For less demanding applications, a less expensive switched or Internet connection option may be more suitable.

Using the guidelines described above, as well as those described by the Cisco Enterprise Architecture, a network administrator should be able to choose an appropriate WAN connection to meet the requirements of different business scenarios.

Refer to
Lab Activity
for this chapter

2.2.4.3   Lab - Researching WAN Technologies
In this lab, you will complete the following objectives:

- Part 1: Investigate Dedicated WAN Technologies and Providers
- Part 2: Investigate a Dedicated Leased Line Service Provider in Your Area

Refer to
Online Course
for Illustration

2.3   Summary

Refer to
Lab Activity
for this chapter

2.3.1.1   Class Activity - WAN Device Modules

WAN Device Modules

Your medium-sized company is upgrading its network. To make the most of the equipment currently in use, you decide to purchase WAN modules instead of new equipment.

All branch offices use either Cisco 1900 or 2911 series ISRs. You will be updating these routers in several locations. Each branch has its own ISP requirements to consider.

To update the devices, focus on the following WAN modules access types:

- Ethernet
- Broadband
- T1/E1 and ISDN PRI
- BRI
- Serial
- T1 and E1 Trunk Voice and WAN
- Wireless LANs and WANs

Refer to
Online Course
for Illustration

2.3.1.2 Summary

A business can use private lines or the public network infrastructure for WAN connections. A public infrastructure connection can be a cost-effective alternative to a private connection between LANs, as long as security is also planned.

WAN access standards operate at Layers 1 and 2 of the OSI model, and are defined and managed by the TIA/EIA, ISO, and IEEE. A WAN may be circuit-switched or packet-switched.

There is common terminology used to identify the physical components of WAN connections and who, the service provider or the customer, is responsible for which components.

Service provider networks are complex and the service provider's backbone networks consist primarily of high-bandwidth fiber-optic media. The device used for interconnection to a customer is specific to the WAN technology that is implemented.

Permanent, dedicated point-to-point connections are provided by using leased lines. Dialup access, although slow, is still viable for remote areas with limited WAN options. Other private connection options include ISDN, Frame Relay, ATM, Ethernet WAN, MPLS, and VSAT.

Public infrastructure connections include DSL, cable, wireless, and 3G/4G cellular. Security over public infrastructure connections can be provided by using remote-access or site-to-site Virtual Private Networks (VPNs).

Go to the online course to take the quiz and exam.

Chapter 2 Quiz

This quiz is designed to provide an additional opportunity to practice the skills and knowledge presented in the chapter and to prepare for the chapter exam. You will be allowed multiple attempts and the grade does not appear in the gradebook.

Chapter 2 Exam

The chapter exam assesses your knowledge of the chapter content.

Your Chapter Notes

Point-to-Point Connections

3.0 Point-to-Point Connections

3.0.1.1 Introduction

One of the most common types of WAN connections, especially in long-distance communications, is a point-to-point connection, also called a serial or leased-line connection. Because these connections are typically provided by a carrier, such as a telephone company, boundaries between what is managed by the carrier and what is managed by the customer must be clearly established.

This chapter covers the terms, technology, and protocols used in serial connections. The HDLC and Point-to-Point Protocols (PPP) are introduced. PPP is a protocol that is able to handle authentication, compression, error detection, monitor link quality, and logically bundles multiple serial connections together to share the load.

Refer to **Lab Activity** for this chapter

3.0.1.2 Class Activity - PPP Persuasion

PPP Persuasion

Your network engineering supervisor recently attended a networking conference where Layer 2 protocols were discussed. He knows that you have Cisco equipment on the premises, but he would also like to offer security and advanced TCP/IP options and controls on that same equipment by using the Point-to-Point Protocol (PPP).

After researching the PPP protocol, you find it offers some advantages over the HDLC protocol, currently used on your network.

Create a matrix listing the advantages and disadvantages of using the HDLC vs. PPP protocols. When comparing the two protocols, include:

- Ease of configuration
- Adaptability to non-proprietary network equipment
- Security options
- Bandwidth usage and compression
- Bandwidth consolidation

Share your chart with another student or class. Justify whether or not you would suggest sharing the matrix with the network engineering supervisor to justify a change being made from HDLC to PPP for Layer 2 network connectivity.

Refer to
Interactive Graphic
in online course.

3.1   Serial Point-to-Point Overview

3.1.1   Serial Communications

3.1.1.1   Serial and Parallel Ports

One of the most common types of WAN connections is the point-to-point connection. As shown in Figure 1, point-to-point connections are used to connect LANs to service provider WANs, and to connect LAN segments within an enterprise network.

A LAN-to-WAN point-to-point connection is also referred to as a serial connection or leased-line connection. This is because the lines are leased from a carrier (usually a telephone company) and are dedicated for use by the company leasing the lines. Companies pay for a continuous connection between two remote sites, and the line is continuously active and available. Leased lines are a frequently used type of WAN access, and they are generally priced based on the bandwidth required and the distance between the two connected points.

Understanding how point-to-point serial communication across a leased line works is important to an overall understanding of how WANs function.

Communications across a serial connection is a method of data transmissions in which the bits are transmitted sequentially over a single channel. This is equivalent to a pipe only wide enough to fit one ball at a time. Multiple balls can only go into the pipe, but only one at a time, and they only have one exit point, the other end of the pipe. A serial port is bidirectional, and often referred to as a bidirectional port or a communications port.

This is in contrast to parallel communications in which bits can be transmitted simultaneously over multiple wires. As shown in Figure 2, a parallel connection theoretically transfers data eight times faster than a serial connection. Based on this theory, a parallel connection sends a byte (eight bits) in the time that a serial connection sends a single bit. However, parallel communications do have issues with crosstalk across wires, especially as the wire length increases. Clock skew is also an issue with parallel communications. Clock skew occurs when data across the various wires does not arrive at the same time, creating synchronization issues. Finally, most parallel communications supports only one-direction, outbound-only communication from the hard drive.

At one time, most PCs included both serial and parallel ports. Parallel ports were used to connect printers, computers, and other devices that required relatively high bandwidth. Parallel ports were also used between interior components. For external communications, a serial bus was primarily used for signal conversion. Because of their bidirectional ability, serial communications are considerably less expensive to implement. Serial communications use fewer wires, cheaper cables, and fewer connector pins.

On most PCs, parallel ports and RS-232 serial ports have been replaced by the higher speed serial Universal Serial Bus (USB) interfaces. However, for long-distance communication, many WANs use still serial transmission.

Refer to
Online Course
for Illustration

3.1.1.2   Serial Communication

The figure shows a simple representation of a serial communication across a WAN. Data is encapsulated by the communications protocol used by the sending router. The encapsulated frame is sent on a physical medium to the WAN. There are various ways to traverse the WAN, but the receiving router uses the same communications protocol to de-encapsulate the frame when it arrives.

There are many different serial communication standards, each one using a different signaling method. There are three important serial communication standards affecting LAN-to-WAN connections:

- **RS-232**- Most serial ports on personal computers conform to the RS-232C or newer RS-422 and RS-423 standards. Both 9-pin and 25-pin connectors are used. A serial port is a general-purpose interface that can be used for almost any type of device, including modems, mice, and printers. These types of peripheral devices for computers have been replaced by new and faster standards such as USB but many network devices use RJ-45 connectors that conform to the original RS-232 standard.

- **V.35**- Typically used for modem-to-multiplexer communication, this ITU standard for high-speed, synchronous data exchange combines the bandwidth of several telephone circuits. In the U.S., V.35 is the interface standard used by most routers and DSUs that connect to T1 carriers. V.35 cables are high-speed serial assemblies designed to support higher data rates and connectivity between DTEs and DCEs over digital lines. There is more on DTEs and DCEs later in this section.

- **HSSI**- A High-Speed Serial Interface (HSSI) supports transmission rates up to 52 Mb/s. Engineers use HSSI to connect routers on LANs with WANs over high-speed lines, such as T3 lines. Engineers also use HSSI to provide high-speed connectivity between LANs, using Token Ring or Ethernet. HSSI is a DTE/DCE interface developed by Cisco Systems and T3 plus Networking to address the need for high-speed communication over WAN links.

Refer to
Online Course
for Illustration

3.1.1.3   Point-to-Point Communication Links

When permanent dedicated connections are required, a point-to-point link is used to provide a single, pre-established WAN communications path from the customer premises, through the provider network, to a remote destination, as shown in the figure.

A point-to-point link can connect two geographically distant sites, such as a corporate office in New York and a regional office in London. For a point-to-point line, the carrier dedicates specific resources for a line that is leased by the customer (leased line).

Note   Point-to-point connections are not limited to connections that cross land. There are hundreds of thousands of miles of undersea fiber-optic cables that connect countries and continents worldwide. An Internet search of "undersea Internet cable map" produces several cable maps of these undersea connections.

Point-to-point links are usually more expensive than shared services. The cost of leased-line solutions can become significant when used to connect many sites over increasing distances. However, there are times when the benefits outweigh the cost of the leased line. The dedicated capacity removes latency or jitter between the endpoints. Constant availability is essential for some applications such as VoIP or video over IP.

Refer to
Online Course
for Illustration

3.1.1.4   Time-Division Multiplexing

With a leased line, despite the fact that customers are paying for dedicated services, and dedicated bandwidth is provided to the customer, the carrier still uses multiplexing technologies within the network. Multiplexing refers to a scheme that allows multiple logical signals to share a single physical channel. Two common types of multiplexing are time-division multiplexing (TDM) and statistical time-division multiplexing (STDM).

TDM

Bell Laboratories originally invented TDM to maximize the amount of voice traffic carried over a medium. Before multiplexing, each telephone call required its own physical link. This was an expensive and unscalable solution. TDM divides the bandwidth of a single link into separate time slots. TDM transmits two or more channels (data stream) over the same link by allocating a different time slot for the transmission of each channel. In effect, the channels take turns using the link.

TDM is a physical layer concept. It has no regard for the nature of the information that is multiplexed on to the output channel. TDM is independent of the Layer 2 protocol that has been used by the input channels.

TDM can be explained by an analogy to highway traffic. To transport traffic from four roads to another city, all traffic can be sent on one lane if the roads are equally serviced and the traffic is synchronized. If each of the four roads puts a car on to the main highway every four seconds, the highway gets a car at the rate of one each second. As long as the speed of all the cars is synchronized, there is no collision. At the destination, the reverse happens and the cars are taken off the highway and fed to the local roads by the same synchronous mechanism.

This is the principle used in synchronous TDM when sending data over a link. TDM increases the capacity of the transmission link by dividing transmission time into smaller, equal intervals so that the link carries the bits from multiple input sources.

In the figure, a multiplexer (MUX) at the transmitter accepts three separate signals. The MUX breaks each signal into segments. The MUX puts each segment into a single channel by inserting each segment into a time slot.

A MUX at the receiving end reassembles the TDM stream into the three separate data streams based only on the timing of the arrival of each bit. A technique called bit interleaving keeps track of the number and sequence of the bits from each specific transmission so that they can be quickly and efficiently reassembled into their original form upon receipt. Byte interleaving performs the same functions, but because there are eight bits in each byte, the process needs a bigger or longer time slot.

Refer to
Online Course
for Illustration

3.1.1.5   Statistical Time-Division Multiplexing

In another analogy, compare TDM to a train with 32 railroad cars. Each car is owned by a different freight company, and every day the train leaves with the 32 cars attached. If one of the companies has cargo to send, the car is loaded. If the company has nothing to send, the car remains empty, but stays on the train. Shipping empty containers is not very efficient. TDM shares this inefficiency when traffic is intermittent, because the time slot is still allocated even when the channel has no data to transmit.

STDM

STDM was developed to overcome this inefficiency. STDM uses a variable time slot length allowing channels to compete for any free slot space. It employs a buffer memory that temporarily stores the data during periods of peak traffic. STDM does not waste high-speed line time with inactive channels using this scheme. STDM requires each transmission to carry identification information or a channel identifier.

Refer to **Online Course** for Illustration

3.1.1.6 TDM Examples

SONET and SDH

On a larger scale, the telecommunications industry uses the Synchronous Optical Networking (SONET) or Synchronous Digital Hierarchy (SDH) standard for optical transport of TDM data. SONET, used in North America, and SDH, used elsewhere, are two closely-related standards that specify interface parameters, rates, framing formats, multiplexing methods, and management for synchronous TDM over fiber.

The figure displays SONET, which is an example of STDM. SONET/SDH takes n bit streams, multiplexes them, and optically modulates the signals. It then sends the signals out using a light emitting device over fiber with a bit rate equal to (incoming bit rate) x n. Thus, traffic arriving at the SONET multiplexer from four places at 2.5 Gb/s goes out as a single stream at 4 x 2.5 Gb/s, or 10 Gb/s. This principle is illustrated in the figure, which shows an increase in the bit rate by a factor of four in time slot T.

Refer to **Online Course** for Illustration

3.1.1.7 Demarcation Point

Prior to deregulation in North America and other countries, telephone companies owned the local loop, including the wiring and equipment on the premises of the customers. The local loop refers to the line from the premises of a telephone subscriber to the telephone company central office. Deregulation forced telephone companies to unbundle their local loop infrastructure to allow other suppliers to provide equipment and services. This led to a need to delineate which part of the network the telephone company owned and which part the customer owned. This point of delineation is the demarcation point, or demarc. The demarcation point marks the point where your network interfaces with a network that is owned by another organization. In telephone terminology, this is the interface between customer premises equipment (CPE) and network service provider equipment. The demarcation point is the point in the network where the responsibility of the service provider ends, as shown in Figure 1.

The differences in demarcation points can best be shown using ISDN. In the United States, a service provider provides the local loop into the customer premises, and the customer provides the active equipment such as the CSU/DSU on which the local loop is terminated. This termination often occurs in a telecommunications closet, and the customer is responsible for maintaining, replacing, or repairing the equipment. In other countries, the network terminating unit (NTU) is provided and managed by the service provider. This allows the service provider to actively manage and troubleshoot the local loop with the demarcation point occurring after the NTU. The customer connects a CPE device, such as a router or Frame Relay access device, to the NTU using a V.35 or RS-232 serial interface.

A router serial port is required for each leased-line connection. If the underlying network is based on the T-carrier or E-carrier technologies, the leased line connects to the network of the carrier through a CSU/DSU. The purpose of the CSU/DSU is to provide a clocking signal to the customer equipment interface from the DSU and terminate the channelized transport media of the carrier on the CSU. The CSU also provides diagnostic functions such as a loopback test.

As shown in Figure 2, most T1 or E1 TDM interfaces on current routers include CSU/DSU capabilities. A separate CSU/DSU is not required because this functionality is embedded in the interface. IOS commands are used to configure the CSU/DSU operations.

Refer to
Online Course
for Illustration

3.1.1.8   DTE-DCE

From the point of view of connecting to the WAN, a serial connection has a DTE device at one end of the connection and a DCE device at the other end. The connection between the two DCE devices is the WAN service provider transmission network, as shown in the figure. In this example:

- The CPE, which is generally a router, is the DTE. The DTE could also be a terminal, computer, printer, or fax machine if they connect directly to the service provider network.

- The DCE, commonly a modem or CSU/DSU, is the device used to convert the user data from the DTE into a form acceptable to the WAN service provider transmission link. This signal is received at the remote DCE, which decodes the signal back into a sequence of bits. The remote DCE then signals this sequence to the remote DTE.

The Electronics Industry Association (EIA) and the International Telecommunication Union Telecommunications Standardization Sector (ITU-T) have been most active in the development of standards that allow DTEs to communicate with DCEs.

Refer to
Online Course
for Illustration

3.1.1.9   Serial Cables

Originally, the concept of DCEs and DTEs was based on two types of equipment: terminal equipment that generated or received data, and the communication equipment that only relayed data. In the development of the RS-232 standard, there were reasons why 25-pin RS-232 connectors on these two types of equipment must be wired differently. These reasons are no longer significant, but there are two different types of cables remaining: one for connecting a DTE to a DCE, and another for connecting two DTEs directly to each other.

The DTE/DCE interface for a particular standard defines the following specifications:

- **Mechanical/physical**- Number of pins and connector type

- **Electrical**- Defines voltage levels for 0 and 1

- **Functional**- Specifies the functions that are performed by assigning meanings to each of the signaling lines in the interface

- **Procedural**- Specifies the sequence of events for transmitting data

The original RS-232 standard only defined the connection of DTEs with DCEs, which were modems. However, to connect two DTEs, such as two computers or two routers in a lab, a special cable called a null modem eliminates the need for a DCE. In other words, the two devices can be connected without a modem. A null modem is a communication method to directly connect two DTEs using a RS-232 serial cable. With a null modem connection, the transmit (Tx) and receive (Rx) lines are cross-linked as shown in Figure 1.

The cable for the DTE to DCE connection is a shielded serial transition cable. The router end of the shielded serial transition cable may be a DB-60 connector, which connects to the DB-60 port on a serial WAN interface card, as shown in Figure 2. The other end of the serial transition cable is available with the connector appropriate for the standard that is to be used. The WAN provider or the CSU/DSU usually dictates this cable type. Cisco devices support the EIA/TIA-232, EIA/TIA-449, V.35, X.21, and EIA/TIA-530 serial standards, as shown in Figure 3.

To support higher port densities in a smaller form factor, Cisco has introduced a Smart Serial cable, as shown in Figure 4. The router interface end of the Smart Serial cable is a 26-pin connector that is significantly more compact than the DB-60 connector.

When using a null modem, synchronous connections require a clock signal. An external device can generate the signal, or one of the DTEs can generate the clock signal. When a DTE and DCE are connected, the serial port on a router is the DTE end of the connection, by default, and the clock signal is typically provided by a CSU/DSU, or similar DCE device. However, when using a null modem cable in a router-to-router connection, one of the serial interfaces must be configured as the DCE end to provide the clock signal for the connection, as shown in Figure 5.

Refer to
Online Course
for Illustration

3.1.1.10 Serial Bandwidth

Bandwidth refers to the rate at which data is transferred over the communication link. The underlying carrier technology depends on the bandwidth available. There is a difference in bandwidth points between the North American (T-carrier) specification and the European (E-carrier) system. Optical networks also use a different bandwidth hierarchy, which again differs between North America and Europe. In the U.S., Optical Carrier (OC) defines the bandwidth points.

In North America, the bandwidth is usually expressed as a digital signal level number (DS0, DS1, etc.), which refers to the rate and format of the signal. The most fundamental line speed is 64 kb/s, or DS-0, which is the bandwidth required for an uncompressed, digitized phone call. Serial connection bandwidths can be incrementally increased to accommodate the need for faster transmission. For example, 24 DS0s can be bundled to get a DS1 line (also called a T1 line) with a speed of 1.544 Mb/s. Also, 28 DS1s can be bundled to get a DS3 line (also called a T3 line) with a speed of 44.736 Mb/s. Leased lines are available in different capacities and are generally priced based on the bandwidth required and the distance between the two connected points.

OC transmission rates are a set of standardized specifications for the transmission of digital signals carried on SONET fiber-optic networks. The designation uses OC, followed by an integer value representing the base transmission rate of 51.84 Mb/s. For example, OC-1 has a transmission capacity of 51.84 Mb/s, whereas an OC-3 transmission medium would be three times 51.84 Mb/s, or 155.52 Mb/s.

The figure lists the most common line types and the associated bit rate capacity of each.

Note E1 (2.048 Mb/s) and E3 (34.368 Mb/s) are European standards like T1 and T3, but with different bandwidths and frame structures.

Refer to
Interactive Graphic
in online course.

3.1.1.11 Activity - Identify the Serial Communications Terminology

Refer to
Online Course
for Illustration

3.1.2 HDLC Encapsulation

3.1.2.1 WAN Encapsulation Protocols

On each WAN connection, data is encapsulated into frames before crossing the WAN link. To ensure that the correct protocol is used, the appropriate Layer 2 encapsulation type must be configured. The choice of protocol depends on the WAN technology and the communicating equipment. The figure displays the more common WAN protocols and where they are used. The following are short descriptions of each type of WAN protocol:

- **HDLC-** The default encapsulation type on point-to-point connections, dedicated links, and circuit-switched connections when the link uses two Cisco devices. HDLC is now the basis for synchronous PPP used by many servers to connect to a WAN, most commonly the Internet.

- **PPP-** Provides router-to-router and host-to-network connections over synchronous and asynchronous circuits. PPP works with several network layer protocols, such as IPv4 and IPv6. PPP uses the HDLC encapsulation protocol, but also has built-in security mechanisms such as PAP and CHAP.

- **Serial Line Internet Protocol (SLIP)-** A standard protocol for point-to-point serial connections using TCP/IP. SLIP has been largely displaced by PPP.

- **X.25/Link Access Procedure, Balanced (LAPB)-** An ITU-T standard that defines how connections between a DTE and DCE are maintained for remote terminal access and computer communications in public data networks. X.25 specifies LAPB, a data link layer protocol. X.25 is a predecessor to Frame Relay.

- **Frame Relay-** An industry standard, switched, data link layer protocol that handles multiple virtual circuits. Frame Relay is a next generation protocol after X.25. Frame Relay eliminates some of the time-consuming processes (such as error correction and flow control) employed in X.25.

- **ATM-** The international standard for cell relay in which devices send multiple service types, such as voice, video, or data, in fixed-length (53-byte) cells. Fixed-length cells allow processing to occur in hardware; thereby, reducing transit delays. ATM takes advantage of high-speed transmission media such as E3, SONET, and T3.

Refer to
Online Course
for Illustration

3.1.2.2 HDLC Encapsulation

HDLC is a bit-oriented synchronous data link layer protocol developed by the International Organization for Standardization (ISO). The current standard for HDLC is ISO 13239. HDLC was developed from the Synchronous Data Link Control (SDLC) standard proposed in the 1970s. HDLC provides both connection-oriented and connectionless service.

HDLC uses synchronous serial transmission to provide error-free communication between two points. HDLC defines a Layer 2 framing structure that allows for flow control and error control through the use of acknowledgments. Each frame has the same format, whether it is a data frame or a control frame.

When frames are transmitted over synchronous or asynchronous links, those links have no mechanism to mark the beginning or end of frames. For this reason, HDLC uses a frame delimiter, or flag, to mark the beginning and the end of each frame.

Cisco has developed an extension to the HLDC protocol to solve the inability to provide multiprotocol support. Although Cisco HLDC (also referred to as cHDLC) is proprietary, Cisco has allowed many other network equipment vendors to implement it. Cisco HDLC frames contain a field for identifying the network protocol being encapsulated. The figure compares standard HLDC to Cisco HLDC.

Refer to
Online Course
for Illustration

3.1.2.3   HDLC Frame Types

HDLC defines three types of frames, each with a different control field format.

Flag

The flag field initiates and terminates error checking. The frame always starts and ends with an 8-bit flag field. The bit pattern is 01111110. Because there is a likelihood that this pattern occurs in the actual data, the sending HDLC system always inserts a 0 bit after every five consecutive 1s in the data field, so in practice the flag sequence can only occur at the frame ends. The receiving system strips out the inserted bits. When frames are transmitted consecutively, the end flag of the first frame is used as the start flag of the next frame.

Address

The address field contains the HDLC address of the secondary station. This address can contain a specific address, a group address, or a broadcast address. A primary address is either a communication source or a destination, which eliminates the need to include the address of the primary.

Control

The control field uses three different formats, depending on the type of HDLC frame used:

- **Information (I) Frame**- I-frames carry upper layer information and some control information. This frame sends and receives sequence numbers, and the poll final (P/F) bit performs flow and error control. The send sequence number refers to the number of the frame to be sent next. The receive sequence number provides the number of the frame to be received next. Both sender and receiver maintain send and receive sequence numbers. A primary station uses the P/F bit to tell the secondary whether it requires an immediate response. A secondary station uses the P/F bit to tell the primary whether the current frame is the last in its current response.

- **Supervisory (S) Frame**- S-frames provide control information. An S-frame can request and suspend transmission, report on status, and acknowledge receipt of I-frames. S-frames do not have an information field.

- **Unnumbered (U) Frame**- U-frames support control purposes and are not sequenced. Depending on the function of the U-frame, its control field is 1 or 2 bytes. Some U-frames have an information field.

Protocol

Only used in Cisco HDLC. This field specifies the protocol type encapsulated within the frame (e.g. 0x0800 for IP).

Data

The data field contains a Path Information Unit (PIU) or Exchange Identification (XID) information.

Frame Check Sequence (FCS)

The FCS precedes the ending flag delimiter and is usually a Cyclic Redundancy Check (CRC) calculation remainder. The CRC calculation is redone in the receiver. If the result differs from the value in the original frame, an error is assumed.

Refer to
Online Course
for Illustration

3.1.2.4   Configuring HDLC Encapsulation

Cisco HDLC is the default encapsulation method used by Cisco devices on synchronous serial lines.

Use Cisco HDLC as a point-to-point protocol on leased lines between two Cisco devices. If connecting non-Cisco devices, use synchronous PPP.

If the default encapsulation method has been changed, use the `encapsulation hdlc` command in privileged EXEC mode to re-enable HDLC.

As shown in the figure, there are two steps to re-enable HDLC encapsulation:

Step 1.   Enter the interface configuration mode of the serial interface.

Step 2.   Enter the `encapsulation hdlc` command to specify the encapsulation protocol on the interface.

Refer to
Online Course
for Illustration

3.1.2.5   Troubleshooting a Serial Interface

The output of the `show interfaces serial` command displays information specific to serial interfaces. When HDLC is configured, encapsulation HDLC should be reflected in the output, as highlighted in Figure 1. Serial 0/0/0 is up, line protocol is up, indicates that the line is up and functioning; encapsulation HDLC, indicates that the default serial encapsulation (HDLC) is enabled.

The `show interfaces serial` command returns one of six possible states:

- Serial x is up, line protocol is up
- Serial x is down, line protocol is down
- Serial x is up, line protocol is down
- Serial x is up, line protocol is up (looped)
- Serial x is up, line protocol is down (disabled)
- Serial x is administratively down, line protocol is down

Of the six possible states, there are five problem states. Figure 2 lists the five problem states, the issues associated with that state, and how to troubleshoot the issue.

The `show controllers` command is another important diagnostic tool when troubleshooting serial lines, as shown in Figure 3. The output indicates the state of the interface channels and whether a cable is attached to the interface. In the figure, interface serial 0/0/0 has a V.35 DCE cable attached. The command syntax varies, depending on the platform. Cisco 7000 series routers use a cBus controller card for connecting serial links. With these routers, use the `show controllers cbus` command.

If the electrical interface output displays as UNKNOWN instead of V.35, EIA/TIA-449, or some other electrical interface type, the likely problem is an improperly connected cable. A problem with the internal wiring of the card is also possible. If the electrical interface is unknown, the corresponding display for the **show interfaces serial** command shows that the interface and line protocol are down.

Refer to **Interactive Graphic** in online course.

3.1.2.6   Syntax Checker - Troubleshooting a Serial Interface

Refer to **Packet Tracer Activity** for this chapter

3.1.2.7   Packet Tracer - Troubleshooting Serial Interfaces

Background/Scenario

You have been asked to troubleshoot WAN connections for a local telephone company (Telco). The Telco router is supposed to communicate with four remote sites, but none of them are working. Use your knowledge of the OSI model and a few general rules to identify and repair the errors in the network.

Refer to **Online Course** for Illustration

3.2   PPP Operation

3.2.1   Benefits of PPP

3.2.1.1   Introducing PPP

Recall that HDLC is the default serial encapsulation method when connecting two Cisco routers. With an added protocol type field, the Cisco version of HDLC is proprietary. Thus, Cisco HDLC can only work with other Cisco devices. However, when there is a need to connect to a non-Cisco router, PPP encapsulation should be used, as shown in the figure.

PPP encapsulation has been carefully designed to retain compatibility with most commonly used supporting hardware. PPP encapsulates data frames for transmission over Layer 2 physical links. PPP establishes a direct connection using serial cables, phone lines, trunk lines, cellular telephones, specialized radio links, or fiber-optic links.

PPP contains three main components:

- HDLC-like framing for transporting multiprotocol packets over point-to-point links.

- Extensible Link Control Protocol (LCP) for establishing, configuring, and testing the data-link connection.

- Family of Network Control Protocols (NCPs) for establishing and configuring different network layer protocols. PPP allows the simultaneous use of multiple network layer protocols. Some of the more common NCPs are Internet Protocol (IPv4) Control Protocol, IPv6 Control Protocol, AppleTalk Control Protocol, Novell IPX Control Protocol, Cisco Systems Control Protocol, SNA Control Protocol, and Compression Control Protocol.

Refer to
Online Course
for Illustration

3.2.1.2   Advantages of PPP

PPP originally emerged as an encapsulation protocol for transporting IPv4 traffic over point-to-point links. PPP provides a standard method for transporting multiprotocol packets over point-to-point links.

There are many advantages to using PPP including the fact that it is not proprietary. PPP includes many features not available in HDLC:

- The link quality management feature, as shown in the figure, monitors the quality of the link. If too many errors are detected, PPP takes the link down.

- PPP supports PAP and CHAP authentication. This feature is explained and practiced in a later section.

Refer to
Online Course
for Illustration

3.2.2   LCP and NCP

3.2.2.1   PPP Layered Architecture

A layered architecture is a logical model, design, or blueprint that aids in communication between interconnecting layers. The figure maps the layered architecture of PPP against the Open System Interconnection (OSI) model. PPP and OSI share the same physical layer, but PPP distributes the functions of LCP and NCP differently.

At the physical layer, you can configure PPP on a range of interfaces, including:

- Asynchronous serial

- Synchronous serial

- HSSI

- ISDN

PPP operates across any DTE/DCE interface (RS-232-C, RS-422, RS-423, or V.35). The only absolute requirement imposed by PPP is a full-duplex circuit, either dedicated or switched, that can operate in either an asynchronous or synchronous bit-serial mode, transparent to PPP link layer frames. PPP does not impose any restrictions regarding transmission rate other than those imposed by the particular DTE/DCE interface in use.

Most of the work done by PPP is at the data link and network layers by the LCP and NCPs. The LCP sets up the PPP connection and its parameters, the NCPs handle higher layer protocol configurations, and the LCP terminates the PPP connection.

Refer to
Online Course
for Illustration

3.2.2.2   PPP – Link Control Protocol (LCP)

The LCP functions within the data link layer and has a role in establishing, configuring, and testing the data-link connection. The LCP establishes the point-to-point link. The LCP also negotiates and sets up control options on the WAN data link, which are handled by the NCPs.

The LCP provides automatic configuration of the interfaces at each end, including:

- Handling varying limits on packet size

- Detecting common misconfiguration errors

■ Terminating the link

■ Determining when a link is functioning properly or when it is failing

After the link is established, PPP also uses the LCP to agree automatically on encapsulation formats such as authentication, compression, and error detection.

Refer to
Online Course
for Illustration

3.2.2.3   PPP – Network Control Protocol (NCP)

PPP permits multiple network layer protocols to operate on the same communications link. For every network layer protocol used, PPP uses a separate NCP, as shown in Figure 1. For example, IPv4 uses the IP Control Protocol (IPCP) and IPv6 uses IPv6 Control Protocol (IPv6CP).

NCPs include functional fields containing standardized codes to indicate the network layer protocol that PPP encapsulates. Figure 2 lists the PPP protocol field numbers. Each NCP manages the specific needs required by its respective network layer protocols. The various NCP components encapsulate and negotiate options for multiple network layer protocols.

Refer to
Online Course
for Illustration

3.2.2.4   PPP Frame Structure

A PPP frame consists of six fields. The following descriptions summarize the PPP frame fields illustrated in the figure:

■ **Flag**- A single byte that indicates the beginning or end of a frame. The flag field consists of the binary sequence 01111110. In successive PPP frames, only a single Flag character is used.

■ **Address**- A single byte that contains the binary sequence 11111111, the standard broadcast address. PPP does not assign individual station addresses.

■ **Control**- A single byte that contains the binary sequence 00000011, which calls for transmission of user data in an unsequenced frame. This provides a connectionless link service that does require the establishment of data links or links stations. On a point-to-point link, the destination node does not need to be addressed. Therefore, for PPP, the Address field is set to 0xFF, the broadcast address. If both PPP peers agree to perform address and control field compression during the LCP negotiation, the Address field is not included.

■ **Protocol**- Two bytes that identify the protocol encapsulated in the information field of the frame. The 2-byte Protocol field identifies the protocol of the PPP payload. If both PPP peers agree to perform protocol field compression during LCP negotiation, the Protocol field is one byte for the protocol identification in the range 0x00-00 to 0x00-FF. The most up-to-date values of the protocol field are specified in the most recent Assigned Numbers Request For Comments (RFC).

■ **Data**- Zero or more bytes that contain the datagram for the protocol specified in the protocol field. The end of the information field is found by locating the closing flag sequence and allowing 2 bytes for the FCS field. The default maximum length of the information field is 1,500 bytes. By prior agreement, consenting PPP implementations can use other values for the maximum information field length.

- **Frame Check Sequence (FCS)**- Normally 16 bits (2 bytes). By prior agreement, consenting PPP implementations can use a 32-bit (4-byte) FCS for improved error detection. If the receiver's calculation of the FCS does not match the FCS in the PPP frame, the PPP frame is silently discarded.

LCPs can negotiate modifications to the standard PPP frame structure. Modified frames, however, are always distinguishable from standard frames.

Refer to
Interactive Graphic
in online course.

3.2.2.5   Activity - Identify PPP Features and Operations

Refer to
Online Course
for Illustration

3.2.3   PPP Sessions

3.2.3.1   Establishing a PPP Session

There are three phases of establishing a PPP session, as shown in the figure:

- **Phase 1: Link establishment and configuration negotiation**- Before PPP exchanges any network layer datagrams, such as IP, the LCP must first open the connection and negotiate configuration options. This phase is complete when the receiving router sends a configuration-acknowledgment frame back to the router initiating the connection.

- **Phase 2: Link quality determination (optional)**- The LCP tests the link to determine whether the link quality is sufficient to bring up network layer protocols. The LCP can delay transmission of network layer protocol information until this phase is complete.

- **Phase 3: Network layer protocol configuration negotiation**- After the LCP has finished the link quality determination phase, the appropriate NCP can separately configure the network layer protocols, and bring them up and take them down at any time. If the LCP closes the link, it informs the network layer protocols so that they can take appropriate action.

The link remains configured for communications until explicit LCP or NCP frames close the link, or until some external event occurs such as an inactivity timer expiring, or an administrator intervening.

The LCP can terminate the link at any time. This is usually done when one of the routers requests termination, but can happen because of a physical event, such as the loss of a carrier or the expiration of an idle-period timer.

Refer to
Online Course
for Illustration

3.2.3.2   LCP Operation

LCP operation includes provisions for link establishment, link maintenance, and link termination. LCP operation uses three classes of LCP frames to accomplish the work of each of the LCP phases:

- Link-establishment frames establish and configure a link (Configure-Request, Configure-Ack, Configure-Nak, and Configure-Reject).

- Link-maintenance frames manage and debug a link (Code-Reject, Protocol-Reject, Echo-Request, Echo-Reply, and Discard-Request).

- Link-termination frames terminate a link (Terminate-Request and Terminate-Ack).

Link Establishment

Link establishment is the first phase of LCP operation, as seen in Figure 1. This phase must complete successfully, before any network layer packets can be exchanged. During link establishment, the LCP opens the connection and negotiates the configuration parameters. The link establishment process starts with the initiating device sending a Configure-Request frame to the responder. The Configure-Request frame includes a variable number of configuration options needed to set up on the link.

The initiator includes the options for how it wants the link created, including protocol or authentication parameters. The responder processes the request:

- If the options are not acceptable or not recognized the responder sends a Configure-Nak or Configure-Reject message. If this occurs and the negotiation fails, the initiator must restart the process with new options.

- If the options are acceptable, the responder responds with a Configure-Ack message and the process moves on to the authentication stage. The operation of the link is handed over to the NCP.

When NCP has completed all necessary configurations, including validating authentication if configured, the line is available for data transfer. During the exchange of data, LCP transitions into link maintenance.

Link Maintenance

During link maintenance, LCP can use messages to provide feedback and test the link, as shown in Figure 2.

- **Echo-Request, Echo-Reply, and Discard-Request**- These frames can be used for testing the link.

- **Code-Reject and Protocol-Reject**- These frame types provide feedback when one device receives an invalid frame due to either an unrecognized LCP code (LCP frame type) or a bad protocol identifier. For example, if an interpretable packet is received from the peer, a Code-Reject packet is sent in response. The sending device will resend the packet.

Link Termination

After the transfer of data at the network layer completes, the LCP terminates the link, as shown in Figure 3. NCP only terminates the network layer and NCP link. The link remains open until the LCP terminates it. If the LCP terminates the link before NCP, the NCP session is also terminated.

PPP can terminate the link at any time. This might happen because of the loss of the carrier, authentication failure, link quality failure, the expiration of an idle-period timer, or the administrative closing of the link. The LCP closes the link by exchanging Terminate packets. The device initiating the shutdown sends a Terminate-Request message. The other device replies with a Terminate-Ack. A termination request indicates that the device sending it needs to close the link. When the link is closing, PPP informs the network layer protocols so that they may take appropriate action.

Refer to
Online Course
for Illustration

3.2.3.3   LCP Packet

Figure 1 shows the fields in an LCP packet:

- **Code**- The code field is 1 byte in length and identifies the type of LCP packet.

- **Identifier**- The identifier field is 1 byte in length and is used to match packet requests and replies.

- **Length**- The length field is 2 bytes in length and indicates the total length (including all fields) of the LCP packet.

- **Data**- The data field is 0 or more bytes as indicated by the length field. The format of this field is determined by the code.

Each LCP packet is a single LCP message consisting of an LCP code field identifying the type of LCP packet, an identifier field so that requests and replies can be matched, and a length field indicating the size of the LCP packet and LCP packet type-specific data.

Each LCP packet has a specific function in the exchange of configuration information depending on its packet type. The code field of the LCP packet identifies the packet type according to Figure 2.

Refer to
Online Course
for Illustration

3.2.3.4   PPP Configuration Options

PPP can be configured to support various optional functions, as shown in Figure 1. These optional functions include:

- Authentication using either PAP or CHAP

- Compression using either Stacker or Predictor

- Multilink that combines two or more channels to increase the WAN bandwidth

To negotiate the use of these PPP options, the LCP link-establishment frames contain option information in the data field of the LCP frame, as shown in Figure 2. If a configuration option is not included in an LCP frame, the default value for that configuration option is assumed.

This phase is complete when a configuration acknowledgment frame has been sent and received.

Refer to
Online Course
for Illustration

3.2.3.5   NCP Explained

NCP Process

After the link has been initiated, the LCP passes control to the appropriate NCP.

Although initially designed for IP packets, PPP can carry data from multiple network layer protocols by using a modular approach in its implementation. PPP's modular model allows LCP to set up the link and then transfer the details of a network protocol to a specific NCP. Each network protocol has a corresponding NCP and each NCP has a corresponding RFC.

There are NCPs for IPv4, IPv6, IPX, AppleTalk, and many others. NCPs use the same packet format as the LCPs.

After the LCP has configured and authenticated the basic link, the appropriate NCP is invoked to complete the specific configuration of the network layer protocol being used. When the NCP has successfully configured the network layer protocol, the network protocol is in the open state on the established LCP link. At this point, PPP can carry the corresponding network layer protocol packets.

IPCP Example

As an example of how the NCP layer works, the NCP configuration of IPv4, which is the most common Layer 3 protocol, is shown in the figure. After LCP has established the link, the routers exchange IPCP messages, negotiating options specific to the IPv4 protocol. IPCP is responsible for configuring, enabling, and disabling the IPv4 modules on both ends of the link. IPV6CP is an NCP with the same responsibilities for IPv6.

IPCP negotiates two options:

- **Compression**- Allows devices to negotiate an algorithm to compress TCP and IP headers and save bandwidth. The Van Jacobson TCP/IP header compression reduces the size of the TCP/IP headers to as few as 3 bytes. This can be a significant improvement on slow serial lines, particularly for interactive traffic.

- **IPv4-Address**- Allows the initiating device to specify an IPv4 address to use for routing IP over the PPP link, or to request an IPv4 address for the responder. Prior to the advent of broadband technologies such as DSL and cable modem services, dialup network links commonly used the IPv4 address option.

After the NCP process is complete, the link goes into the open state and LCP takes over again in a link maintenance phase. Link traffic consists of any possible combination of LCP, NCP, and network layer protocol packets. When data transfer is complete, NCP terminates the protocol link; LCP terminates the PPP connection.

Refer to **Interactive Graphic** in online course.

3.2.3.6   Activity - Identify the Steps in the LCP Link Negotiation Process

Refer to **Online Course** for Illustration

3.3   Configure PPP

3.3.1   Configure PPP

3.3.1.1   PPP Configuration Options

In the previous section, configurable LCP options were introduced to meet specific WAN connection requirements. PPP may include the following LCP options:

- **Authentication**- Peer routers exchange authentication messages. Two authentication choices are Password Authentication Protocol (PAP) and Challenge Handshake Authentication Protocol (CHAP).

- **Compression**- Increases the effective throughput on PPP connections by reducing the amount of data in the frame that must travel across the link. The protocol decompresses the frame at its destination. Two compression protocols available in Cisco routers are Stacker and Predictor.

- **Error detection**- Identifies fault conditions. The Quality and Magic Number options help ensure a reliable, loop-free data link. The Magic Number field helps in detecting links that are in a looped-back condition. Until the Magic-Number Configuration Option has been successfully negotiated, the Magic-Number must be transmitted as zero. Magic numbers are generated randomly at each end of the connection.

- **PPP Callback**- PPP callback is used to enhance security. With this LCP option, a Cisco router can act as a callback client or a callback server. The client makes the initial call, requests that the server call it back, and terminates its initial call. The callback router answers the initial call and makes the return call to the client based on its configuration statements. The command is `ppp callback [accept | request]`.

- **Multilink**- This alternative provides load balancing over the router interfaces that PPP uses. Multilink PPP, also referred to as MP, MPPP, MLP, or Multilink, provides a method for spreading traffic across multiple physical WAN links while providing packet fragmentation and reassembly, proper sequencing, multivendor interoperability, and load balancing on inbound and outbound traffic.

When options are configured, a corresponding field value is inserted into the LCP option field.

Refer to
Online Course
for Illustration

3.3.1.2 PPP Basic Configuration Command

Enabling PPP on an Interface

To set PPP as the encapsulation method used by a serial interface, use the `encapsulation ppp` interface configuration command.

The following example enables PPP encapsulation on interface serial 0/0/0:

```
R3# configure terminal
R3(config)# interface serial 0/0/0
R3(config-if)# encapsulation ppp
```

The `encapsulation ppp` interface command has no arguments. Remember that if PPP is not configured on a Cisco router, the default encapsulation for serial interfaces is HDLC.

The figure shows that routers R1 and R2 have been configured with both an IPv4 and an IPv6 address on the serial interfaces. PPP is a Layer 2 encapsulation that supports various Layer 3 protocols including IPv4 and IPv6.

Refer to
Online Course
for Illustration

3.3.1.3 PPP Compression Commands

Point-to-point software compression on serial interfaces can be configured after PPP encapsulation is enabled. Because this option invokes a software compression process, it can affect system performance. If the traffic already consists of compressed files, such as .zip, .tar, or .mpeg, do not use this option. The figure shows the command syntax for the `compress` command.

To configure compression over PPP, enter the following commands:

```
R3(config)# interface serial 0/0/0
R3(config-if)# encapsulation ppp
R3(config-if)# compress [ predictor | stac ]
```

Refer to
Online Course
for Illustration

3.3.1.4 PPP Link Quality Monitoring Command

Recall that LCP provides an optional link quality determination phase. In this phase, LCP tests the link to determine whether the link quality is sufficient to use Layer 3 protocols.

The **ppp quality** percentage command ensures that the link meets the quality requirement set; otherwise, the link closes down.

The percentages are calculated for both incoming and outgoing directions. The outgoing quality is calculated by comparing the total number of packets and bytes sent to the total number of packets and bytes received by the destination node. The incoming quality is calculated by comparing the total number of packets and bytes received to the total number of packets and bytes sent by the destination node.

If the link quality percentage is not maintained, the link is deemed to be of poor quality and is taken down. Link Quality Monitoring (LQM) implements a time lag so that the link does not bounce up and down.

The following configuration example monitors the data dropped on the link and avoids frame looping, as shown in Figure 1:

```
R3(config)# interface serial 0/0/0
R3(config-if)# encapsulation ppp
R3(config-if)# ppp quality 80
```

Use the **no ppp quality** command to disable LQM.

Use the Syntax Checker in Figure 2 to configure PPP encapsulation, compression, and LQM on router R1's Serial 0/0/1 interface.

Refer to
Online Course
for Illustration

3.3.1.5 PPP Multilink Commands

Multilink PPP (also referred to as MP, MPPP, MLP, or Multilink) provides a method for spreading traffic across multiple physical WAN links. Multilink PPP also provides packet fragmentation and reassembly, proper sequencing, multivendor interoperability, and load balancing on inbound and outbound traffic.

MPPP allows packets to be fragmented and sends these fragments simultaneously over multiple point-to-point links to the same remote address. The multiple physical links come up in response to a user-defined load threshold. MPPP can measure the load on just inbound traffic, or on just outbound traffic, but not on the combined load of both inbound and outbound traffic.

Configuring MPPP requires two steps, as shown in the figure.

Step 1. Create a multilink bundle.

- The **interface multilink** number command creates the multilink interface.

- In interface configuration mode, an IP address is assigned to the multilink interface. In this example, both IPv4 and IPv6 addresses are configured on routers R3 and R4.

- The interface is enabled for multilink PPP.

- The interface is assigned a multilink group number.

Step 2.   Assign interfaces to the multilink bundle. Each interface that is part of the multilink group:

- Is enabled for PPP encapsulation.

- Is enabled for multilink PPP.

- Is bound to the multilink bundle using the multilink group number configured in Step 1.

To disable PPP multilink, use the `no ppp multilink` command.

3.3.1.6   Verifying PPP Configuration

Use the `show interfaces serial` command to verify proper configuration of HDLC or PPP encapsulation. The command output in Figure 1 shows a PPP configuration.

When you configure HDLC, the output of the `show interfaces serial` command should display `encapsulation HDLC`. When PPP is configured, the LCP and NCP states also display. Notice that NCPs IPCP and IPV6CP are open for IPv4 and IPv6 because R1 and R2 were configured with both IPv4 and IPv6 addresses.

Figure 2 summarizes commands used when verifying PPP.

The `show ppp multilink` command verifies that PPP multilink is enabled on R3, as shown in Figure 3. The output indicates the interface Multilink 1, the hostnames of both the local and remote endpoints, and the serial interfaces assigned to the multilink bundle.

3.3.2   PPP Authentication

3.3.2.1   PPP Authentication Protocols

PPP defines an extensible LCP that allows negotiation of an authentication protocol for authenticating its peer before allowing network layer protocols to transmit over the link. RFC 1334 defines two protocols for authentication, PAP and CHAP, as shown in the figure.

PAP is a very basic two-way process. There is no encryption. The username and password are sent in plaintext. If it is accepted, the connection is allowed. CHAP is more secure than PAP. It involves a three-way exchange of a shared secret.

The authentication phase of a PPP session is optional. If used, the peer is authenticated after LCP establishes the link and chooses the authentication protocol. If it is used, authentication takes place before the network layer protocol configuration phase begins.

The authentication options require that the calling side of the link enter authentication information. This helps to ensure that the user has the permission of the network administrator to make the call. Peer routers exchange authentication messages.

3.3.2.2   Password Authentication Protocol (PAP)

One of the many features of PPP is that it performs Layer 2 authentication in addition to other layers of authentication, encryption, access control, and general security procedures.

Initiating PAP

PAP provides a simple method for a remote node to establish its identity using a two-way handshake. PAP is not interactive. When the `ppp authentication pap` command is used, the username and password are sent as one LCP data package, rather than the server sending a login prompt and waiting for a response, as shown in Figure 1. After PPP completes the link establishment phase, the remote node repeatedly sends a username-password pair across the link until the receiving node acknowledges it or terminates the connection.

Completing PAP

At the receiving node, the username-password is checked by an authentication server that either allows or denies the connection. An accept or reject message is returned to the requester, as shown in Figure 2.

PAP is not a strong authentication protocol. Using PAP, passwords are sent across the link in plaintext and there is no protection from playback or repeated trial-and-error attacks. The remote node is in control of the frequency and timing of the login attempts.

Nonetheless, there are times when using PAP can be justified. For example, despite its shortcomings, PAP may be used in the following environments:

- A large installed base of client applications that do not support CHAP

- Incompatibilities between different vendor implementations of CHAP

- Situations where a plaintext password must be available to simulate a login at the remote host

Refer to
Online Course
for Illustration

3.3.2.3   Challenge Handshake Authentication Protocol (CHAP)

After authentication is established with PAP, it does not re-authenticate. This leaves the network vulnerable to attack. Unlike PAP, which only authenticates once, CHAP conducts periodic challenges to make sure that the remote node still has a valid password value. The password value is variable and changes unpredictably while the link exists.

After the PPP link establishment phase is complete, the local router sends a challenge message to the remote node, as shown in Figure 1.

The remote node responds with a value calculated using a one-way hash function, which is typically Message Digest 5 (MD5) based on the password and challenge message, as shown in Figure 2.

The local router checks the response against its own calculation of the expected hash value. If the values match, the initiating node acknowledges the authentication, as shown in Figure 3. If the value does not match, the initiating node immediately terminates the connection.

CHAP provides protection against playback attack by using a variable challenge value that is unique and unpredictable. Because the challenge is unique and random, the resulting hash value is also unique and random. The use of repeated challenges limits the time of exposure to any single attack. The local router or a third-party authentication server is in control of the frequency and timing of the challenges.

Refer to
Online Course
for Illustration

3.3.2.4   PPP Encapsulation and Authentication Process

The flowchart in Figure 1 can be used to help understand the PPP authentication process when configuring PPP. The flowchart provides a visual example of the logic decisions made by PPP.

For example, if an incoming PPP request requires no authentication, then PPP progresses to the next level. If an incoming PPP request requires authentication, then it can be authenticated using either the local database or a security server. As illustrated in the flowchart, successful authentication progresses to the next level, while an authentication failure disconnects and drops the incoming PPP request.

Follow the steps as the animation progresses in Figure 2 to view R1 establishing an authenticated PPP CHAP connection with R2.

Step 1.   R1 initially negotiates the link connection using LCP with router R2 and the two systems agree to use CHAP authentication during the PPP LCP negotiation.

Step 2.   R2 generates an ID and a random number, and sends that and its username as a CHAP challenge packet to R1.

Step 3.   R1 uses the username of the challenger (R2) and cross references it with its local database to find its associated password. R1 then generates a unique MD5 hash number using the R2's username, ID, random number and the shared secret password. In this example, the shared secret password is boardwalk.

Step 4.   Router R1 then sends the challenge ID, the hashed value, and its username (R1) to R2.

Step 5.   R2 generates its own hash value using the ID, the shared secret password, and the random number it originally sent to R1.

Step 6.   R2 compares its hash value with the hash value sent by R1. If the values are the same, R2 sends a link established response to R1.

If the authentication failed, a CHAP failure packet is built from the following components:

- 04 = CHAP failure message type

- id = copied from the response packet

- "Authentication failure" or some similar text message, which is meant to be a user-readable explanation

The shared secret password must be identical on R1 and R2.

Refer to
Online Course
for Illustration

3.3.2.5   Configuring PPP Authentication

To specify the order in which the CHAP or PAP protocols are requested on the interface, use the `ppp authentication` interface configuration command, as shown in the figure. Use the `no` form of the command to disable this authentication.

After you have enabled CHAP or PAP authentication, or both, the local router requires the remote device to prove its identity before allowing data traffic to flow. This is done as follows:

■ PAP authentication requires the remote device to send a name and password to be checked against a matching entry in the local username database or in the remote TACACS/TACACS+ database.

■ CHAP authentication sends a challenge to the remote device. The remote device must encrypt the challenge value with a shared secret and return the encrypted value and its name to the local router in a response message. The local router uses the name of the remote device to look up the appropriate secret in the local username or remote TACACS/TACACS+ database. It uses the looked-up secret to encrypt the original challenge and verify that the encrypted values match.

Note   Authentication, authorization and accounting (AAA)/TACACS is a dedicated server used to authenticate users. TACACS clients send a query to a TACACS authentication server. The server can authenticate the user, authorize what the user can do, and track what the user has done.

Either PAP or CHAP or both can be enabled. If both methods are enabled, the first method specified is requested during link negotiation. If the peer suggests using the second method or simply refuses the first method, the second method should be tried. Some remote devices support CHAP only and some PAP only. The order in which you specify the methods is based on your concerns about the ability of the remote device to correctly negotiate the appropriate method as well as your concern about data line security. PAP usernames and passwords are sent as plaintext strings and can be intercepted and reused. CHAP has eliminated most of the known security holes.

Refer to
Online Course
for Illustration

3.3.2.6   Configuring PPP with Authentication

The procedure outlined in the table describes how to configure PPP encapsulation and PAP/CHAP authentication protocols. Correct configuration is essential, because PAP and CHAP use these parameters to authenticate.

Configuring PAP Authentication

Figure 1 is an example of a two-way PAP authentication configuration. Both routers authenticate and are authenticated, so the PAP authentication commands mirror each other. The PAP username and password that each router sends must match those specified with the `username` name `password` password command of the other router.

PAP provides a simple method for a remote node to establish its identity using a two-way handshake. This is done only on initial link establishment. The hostname on one router must match the username the other router has configured for PPP. The passwords must also match. Specify the username and password parameters, use the following command: `ppp pap sent-username` name `password` password.

Use the Syntax Checker in Figure 2 to configure PAP authentication on router R1's serial 0/0/1 interface.

Configuring CHAP Authentication

CHAP periodically verifies the identity of the remote node using a three-way handshake. The hostname on one router must match the username the other router has configured. The passwords must also match. This occurs on initial link establishment and can be repeated any time after the link has been established. Figure 3 is an example of a CHAP configuration.

Use the Syntax Checker in Figure 4 to configure CHAP authentication on router R1's serial 0/0/1 interface.

Refer to **Packet Tracer Activity** for this chapter

3.3.2.7   Packet Tracer - Configuring PAP and CHAP Authentication

Background/Scenario

In this activity, you will practice configuring PPP encapsulation on serial links. You will also configure PPP PAP authentication and PPP CHAP authentication.

Refer to **Lab Activity** for this chapter

3.3.2.8   Lab - Configuring Basic PPP with Authentication

In this lab, you will complete the following objectives:

- Part 1: Configure Basic Device Settings
- Part 2: Configure PPP Encapsulation
- Part 3: Configure PPP CHAP Authentication

Refer to **Online Course** for Illustration

3.4   Troubleshoot WAN Connectivity

3.4.1   Troubleshoot PPP

3.4.1.1   Troubleshooting PPP Serial Encapsulation

Recall that the `debug` command is used for troubleshooting and is accessed from privileged EXEC mode of the command-line interface. A `debug` output displays information about various router operations, related traffic generated or received by the router, and any error messages. It can consume a significant amount of resources, and the router is forced to process-switch the packets being debugged. The `debug` command must not be used as a monitoring tool; rather, it is meant to be used for a short period of time for troubleshooting.

Use the `debug ppp` command to display information about the operation of PPP. The figure shows the command syntax. Use the `no` form of this command to disable debugging output.

Use the `debug ppp` command when trying to search the following:

- NCPs that are supported on either end of a PPP connection
- Any loops that might exist in a PPP internetwork
- Nodes that are (or are not) properly negotiating PPP connections
- Errors that have occurred over the PPP connection

- Causes for CHAP session failures

- Causes for PAP session failures

- Information specific to the exchange of PPP connections using the Callback Control Protocol (CBCP), used by Microsoft clients

- Incorrect packet sequence number information where MPPC compression is enabled

Refer to
Online Course
for Illustration

3.4.1.2   Debug PPP

In addition to the `debug ppp` command, there are other commands that are available for troubleshooting a PPP connection.

A good command to use when troubleshooting serial interface encapsulation is the `debug ppp packet` command, as shown in Figure 1. The figure example depicts packet exchanges under normal PPP operation, including LCP state, LQM procedures, and the LCP magic number.

Figure 2 displays the output of the `debug ppp negotiation` command in a normal negotiation, where both sides agree on NCP parameters. In this case, protocol types IPv4 and IPv6 are proposed and acknowledged. The `debug ppp negotiation` command enables the network administrator to view the PPP negotiation transactions, identify the problem or stage when the error occurs, and develop a resolution. The output includes the LCP negotiation, authentication, and NCP negotiation.

The `debug ppp error` command is used to display protocol errors and error statistics associated with PPP connection negotiation and operation, as shown in Figure 3. These messages might appear when the Quality Protocol option is enabled on an interface that is already running PPP.

Refer to
Online Course
for Illustration

3.4.1.3   Troubleshooting a PPP Configuration with Authentication

Authentication is a feature that needs to be implemented correctly or the security of your serial connection may be compromised. Always verify your configuration with the `show interfaces serial` command, in the same way as you did without authentication.

Note   Never assume your authentication configuration works without testing it. Debugging allows you to confirm your configuration and correct any deficiencies. For debugging PPP authentication, use the `debug ppp authentication` command.

The figure shows an example output of the `debug ppp authentication` command. The following is an interpretation of the output:

Line 1 says that the router is unable to authenticate on interface Serial0 because the peer did not send a name.

Line 2 says the router was unable to validate the CHAP response because USERNAME `pioneer` was not found.

Line 3 says no password was found for `pioneer`. Other possible responses at this line might have been no name received to authenticate, unknown name, no secret for given name, short MD5 response received, or MD5 compare failed.

In the last line, the code 4 means that a failure has occurred. Other code values are as follows:

- 1 - Challenge
- 2 - Response
- 3 - Success
- 4 - Failure
- id - 3 is the ID number per LCP packet format
- len - 48 is the packet length without the header

Refer to **Packet Tracer Activity** for this chapter

3.4.1.4   Packet Tracer - Troubleshooting PPP with Authentication

Background/Scenario

The routers at your company were configured by an inexperienced network engineer. Several errors in the configuration have resulted in connectivity issues. Your boss has asked you to troubleshoot and correct the configuration errors and document your work. Using your knowledge of PPP and standard testing methods, find and correct the errors. Make sure that all of the serial links use PPP CHAP authentication, and that all of the networks are reachable. The passwords are "cisco" and "class".

Refer to **Lab Activity** for this chapter

3.4.1.5   Lab - Troubleshooting Basic PPP with Authentication

In this lab, you will complete the following objectives:

- Part 1: Build the Network and Load Device Configurations
- Part 2: Troubleshoot the Data Link Layer
- Part 3: Troubleshoot the Network Layer

Refer to **Online Course** for Illustration

Refer to **Lab Activity** for this chapter

3.5   Summary

3.5.1.1   Class Activity - PPP Validation

PPP Validation

Three friends who are enrolled in the Cisco Networking Academy want to check their knowledge of PPP network configuration.

They set up a contest where each person will be tested on configuring PPP with defined PPP scenario requirements and varying options. Each person devises a different configuration scenario.

The next day they get together and test each other's configuration using their PPP scenario requirements.

Refer to **Packet Tracer Activity** for this chapter

3.5.1.2   Packet Tracer - Skills Integration Challenge

Background/Scenario

This activity allows you to practice a variety of skills including configuring VLANs, PPP with CHAP, static and default routing, using IPv4 and IPv6. Due to the sheer number of graded elements, feel free to click Check Results and Assessment Items to see if you correctly entered a graded command. Use the passwords "cisco" and "class" to access EXEC modes of the CLI for routers and switches.

Refer to **Online Course** for Illustration

3.5.1.3   Summary

Serial transmissions sequentially send one bit at a time over a single channel. A serial port is bidirectional. Synchronous serial communications require a clocking signal.

Point-to-Point links are usually more expensive than shared services; however, the benefits may outweigh the costs. Constant availability is important for some protocols, such as VoIP.

SONET is an optical network standard that uses STDM for efficient use of bandwidth. In the United States, OC transmission rates are standardized specifications for SONET.

The bandwidth hierarchy used by carriers is different in North America (T-carrier) and Europe (E-carrier). In North America, the fundamental line speed is 64 kbps, or DS0. Multiple DS0s are bundled together to provide higher line speeds.

The demarcation point is the point in the network where the responsibility of the service provider ends and the responsibility of the customer begins. The CPE, usually a router, is the DTE device. The DCE is usually a modem or CSU/DSU.

A null modem cable is used to connect two DTE devices together without the need for a DCE device by crossing the Tx and Rx lines. When using this cable between routers in a lab, one of the routers must provide the clocking signal.

Cisco HDLC is a bit-oriented synchronous data link layer protocol extension of HDLC and is used by many vendors to provide multiprotocol support. This is the default encapsulation method used on Cisco synchronous serial lines.

Synchronous PPP is used to connect to non-Cisco devices, to monitor link quality, provide authentication, or bundle links for shared use. PPP uses HDLC for encapsulating datagrams. LCP is the PPP protocol used to establish, configure, test, and terminate the data link connection. LCP can optionally authenticate a peer using PAP or CHAP. A family of NCPs are used by the PPP protocol to simultaneously support multiple network layer protocols. Multilink PPP spreads traffic across bundled links by fragmenting packets and simultaneously sending these fragments over multiple links to same remote address, where they are reassembled.

Go to the online
course to take the
quiz and exam.

Chapter 3 Quiz

This quiz is designed to provide an additional opportunity to practice the skills and knowledge presented in the chapter and to prepare for the chapter exam. You will be allowed multiple attempts and the grade does not appear in the gradebook.

Chapter 3 Exam

The chapter exam assesses your knowledge of the chapter content.

Your Chapter Notes

Frame Relay

4.0   Frame Relay

4.0.1.1   Introduction

An alternative to dedicated, expensive, leased WAN lines is Frame Relay. Frame Relay is a high-performance WAN protocol that operates at the physical and data link layers of the OSI reference model. Although newer services such as broadband and metro Ethernet have reduced the need for Frame Relay in many locations, Frame Relay is still a viable option in many locales around the world. Frame Relay provides a cost-efficient solution for communications between multiple remote sites by using a single access circuit from each site to the provider.

This chapter introduces the fundamental concepts of Frame Relay. It also covers Frame Relay configuration, verification, and troubleshooting tasks.

> Refer to
> **Lab Activity**
> for this chapter

4.0.1.2   Class Activity - Emerging WAN Technologies

Emerging WAN Technologies

As the network administrator, in your small- to medium-sized business, you have already moved from leased-line WAN to Frame Relay connectivity for WAN network communication. You are responsible to keep current with all future network upgrades.

To stay current with emerging and developing technologies, you find that there are some alternate options available for WAN connectivity. Some of these include:

- Frame Relay
- Broadband DSL
- Broadband cable modem
- GigaMAN
- VPN
- MPLS

Because you want to offer the best quality, lowest-cost WAN network service to your company, you decide to research, at least, two emerging and developing technologies. It is your intent to gather information about these two alternate WAN options to intelligently discuss the future goals of your network with your business manager and other network administrators.

Refer to
Interactive Graphic
in online course.

4.1   Introduction to Frame Relay

4.1.1   Benefits of Frame Relay

4.1.1.1   Introducing Frame Relay

Leased lines provide permanent dedicated capacity and are used extensively for building WANs. They have been the traditional connection of choice, but have a number of disadvantages. One disadvantage is that customers pay for leased lines with a fixed capacity. However, WAN traffic is often variable and leaves some of the capacity unused. In addition, each endpoint needs a separate physical interface on the router, which increases equipment costs. Any change to the leased line generally requires a site visit by the carrier personnel.

Frame Relay is a high-performance WAN protocol that operates at the physical and data link layers of the OSI reference model. Unlike leased lines, Frame Relay requires only a single access circuit to the Frame Relay provider to communicate with other sites connected to the same provider. The capacity between any two sites can vary.

Eric Scace, an engineer at Sprint International, invented Frame Relay as a simpler version of the X.25 protocol to use across Integrated Services Digital Network (ISDN) interfaces. Today, it is also used over a variety of other network interfaces. When Sprint first implemented Frame Relay in its public network, they used StrataCom switches. Cisco's acquisition of StrataCom in 1996 marked their entry into the carrier market.

Network providers implement Frame Relay to support voice and data traffic between LANs over a WAN. Each end user gets a private line, or leased line, to a Frame Relay node. The Frame Relay network handles the transmission over a frequently changing path transparent to all end users. As shown in the figure, Frame Relay provides a solution to allow the communications between multiple sites using a single access circuit to the provider.

Historically, Frame Relay was used extensively as a WAN protocol because it was inexpensive compared to dedicated leased lines. In addition, configuring user equipment in a Frame Relay network is very simple. Frame Relay connections are created by configuring customer premise equipment (CPE) routers or other devices to communicate with a service provider Frame Relay switch. The service provider configures the Frame Relay switch, which helps keep end-user configuration tasks to a minimum.

Refer to
Online Course
for Illustration

4.1.1.2   Benefits of Frame Relay WAN Technology

With the advent of broadband services such as DSL and cable modem, Ethernet WAN (point-to-point Ethernet service over fiber optic cable), VPN, and Multiprotocol Label Switching (MPLS), Frame Relay has become a less suitable solution for accessing the WAN. However, there are still locations in the world which rely on Frame Relay for connectivity to the WAN.

Frame Relay provides greater bandwidth, reliability, and resiliency than private or leased lines.

Using an example of a large enterprise network helps illustrate the benefits of using a Frame Relay WAN. In the example shown in the figure, SPAN Engineering Company has five campuses across North America. Like most organizations, SPAN's bandwidth requirements are varied.

The first thing to consider is the bandwidth requirement of each site. Working from the headquarters, the Chicago-to-New York connection requires a maximum speed of 256 kb/s. Three other sites need a maximum speed of 48 kb/s connecting to the headquarters, while the connection between the New York and Dallas branch offices requires only 12 kb/s.

Before Frame Relay became available, SPAN Engineering Company leased dedicated lines.

Note   The bandwidth values used in the leased line and Frame Relay examples throughout this chapter do not necessarily reflect current bandwidths used by many customers today. The bandwidth values used in this chapter are only for comparison purposes.

Refer to
Online Course
for Illustration

4.1.1.3   Dedicated Line Requirements

Using leased lines, each of SPAN's sites is connected through a switch at the local telephone company's central office (CO) through the local loop, and then across the entire network. The Chicago and New York sites each use a dedicated T1 line (equivalent to 24 DS0 channels) to connect to the switch, while other sites use ISDN connections (56 kb/s), as shown in the figure. Because the Dallas site connects with both New York and Chicago, it has two locally leased lines. The network providers have provided SPAN with one DS0 between the respective COs, except for the larger pipe connecting Chicago to New York, which has four DS0s. DS0s are priced differently from region to region, and usually are offered at a fixed price. These lines are truly dedicated in that the network provider reserves that line for SPAN's own use. There is no sharing, and SPAN is paying for the end-to-end circuit regardless of how much bandwidth it uses.

A dedicated line provides little practical opportunity for a one-to-many connection without getting more lines from the network provider. In the example, almost all communication must flow through the corporate headquarters, simply to reduce the cost of additional lines.

Upon further examination of the bandwidth requirements for each site, it becomes apparent that there is a lack of efficiency:

- Of the 24 DS0 channels available in the T1 connection, the Chicago site only uses seven. Some carriers offer fractional T1 connections in increments of 64 kb/s, but this requires a specialized device called a multiplexer at the customer end to channelize the signals. In this case, SPAN has opted for the full T1 service.

- Similarly, the New York site only uses five of its available 24 DS0s.

- Because Dallas must connect to Chicago and New York, there are two lines connecting through the CO to each site.

The leased-line design also limits flexibility. Unless circuits are already installed, connecting new sites typically requires new circuit installations and takes considerable time to implement. From a network reliability point of view, imagine the additional costs in money and complexity of adding spare and redundant circuits.

Refer to
Online Course
for Illustration

4.1.1.4   Cost Effectiveness and Flexibility of Frame Relay

SPAN's Frame Relay network uses Permanent Virtual Circuits (PVCs), as shown in the figure. A PVC is the logical path along an originating Frame Relay link, through the network, and along a terminating Frame Relay link to its ultimate destination. Compare this to the physical path used by a dedicated connection. In a network with Frame Relay access, a PVC uniquely defines the path between two endpoints. The concept of virtual circuits (VCs) is discussed in more detail later in this section.

SPAN's Frame Relay solution provides both cost effectiveness and flexibility.

Cost Effectiveness of Frame Relay

Frame Relay is a more cost-effective option for two reasons. First, with dedicated lines, customers pay for an end-to-end connection, which includes the local loop and the network link. With Frame Relay, customers only pay for the local loop, and for the bandwidth they purchase from the network provider. Distance between nodes is not important. While in a dedicated-line model, customers use dedicated lines provided in increments of 64 kb/s, and Frame Relay customers can define their virtual circuit needs in far greater granularity, often in increments as small as 4 kb/s.

The second reason for Frame Relay's cost effectiveness is that it shares bandwidth across a larger base of customers. Typically, a network provider can service 40 or more 56 kb/s customers over one T1 circuit. Using dedicated lines would require more CSU/DSUs (one for each line) and more complicated routing and switching. Network providers save because there is less equipment to purchase and maintain.

Note   Cost can vary significantly depending on location.

The Flexibility of Frame Relay

A virtual circuit provides considerable flexibility in network design. Examining the figure, you can see that SPAN's offices all connect to the Frame Relay cloud over their respective local loops. What happens in the cloud is really of no concern at this time. All that matters is that when any SPAN office wants to communicate with any other SPAN office, all it needs to do is connect to a virtual circuit leading to the other office. In Frame Relay, the end of each connection has a number to identify it called a data link connection identifier (DLCI). Any station can connect with any other simply by stating the address of that station and DLCI number of the line it must use. In a later section, you will learn that when Frame Relay is configured, all data from all configured DLCIs flows through the same port of the router. Imagine the same flexibility using dedicated lines. Not only is it complicated, but it also requires considerably more equipment.

Refer to
Interactive Graphic
in online course.

4.1.1.5   Activity - Identify Frame Relay Terminology and Concepts

Refer to
Online Course
for Illustration

4.1.2   Frame Relay Operation

4.1.2.1   Virtual Circuits

The connection through a Frame Relay network between two DTEs is a VC. The circuits are virtual because there is no direct electrical connection from end to end. The connection is logical, and data moves from end to end, without a direct electrical circuit. With

VCs, Frame Relay shares the bandwidth among multiple users and any single site can communicate with any other single site without using multiple dedicated physical lines.

There are two ways to establish VCs:

■ **Switched Virtual Circuits (SVC)**- Established dynamically by sending signaling messages to the network (CALL SETUP, DATA TRANSFER, IDLE, CALL TERMINATION).

■ **Permanent Virtual Circuits (PVCs)** - preconfigured by the carrier, and after they are set up, only operate in DATA TRANSFER and IDLE modes. Note that some publications refer to PVCs as private VCs.

Note   PVCs are more commonly implemented than SVCs.

Click Play in Figure 1 to view an animation on a VC between the sending and receiving nodes. The VC follows the path A, B, C, and D. Frame Relay creates a VC by storing input-port to output-port mapping in the memory of each switch and thus links one switch to another until a continuous path from one end of the circuit to the other is identified. A VC can pass through any number of intermediate devices (switches) located within the Frame Relay network.

VCs provide a bidirectional communication path from one device to another. VCs are identified by DLCIs, as shown in Figure 2. DLCI values typically are assigned by the Frame Relay service provider. Frame Relay DLCIs have local significance, which means that the values themselves are not unique in the Frame Relay WAN. A DLCI identifies a VC to the equipment at an endpoint. A DLCI has no significance beyond the single link. Two devices connected by a VC may use a different DLCI value to refer to the same connection.

Locally significant DLCIs have become the primary method of addressing, because the same address can be used in several different locations while still referring to different connections. Local addressing prevents a customer from running out of DLCIs as the network grows.

Click Play in Figure 3. This is the same network as presented in the previous figure, but this time, as the frame moves across the network, Frame Relay labels each VC with a DLCI. The DLCI is stored in the address field of every frame transmitted to tell the network how the frame should be routed. The Frame Relay service provider assigns DLCI numbers. Usually, DLCIs 0 to 15 and 1,008 to 1,023 are reserved. Therefore, service providers typically assign DLCIs in the range of 16 to 1,007.

In this example, the frame uses DLCI 102. It leaves the router (R1) using Port 0 and VC 102. At switch A, the frame exits Port 1 using VC 432. This process of VC-port mapping continues through the WAN until the frame reaches its destination at DLCI 201. The DLCI is stored in the address field of every frame transmitted.

Refer to
Online Course
for Illustration

4.1.2.2 Multiple Virtual Circuits

Multiple VCs

Frame Relay is statistically multiplexed, meaning that it transmits only one frame at a time, but that many logical connections can co-exist on a single physical line. The Frame Relay

Access Device (FRAD), or router connected to the Frame Relay network, may have multiple VCs connecting it to various endpoints. Multiple VCs on a single physical line are distinguished because each VC has its own DLCI. Keep in mind that the DLCI has only local significance and may be different at each end of a VC.

Figure 1 shows an example of two VCs on a single access line, each with its own DLCI, attaching to a router (R1).

This capability often reduces the equipment and network complexity required to connect multiple devices, making it a very cost-effective replacement for a mesh of access lines. With this configuration, each endpoint needs only a single access line and interface. More savings arise as the capacity of the access line is based on the average bandwidth requirement of the VCs, rather than on the maximum bandwidth requirement.

In the example in Figure 2, SPAN Engineering Co. has five remote locations, with its headquarters in Chicago. Chicago is connected to the network using five VCs and each VC is given a DLCI. To see Chicago's respective DLCI mappings, click on the location in the table. Notice that SPAN has grown and recently opened an office in San Jose. Using Frame Relay made this expansion relatively easy.

Cost Benefits of Multiple VCs

With Frame Relay, customers pay for the bandwidth they use. In effect, they pay for a Frame Relay port. When the customer increases the number of ports, as described above, they pay for more bandwidth, but they do not pay for more equipment because the ports are virtual. There is no change to the physical infrastructure. Compare this to purchasing more bandwidth using dedicated lines.

Refer to
Online Course
for Illustration

4.1.2.3   Frame Relay Encapsulation

Frame Relay takes data packets from a network layer protocol, such as IPv4 or IPv6, encapsulates them as the data portion of a Frame Relay frame, and then passes the frame to the physical layer for delivery on the wire. To understand how this works, it is helpful to understand how it relates to the lower levels of the OSI model.

Frame Relay encapsulates data for transport and moves it down to the physical layer for delivery, as shown in Figure 1.

First, Frame Relay accepts a packet from a network layer protocol, such as IPv4. It then wraps it with an address field that contains the DLCI and a checksum. Flag fields are added to indicate the beginning and end of the frame. The flag fields mark the start and end of the frame and are always the same. The flags are represented either as the hexadecimal number 7E or as the binary number 01111110. After the packet is encapsulated, Frame Relay passes the frame to the physical layer for transport.

The CPE router encapsulates each Layer 3 packet inside a Frame Relay header and trailer before sending it across the VC. The header and trailer are defined by the Link Access Procedure for Frame Relay (LAPF) Bearer Services specification, ITU Q.922-A. As shown in Figure 2, the Frame Relay header (address field) specifically contains the following:

■ **DLCI-** The 10-bit DLCI is one of the most important fields in the Frame Relay header. This value represents the virtual connection between the DTE device and the switch. Each virtual connection that is multiplexed on to the physical channel is represented by a unique DLCI. The DLCI values have local significance only, which means that they are unique only to the physical channel on which they reside. Therefore, devices at opposite ends of a connection can use different DLCI values to refer to the same virtual connection.

- **C/R**- The bit that follows the most significant DLCI byte in the Address field. The C/R bit is not currently defined.

- **Extended Address (EA)**- If the value of the EA field is 1, the current byte is determined to be the last DLCI octet. Although current Frame Relay implementations all use a two-octet DLCI, this capability does allow longer DLCIs in the future. The eighth bit of each byte of the Address field indicates the EA.

- **Congestion Control**- Consists of three Frame Relay congestion-notification bits. These three bits are specifically referred to as the Forward Explicit Congestion Notification (FECN), Backward Explicit Congestion Notification (BECN), and Discard Eligible bits.

The physical layer is typically EIA/TIA-232, 449 or 530, V.35, or X.21. The Frame Relay frame is a subset of the HDLC frame type; therefore, it is delimited with flag fields. The 1-byte flag uses the bit pattern 01111110. The FCS determines whether any errors in the Layer 2 address field occurred during transmission. The FCS is calculated prior to transmission by the sending node, and the result is inserted in the FCS field. At the distant end, a second FCS value is calculated and compared to the FCS in the frame. If the results are the same, the frame is processed. If there is a difference, the frame is discarded. Frame Relay does not notify the source when a frame is discarded. Error control is left to the upper layers of the OSI model.

Refer to **Online Course** for Illustration

4.1.2.4   Frame Relay Topologies

When more than two sites must be connected, the Frame Relay topology, or map, of the connections between the sites must be planned. A network designer must consider the topology from several perspectives to understand the network and the equipment used to build the network. Complete topologies for design, implementation, operation, and maintenance include overview maps, logical connection maps, functional maps, and address maps showing the detailed equipment and channel links.

Cost-effective Frame Relay networks link dozens and even hundreds of sites. Considering that a corporate network might span any number of service providers and include networks from acquired businesses differing in basic design, documenting topologies can be a very complicated process. However, every network or network segment can be viewed as being one of three topology types: star, full mesh, or partial mesh.

Star Topology (Hub and Spoke)

The simplest WAN topology is a star, as shown in Figure 1. In this topology, SPAN Engineering Company has a central site in Chicago that acts as a hub and hosts the primary services.

Connections to each of the five remote sites act as spokes. In a star topology, the location of the hub is usually chosen by the lowest leased-line cost. When implementing a star topology with Frame Relay, each remote site has an access link to the Frame Relay cloud with a single VC.

Figure 2 shows the star topology in the context of a Frame Relay cloud. The hub at Chicago has an access link with multiple VCs, one for each remote site. The lines going out from the cloud represent the connections from the Frame Relay service provider and terminate at the customer premises. These are typically lines ranging in speed from 56 kb/s to a T1 (1.544 Mb/s) and faster. One or more DLCI numbers are assigned to each line endpoint. Because Frame Relay costs are not distance-related, the hub does not need to be in the geographical center of the network.

Refer to **Online Course** for Illustration

4.1.2.5   Frame Relay Topologies (Cont.)

Full Mesh Topology

Figure 1 represents a full mesh topology using dedicated lines. A full mesh topology suits a situation in which the services to be accessed are geographically dispersed and highly reliable access to them is required. A full mesh topology connects every site to every other site. Using leased-line interconnections, additional serial interfaces and lines add costs. In this example, 10 dedicated lines are required to interconnect each site in a full mesh topology.

Using Frame Relay Mesh, a network designer can build multiple connections simply by configuring additional VCs on each existing link, as shown in Figure 2. This software upgrade grows the star topology to a full mesh topology without the expense of additional hardware or dedicated lines. Because VCs use statistical multiplexing, multiple VCs on an access link generally make better use of Frame Relay than single VCs. Figure 2 shows how SPAN has used four VCs on each link to scale its network without adding new hardware. Service providers will charge for the additional bandwidth, but this solution is usually more cost effective than using dedicated lines.

Partial Mesh Topology

For large networks, a full mesh topology is seldom affordable because the number of links required increases exponentially. The issue is not with the cost of the hardware, but because there is a theoretical limit of less than 1,000 VCs per link. In practice, the limit is less than that.

For this reason, larger networks are generally configured in a partial mesh topology. With partial mesh, there are more interconnections than required for a star arrangement, but not as many as for a full mesh. The actual pattern is dependent on the data flow requirements.

Refer to **Online Course** for Illustration

4.1.2.6   Frame Relay Address Mapping

Before a Cisco router is able to transmit data over Frame Relay, it needs to know which local DLCI maps to the Layer 3 address of the remote destination. Cisco routers support all network layer protocols over Frame Relay, such as IPv4, IPv6, IPX, and AppleTalk. This address-to-DLCI mapping can be accomplished either by static or dynamic mapping. Figure 1 shows an example topology with DLCI mapping.

Inverse ARP

A primary tool of Frame Relay is Inverse Address Resolution Protocol (ARP). Whereas ARP translates Layer 3 IPv4 addresses to Layer 2 MAC addresses, Inverse ARP does the opposite. The corresponding Layer 3 IPv4 addresses must be available before VCs can be used.

Note Frame Relay for IPv6 uses Inverse Neighbor Discovery (IND) to obtain a Layer 3 IPv6 address from a Layer 2 DLCI. A Frame Relay router sends an IND Solicitation message to request a Layer 3 IPv6 address corresponding to a Layer 2 DLCI address of the remote Frame Relay router. At the same time the IND Solicitation message provides the sender's Layer 2 DLCI address to the remote Frame Relay router.

Dynamic Mapping

Dynamic address mapping relies on Inverse ARP to resolve a next-hop network layer IPv4 address to a local DLCI value. The Frame Relay router sends out Inverse ARP requests on its PVC to discover the protocol address of the remote device connected to the Frame Relay network. The router uses the responses to populate an address-to-DLCI mapping table on the Frame Relay router or access server. The router builds and maintains this mapping table, which contains all resolved Inverse ARP requests, including both dynamic and static mapping entries.

On Cisco routers, Inverse ARP is enabled, by default, for all protocols enabled on the physical interface. Inverse ARP packets are not sent out for protocols that are not enabled on the interface.

Static Frame Relay Mapping

The user can choose to override dynamic Inverse ARP mapping by supplying a manual static map for the next-hop protocol address to a local DLCI. A static map works similarly to dynamic Inverse ARP by associating a specified next-hop protocol address to a local Frame Relay DLCI. You cannot use Inverse ARP and a map statement for the same DLCI and protocol.

An example of using static address mapping is a situation in which the router at the other side of the Frame Relay network does not support dynamic Inverse ARP for a specific network protocol. To provide connectivity, a static mapping is required to complete the remote network layer address to local DLCI resolution.

Another example is on a hub-and-spoke Frame Relay network. Use static address mapping on the spoke routers to provide spoke-to-spoke reachability. Because the spoke routers do not have direct connectivity with each other, dynamic Inverse ARP would not work between them. Dynamic Inverse ARP relies on the presence of a direct point-to-point connection between two ends. In this case, dynamic Inverse ARP only works between hub and spoke, and the spokes require static mapping to provide reachability to each other.

Configuring Static Mapping

Establishing static mapping depends on your network needs. To map between a next hop protocol address and DLCI destination address, use this command: `frame-relay map` protocol protocol-addressdlci [`broadcast`] [`ietf`] [`cisco`].

Use the keyword `ietf` when connecting to a non-Cisco router.

The configuration of Open Shortest Path First (OSPF) protocol can be greatly simplified by adding the optional `broadcast` keyword when doing this task. The `broadcast` keyword specifies that broadcast and multicast traffic is allowed over the VC. This configuration permits the use of dynamic routing protocols over the VC.

Figure 2 provides an example of static mapping on a Cisco router. In this example, static address mapping is performed on interface serial 0/0/1. The Frame Relay encapsulation used on DLCI 102 is CISCO. As seen in the configuration steps, static mapping of the address using the `frame-relay map` command allows users to select the type of Frame Relay encapsulation used on a per-VC basis.

Figure 3 shows the output of the `show frame-relay map` command. Notice that the interface is up and the destination IPv4 address is 10.1.1.2. The DLCI identifies the logical connection being used to reach this interface. This value is displayed in decimal value (102), in hexadecimal value (0x66), and as its value as it would appear on the wire (0x1860). This is a static entry, not a dynamic entry. The link is using Cisco encapsulation as opposed to IETF encapsulation.

Refer to **Online Course** for Illustration

4.1.2.7 Local Management Interface (LMI)

Another important concept in Frame Relay is the Local Management Interface (LMI). The Frame Relay design provides packet-switched data transfer with minimum end-to-end delays. The original design omits anything that might contribute to delay.

When vendors implemented Frame Relay as a separate technology rather than as one component of ISDN, they decided that there was a need for DTEs to dynamically acquire information about the status of the network. However, the original design did not include this feature. A consortium of Cisco, Digital Equipment Corporation (DEC), Northern Telecom, and StrataCom extended the Frame Relay protocol to provide additional capabilities for complex internetworking environments. These extensions are referred to collectively as the LMI.

Refer to the Frame Relay topology in Figure 1. Basically, the LMI is a keepalive mechanism that provides status information about Frame Relay connections between the router (DTE) and the Frame Relay switch (DCE). Every 10 seconds or so, the end device polls the network, either requesting a dumb sequenced response or channel status information. If the network does not respond with the requested information, the user device may consider the connection to be down. When the network responds with a FULL STATUS response, it includes status information about DLCIs that are allocated to that line. The end device can use this information to determine whether the logical connections are able to pass data.

Figure 2 shows the output of the `show frame-relay lmi` command. The output shows the LMI type used by the Frame Relay interface and the counters for the LMI status exchange sequence, including errors such as LMI timeouts.

It is easy to confuse the LMI and encapsulation. The LMI is a definition of the messages used between the DTE (R1) and the DCE (the Frame Relay switch owned by the service provider). Encapsulation defines the headers used by a DTE to communicate information to the DTE at the other end of a VC. The switch and its connected router care about using the same LMI. The switch does not care about the encapsulation. The endpoint routers (DTEs) do care about the encapsulation.

Refer to **Online Course** for Illustration

4.1.2.8 LMI Extensions

In addition to the Frame Relay protocol functions for transferring data, the Frame Relay specification includes optional LMI extensions. Some of the extensions include:

- **VC status messages**- Provide information about PVC integrity by communicating and synchronizing between devices, periodically reporting the existence of new PVCs and the deletion of already existing PVCs. VC status messages prevent data from being sent into black holes (PVCs that no longer exist).

- **Multicasting**- Allows a sender to transmit a single frame that is delivered to multiple recipients. Multicasting supports the efficient delivery of routing protocol messages and address resolution procedures that are typically sent to many destinations simultaneously.

- **Global addressing**- Provides connection IDs with global rather than local significance, allowing them to be used to identify a specific interface to the Frame Relay network. Global addressing makes the Frame Relay network resemble a LAN in terms of addressing, and ARPs are used as on a LAN.

- **Simple flow control**- Provides for an XON/XOFF flow control mechanism that applies to the entire Frame Relay interface. It is intended for devices that cannot use the congestion notification bits (i.e., FECN and BECN) that would be leveraged by higher layers, but still require some level of flow control.

LMI is used to manage Frame Relay links. Each LMI message is classified by a DLCI appearing in the LMI frame. The 10-bit DLCI field supports 1,024 VC IDs: 0 to 1,023, as shown in Figure 1. The LMI extensions reserve some of these VC IDs, thereby reducing the number of permitted VCs. LMI messages are exchanged between the DTE and DCE using these reserved DLCIs.

There are several LMI types, each of which is incompatible with the others. The LMI type configured on the router must match the type used by the service provider. Three types of LMIs are supported by Cisco routers:

- **CISCO**- Original LMI extension

- **ANSI**- Corresponding to the ANSI standard T1.617 Annex D

- **Q933A**- Corresponding to the ITU standard Q933 Annex A

To display the LMI message information and the associated DLCI numbers, use the `show interfaces` [type number] command, as shown in Figure 2. Cisco uses DLCI 1023 to identify LMI messages used for Frame Relay link management.

Starting with the Cisco IOS software Release 11.2, the default LMI autosense feature detects the LMI type supported by the directly connected Frame Relay switch. Based on the LMI status messages it receives from the Frame Relay switch, the router automatically configures its interface with the supported LMI type acknowledged by the Frame Relay switch. If it is necessary to set the LMI type, use the `frame-relay lmi-type` [`cisco` | `ansi` | `q933a`] interface configuration command. Configuring the LMI type disables the autosense feature.

In cases where a Frame Relay switch uses non-default timeout settings, the keepalive interval must also be configured on the Frame Relay interface to prevent status exchange messages from timing out. The LMI status exchange messages determine the status of the PVC connection. A large mismatch in the keepalive interval on the router and the switch can cause the switch to declare the router dead. It is important to consult the Frame Relay service provider for information on how to modify the keepalive setting. By default, the keepalive time interval is 10 seconds on Cisco serial interfaces. You can change the keepalive interval with the `keepalive` interface configuration command.

Status messages help verify the integrity of logical and physical links. This information is critical in a routing environment because routing protocols make decisions based on link integrity.

As shown in Figure 3, LMI status messages are similar to the Frame Relay frame. In place of the Address field of a Frame Relay frame that is used for data transmission, is an LMI DLCI field. Following the DLCI field are the Control, Protocol Discriminator, and Call Reference fields. These are the same as with standard Frame Relay data frames. The fourth field indicates the LMI message type and includes one of the three LMI message types supported by Cisco.

Refer to
Online Course
for Illustration

4.1.2.9 Using LMI and Inverse ARP to Map Addresses

LMI status messages combined with Inverse ARP messages allow a router to associate network layer and data link layer addresses.

Play the animation in Figure 1 to watch how the LMI process begins.

In this example, when R1 connects to the Frame Relay network, it sends an LMI status inquiry message to the network. The network replies with an LMI status message containing details of every VC configured on the access link.

Periodically, the router repeats the status inquiry, but subsequent responses include only status changes. After a set number of these abbreviated responses, the network sends a full status message.

If the router needs to map VCs to network layer addresses, it sends an Inverse ARP message on each VC. Inverse ARP operates similarly to ARP on an Ethernet local network, with the exception that Inverse ARP does not broadcast requests. With ARP, the sending device knows the Layer 3 IP address and sends a broadcast to learn the destination Layer 2 MAC address. With Inverse ARP, the router knows the Layer 2 address, which is the local DLCI, and sends a request for the destination Layer 3 IP address.

Inverse ARP operation

When an interface supporting Inverse ARP becomes active, it initiates the Inverse ARP protocol and formats an Inverse ARP request for the active VC. The Inverse ARP request includes the source hardware, source Layer 3 protocol address, and the known target hardware address. It then fills the target Layer 3 protocol address field with all zeroes. It encapsulates the packet for the specific network and sends it directly to the destination device using the VC.

Upon receiving an Inverse ARP request, the destination device will use the address of the source device to create its own DLCI-to-Layer 3 map. It will then send an Inverse ARP response that includes its Layer 3 address information. When the source device receives the Inverse ARP response, it completes the DLCI-to-Layer 3 map using the provided information.

When an interface on a Cisco router is configured to use Frame Relay encapsulation, Inverse ARP is enabled by default.

Play the animation in Figure 2 to see Inverse ARP operation.

Refer to
Interactive Graphic
in online course.

4.1.2.10 Activity - Map the Virtual Circuit to the Port Number

Refer to
Interactive Graphic
in online course.

4.1.2.11 Activity - Match Frame Relay Fields to the Definition

Refer to
Interactive Graphic
in online course.

4.1.2.12 Activity - Identify LMI Terminology and Concepts

Refer to
Online Course
for Illustration

4.1.3   Advanced Frame Relay Concepts

4.1.3.1   Access Rate and Committed Information Rate

Service providers build Frame Relay networks using very large and very powerful switches, but devices only see the switch interface of the service provider. Customers are usually not exposed to the inner workings of the network, which may be built on very high-speed technologies, such as SONET or SDH.

From a customer's point of view, Frame Relay is a single interface configured with one or more PVCs. Customers buy Frame Relay services from a service provider. Before considering how to pay for Frame Relay services, there are some terms and concepts to learn, as shown in the figure:

- **Access rate**- Access rate refers to the port speed. From a customer's point of view, the service provider provides a serial connection or access link to the Frame Relay network over a leased line. The access rate is the rate at which your access circuits join the Frame Relay network. These may be 56 kb/s, T1 (1.544 Mb/s), or Fractional T1 (a multiple of 56 kb/s or 64 kb/s). Access rates are clocked on the Frame Relay switch. It is not possible to send data at higher than the access rate.

- **Committed Information Rate (CIR)**- Customers negotiate CIRs with service providers for each PVC. The CIR is the amount of data that the network receives from the access circuit. The service provider guarantees that the customer can send data at the CIR. All frames received at or below the CIR are accepted.

The CIR specifies the maximum average data rate that the network undertakes to deliver under normal conditions. When subscribing to a Frame Relay service, the local access rate is specified, for example 56 kb/s or T1. Typically, the provider asks the customer to specify a CIR for each DLCI.

If the customer sends information faster than the CIR on a given DLCI, the network marks some frames with a Discard Eligibility (DE) bit. The network does its best to deliver all packets; however it discards DE packets first if there is congestion.

Note   Many inexpensive Frame Relay services are based on a CIR of zero (0). A CIR of zero means that every frame is a DE frame and the network throws away any frame when it needs to. The DE bit is within the address field of the Frame Relay frame header.

Refer to
Online Course
for Illustration

4.1.3.2   Frame Relay Example

Aside from any CPE costs, the customer pays for three Frame Relay cost components as follows:

- **Access rate**- The cost of the access line from the DTE to the DCE (customer to service provider). This line is charged based on the port speed that has been negotiated and installed.

- **PVC**- This cost component is based on the PVCs. After a PVC is established, the additional cost to increase CIR is typically small and can be done in small (4 kb/s) increments.

■ **CIR**- Customers normally choose a CIR lower than the access rate. This allows them to take advantage of bursts.

In the example in the figure, the customer is paying for the following:

■ An access line with a rate of 64 kb/s connecting their DTE to the DCE of the service provider through serial port S0/0/1.

■ Two virtual ports, one at 32 kb/s and the other at 16 kb/s.

■ A CIR of 48 kb/s across the entire Frame Relay network. This is usually a flat charge and not connected to the distance.

Note   The bandwidth values used throughout this chapter are for comparative purposes only. They do not necessarily reflect actual implementations.

Oversubscription

Service providers sometimes sell more capacity than they have on the assumption that not everyone will demand their entitled capacity all of the time. This oversubscription is analogous to airlines selling more seats than they have in the expectation that some of the booked customers will not show up. Because of oversubscription, there are instances when the sum of CIRs from multiple PVCs to a given location is higher than the port or access channel rate. This can cause congestion and dropped traffic.

Refer to
Online Course
for Illustration

4.1.3.3   Bursting

A great advantage of Frame Relay is that any network capacity that is being unused is made available or shared with all customers, usually at no extra charge. This allows customers to burst over their CIR as a bonus.

Using the previous example, Figure 1 shows an access rate on serial port S0/0/1 of router R1 to be 64 kb/s. This is higher than the combined CIRs of the two PVCs. Under normal circumstances, the two PVCs should not transmit more than 32 kb/s and 16 kb/s, respectively. As long as the amount of data the two PVCs send does not exceed the CIR, it should get through the network.

Because the physical circuits of the Frame Relay network are shared between subscribers, there are often times where there is excess bandwidth available. Frame Relay can allow customers to dynamically access this extra bandwidth and burst over their CIR for free.

Bursting allows devices that temporarily need additional bandwidth to borrow it at no extra cost from other devices not using it. For example, if PVC 102 is transferring a large file, it could use any of the 16 kb/s not being used by PVC 103. A device can burst up to the access rate and still expect the data to get through. The duration of a burst transmission should be less than three or four seconds.

Various terms are used to describe burst rates, including the Committed Burst Size (Bc) and Excess Burst Size (Be).

The Bc is a negotiated rate above the CIR that the customer can use to transmit for short burst, and represents the maximum allowed traffic under normal working conditions. It allows traffic to burst to higher speeds, as available network bandwidth permits. However, it cannot exceed the access rate of the link. A device can burst up to the Bc and still expect the data to get through. If long bursts persist, then a higher CIR should be purchased.

For example, DLCI 102 has a CIR of 32 kb/s with an additional Bc of 16 kb/s for a total of up to 48 kb/s. DLCI 103 has a CIR of 16 kb/s. However, DLCI 103 does not have a Bc negotiated; therefore, the Bc is set to 0 kb/s. Frames within the negotiated CIR are not eligible for discard (DE = 0). Frames above the CIR have the DE bit set to 1, marking it as eligible to be discarded, should the network be congested. Frames submitted in the Bc level are marked as Discard Eligible (DE) in the frame header but will most likely be forwarded.

The Be describes the bandwidth available above the CIR up to the access rate of the link. Unlike the Bc, it is not negotiated. Frames may be transmitted at this level but are most likely dropped.

Figure 2 illustrates the relationship between the various bursting terms.

4.1.3.4   Frame Relay Flow Control

Refer to
Online Course
for Illustration

Frame Relay reduces network overhead by implementing simple congestion-notification mechanisms, rather than explicit, per-VC flow control. These congestion-notification mechanisms are the Forward Explicit Congestion Notification (FECN) and the Backward Explicit Congestion Notification (BECN).

To help understand the mechanisms, Figure 1 shows the structure of the Standard Frame Relay frame for review. FECN and BECN are each controlled by a single bit contained in the frame header. They let the router know that there is congestion and that the router should stop transmission until the condition is reversed. When the DCE sets the BECN bit to 1, it notifies devices in the direction of the source (upstream) that there is congestion on the network. When the DCE sets the FECN bit to 1, it notifies devices in the direction of the destination (downstream) that there is congestion on the network.

The frame header also contains the DE bit, which identifies less important traffic that can be dropped during periods of congestion. DTE devices can set the value of the DE bit to 1 to indicate that the frame has lower importance than other frames. When the network becomes congested, DCE devices discard the frames with the DE bit set to 1 before discarding those that do not. This reduces the likelihood of critical data being dropped during periods of congestion.

In periods of congestion, the service provider's Frame Relay switch applies the following logic rules to each incoming frame based on whether the CIR is exceeded:

- If the incoming frame does not exceed the Bc, the frame is passed.
- If an incoming frame exceeds the Bc, it is marked as DE.
- If an incoming frame exceeds the Bc and the Be, it is discarded.

Click the play button in the Figure 2 animation to view how the FECN and BECN are used.

Frames arriving at a switch are queued or buffered prior to forwarding. As in any queuing system, it is possible that there will be an excessive buildup of frames at a switch. This causes delays, which lead to unnecessary retransmissions that occur when higher level protocols receive no acknowledgment within a set time. In severe cases, this can cause a serious drop in network throughput. To avoid this problem, Frame Relay incorporates a flow control feature.

The animation shows a switch with a filling queue. To reduce the flow of frames to the queue, the switch notifies DTEs of the problem using the Explicit Congestion Notification bits in the frame address field.

- The FECN bit, indicated by F, is set on every frame that the switch receives on the congested link.

- The BECN bit, indicated by B, is set on every frame that the switch places onto the congested link.

DTEs receiving frames with the ECN bits set are expected to try to reduce the flow of frames until the congestion clears. If the congestion occurs on an internal trunk, DTEs may receive notification even though they are not the cause of the congestion.

Refer to
Interactive Graphic
in online course.

4.1.3.5   Activity - Identify Frame Relay Bandwidth and Flow Control Terminology

Refer to
Online Course
for Illustration

4.2   Configure Frame Relay

4.2.1   Configure Basic Frame Relay

4.2.1.1   Basic Frame Relay Configuration Commands

Frame Relay is configured on a Cisco router from the Cisco IOS command-line interface (CLI). Figure 1 shows the required and optional steps for configuring Frame Relay.

Figure 2 shows the three router topology that will be used in this section, though initial focus will be on the Frame Relay link between R1 and R2, network 10.1.1.0/24. Notice that all routers have been configured with both IPv4 and IPv6 addresses.

Step 1.   Set the IP Address on the InterfaceOn a Cisco router, Frame Relay is most commonly supported on synchronous serial interfaces. Use the `ip address` command to set the IPv4 address of the interface.On the link between R1 and R2, R1 S0/0/1 has been assigned 10.1.1.1/24, and R2 S0/0/1 has been assigned IPv4 address 10.1.1.2/24.Using the `ipv6 address` command, routers R1 and R2 have also both been configured with the following IPv6 addresses:

- R1 has been configured with the IPv6 global unicast address, 2001:DB8:CAFE:1::1/64 and the static link-local address FE80::1.

- R2 has been configured with the IPv6 global unicast address, 2001:DB8:CAFE:1::2/64 and the static link-local address FE80::2.

Note   By default, Cisco IOS uses EUI-64 to automatically generate the IPv6 link-local address on an interface. Configuring static link-local addresses makes it easier to remember and identify the link-local addresses. IPv6 link-local addresses are used by IPv6 routing protocols for routing messages and next-hop addresses in the IPv6 routing table.

Step 2.   Configure Encapsulation

The `encapsulation frame-relay` [`cisco` | `ietf`] interface configuration command enables Frame Relay encapsulation and allows Frame Relay processing on the supported interface. There are two encapsulation options to choose from, `cisco` and `ietf`.

- The `cisco` encapsulation type is the default Frame Relay encapsulation enabled on supported interfaces. Use this option if connecting to another Cisco router. Many non-Cisco devices also support this encapsulation type. It uses a 4-byte header, with 2 bytes to identify the DLCI and 2 bytes to identify the packet type.

- The `ietf` encapsulation type complies with RFC 1490 and RFC 2427. Use this option if connecting to a non-Cisco router.

Step 3.   Set the Bandwidth

Use the `bandwidth` command to set the bandwidth of the serial interface. Specify bandwidth in kb/s. This command notifies the routing protocol that bandwidth is statically configured on the link. The EIGRP and OSPF routing protocols use the bandwidth value to calculate and determine the metric of the link.

Step 4.   Set the LMI Type (optional)

Manually setting the LMI type is optional, as Cisco routers autosense the LMI type by default. Recall that Cisco supports three LMI types: `cisco`, `ANSI Annex D`, and `Q933-A Annex A`. The default LMI type for Cisco routers is `cisco`.

Figure 3 shows the R1 and R2 configurations for enabling Frame Relay.

The `show interfaces serial` command verifies the configuration, including the Layer 2 encapsulation of Frame Relay and the default LMI type of `cisco`, as shown in Figure 4. Notice that this command shows the IPv4 address, but does not include any of the IPv6 addresses. Use the `show ipv6 interface` or the `show ipv6 interface brief` command to verify IPv6.

Note   The `no encapsulation frame-relay` command removes the Frame Relay encapsulation on the interface and returns the interface to the default HDLC encapsulation.

4.2.1.2   Configuring a Static Frame Relay Map
Configuring a Static Frame Relay Map

Cisco routers support all network layer protocols over Frame Relay, such as IPv4, IPv6, IPX, and AppleTalk. The address-to-DLCI mapping can be accomplished either by dynamic or static address mapping.

Dynamic mapping is performed by the Inverse ARP feature. Because Inverse ARP is enabled by default, no additional command is required to configure dynamic mapping on an interface. Figure 1 shows the topology used for this topic.

Static mapping is manually configured on a router. Establishing static mapping depends on your network needs. To map between a next hop protocol address and a DLCI destination address, use the `frame-relay map` protocol protocol-address dlci [`broadcast`] command, as shown in Figure 2. Notice the `broadcast` keyword at the end of the command.

Frame Relay, ATM, and X.25 are non-broadcast multiaccess (NBMA) networks. NBMA networks allow only data transfer from one computer to another, over a VC, or across a switching device. NBMA networks do not support multicast or broadcast traffic, so a single packet cannot reach all destinations. This requires you to replicate the packets manually to all destinations. Using the `broadcast` keyword is a simplified way to forward routing updates. The `broadcast` keyword allows IPv4 broadcasts and multicasts to be propagated to all nodes. It also allows IPv6 multicasts over the PVC. When the keyword is enabled, the router converts the broadcast or multicast traffic into unicast traffic so that other nodes receive the routing updates.

Figure 3 shows how to use the keywords when configuring static address maps. Notice that the first IPv6 Frame Relay map to a global unicast address does not include the `broadcast` keyword. However, the `broadcast` keyword is used in the mapping to the link-local address. IPv6 routing protocols use link-local addresses for multicast routing updates; therefore, only the link-local address map requires the `broadcast` keyword to forward multicast packets.

The example only shows the configurations to map the VCs between R1 and R2.

Note Some routing protocols may require additional configuration options. For example, RIP, EIGRP, and OSPF require additional configurations to be supported on NBMA networks.

Refer to **Online Course** for Illustration

4.2.1.3 Verify a Static Frame Relay Map

To verify the Frame Relay mapping, use the `show frame-relay map` command, as shown in Figure 1. Notice that there are three Frame Relay maps. There is one map for IPv4 and two for IPv6, one for each of the IPv6 addresses.

Use the Syntax Checker in Figure 2 to configure the static Frame Relay maps on R1 to R3.

Refer to **Packet Tracer Activity** for this chapter

4.2.1.4 Packet Tracer - Configuring Static Frame Relay Maps

Background/Scenario

In this activity, you will configure two static Frame Relay maps on each router to reach two other routers. Although the LMI type is autosensed on the routers, you will statically assign the type by manually configuring the LMI.

Refer to
Online Course
for Illustration

4.2.2   Configure Subinterfaces

4.2.2.1   Reachability Issues

By default, most Frame Relay networks provide NBMA connectivity, using a hub-and-spoke topology, between remote sites. In an NBMA Frame Relay topology, when a single multipoint interface must be used to interconnect multiple sites, routing update reachability issues may result. With distance vector routing protocols, reachability issues may result from split horizon and multicast or broadcast replication. With link state routing protocols, issues with the DR/BDR election may result in reachability issues.

Split Horizon

The split horizon rule is a loop prevention mechanism for distance vector routing protocols such as EIGRP and RIP. It is not applicable to link-state routing protocols. Split horizon rule reduces routing loops by preventing a routing update that is received on an interface from being forwarded out the same interface.

For example, in Figure 1, which is a hub-and-spoke Frame Relay topology, a remote router R2 (a spoke router) sends an update to the headquarters router R1 (the hub router). R1 is connecting multiple PVCs over a single physical interface. R1 receives the multicast on its physical interface; however, split horizon cannot forward that routing update through the same interface to other remote (spoke) routers.

Note   Split horizon is not an issue if only one PVC (a single remote connection) is configured on a physical interface. This type of connection is point-to-point.

Figure 2 displays a similar example using the reference topology used throughout this chapter. R2, a spoke router, sends a routing update to R1, a hub router. R1 has multiple PVCs on a single physical interface. The split horizon rule prevents R1 from forwarding that routing update through the same physical interface to the other remote spoke router (R3).

Multicast and Broadcast Replication

As shown in Figure 3, due to split horizon, when a router supports multipoint connections over a single interface, the router must replicate broadcast or multicast packets. In the case of routing updates, the updates must be replicated and sent on each PVC to the remote routers. These replicated packets consume bandwidth and cause significant latency variations in user traffic. The amount of broadcast traffic and the number of VCs terminating at each router should be evaluated during the design phase of a Frame Relay network. Overhead traffic, such as routing updates, can affect the delivery of critical user data, especially when the delivery path contains low-bandwidth (56 kb/s) links.

Neighbor Discovery: DR and BDR

Link-state routing protocols, such as OSPF, does not use the split horizon rule for loop prevention. However, reachability issues can arise with the DR/BDR. OSPF over NBMA networks works in non-broadcast network mode, by default, and neighbors are not automatically discovered. Neighbors can be statically configured. However, ensure that the hub router becomes a DR, as shown in Figure 4. Recall that a NBMA network behaves like

Ethernet, and on Ethernet, a DR is needed to exchange routing information between all routers on a segment. Therefore, only the hub router can act as a DR, because it is the only router that has PVCs with all other routers.

Refer to
Online Course
for Illustration

4.2.2.2   Solving Reachability Issues

There are several ways to solve the routing reachability issue:

- **Disable split horizon**- One method for solving the reachability issues that are produced by split horizon may be to turn off split horizon. However, disabling split horizon increases the chances of routing loops in your network. Additionally, only IP allows the ability to disable split horizon; IPX and AppleTalk do not.

- **Full meshed topology**- Another method is to use a fully meshed topology; however, this topology increases costs.

- **Subinterfaces**- In a hub-and-spoke Frame Relay topology, the hub router can be configured with logically assigned interfaces called subinterfaces.

Frame Relay Subinterfaces

Frame Relay can partition a physical interface into multiple virtual interfaces called subinterfaces, as shown in Figure 1. A subinterface is simply a logical interface that is directly associated with a physical interface. Therefore, a Frame Relay subinterface can be configured for each of the PVCs coming into a physical serial interface.

To enable the forwarding of broadcast routing updates in a Frame Relay network, you can configure the router with logically assigned subinterfaces. Using a subinterface configuration, each VC can be configured as a point-to-point connection. A partially meshed network can be divided into a number of smaller, fully meshed, point-to-point networks. Each point-to-point subnetwork can be assigned a unique network address. This allows each subinterface to act similarly to a leased line. Using a Frame Relay point-to-point subinterface, each pair of the point-to-point routers is on its own subnet. This allows packets received on one subinterface to be sent out another subinterface, even though the packets are being forwarded out the same physical interface.

Frame Relay subinterfaces can be configured in either point-to-point or multipoint mode:

- **Point-to-point** (Figure 2) - A single point-to-point subinterface establishes one PVC connection to another physical interface or subinterface on a remote router. In this case, each pair of the point-to-point routers is on its own subnet, and each point-to-point subinterface has a single DLCI. In a point-to-point environment, each subinterface is acting like a point-to-point interface. For each point-to-point VC, there is a separate subnet. Therefore, routing update traffic is not subject to the split horizon rule.

- **Multipoint** (Figure 3) - A single multipoint subinterface establishes multiple PVC connections to multiple physical interfaces or subinterfaces on remote routers. All the participating interfaces are in the same subnet. The subinterface acts like an NBMA Frame Relay interface, so routing update traffic is subject to the split horizon rule. All multipoint VCs belong to the same subnet.

When configuring subinterfaces, the `encapsulation frame-relay` command is assigned to the physical interface. All other configuration items, such as the network layer address and DLCIs, are assigned to the subinterface.

The multipoint subinterface configurations can be used to conserve addresses. This can be especially helpful if Variable Length Subnet Masking (VLSM) is not being used. However, multipoint configurations may not work properly given the broadcast traffic and split horizon considerations. The point-to-point subinterface option was created to avoid these issues.

Refer to
Online Course
for Illustration

4.2.2.3   Configuring Point-to-Point Subinterfaces

Subinterfaces address the limitations of Frame Relay networks by providing a way to subdivide a partially meshed Frame Relay network into a number of smaller, fully meshed, or point-to-point, subnetworks. Each subnetwork is assigned its own network number and appears to the protocols as if it were reachable through a separate interface.

To create a subinterface, in global configuration mode, use the `interface serial` command followed by the physical port number, a period (.), and the subinterface number. To make troubleshooting easier, use the DLCI as the subinterface number. You must also specify whether the interface is point-to-multipoint or point-to-point using either the `multipoint` or `point-to-point` keyword because there is no default. These keywords are defined in Figure 1.

The following command creates a point-to-point subinterface for PVC 103 to R3:

```
R1(config-if)# interface serial 0/0/0.103 point-to-point
```

Note   For simplicity, only IPv4 addresses are used in this section to illustrate subinterfaces. The same concepts and commands also apply when using IPv6 addressing.

If the subinterface is configured as point-to-point, the local DLCI for the subinterface must also be configured to distinguish it from the physical interface. The DLCI is also required for multipoint subinterfaces for which Inverse ARP is enabled for IPv4. It is not required for multipoint subinterfaces configured with static route maps.

The Frame Relay service provider assigns the DLCI numbers. These numbers range from 16 to 992, and usually have only local significance. The range varies depending on the LMI used.

The `frame-relay interface-dlci` command configures the local DLCI on the subinterface, as shown in Figure 2:

```
R1(config-subif)# frame-relay interface-dlci 103
```

Note   Unfortunately, altering an existing Frame Relay subinterface configuration may fail to provide the expected result. In these situations, shut down the physical interface, make the appropriate changes to the subinterfaces and then re-enable the physical interface. If the corrected configuration produces unexpected results, then it may be necessary to save the configuration and reload the router.

Refer to
Online Course
for Illustration

4.2.2.4   Example: Configuring Point-to-Point Subinterfaces

Figure 1 shows the previous topology but using point-to-point subinterfaces. Each PVC is a separate subnetwork. The router's physical interfaces are divided into subinterfaces, with each subinterface on a separate subnetwork.

In Figure 2, R1 has two point-to-point subinterfaces. The s0/0/1.102 subinterface connects to R2, and the s0/0/1.103 subinterface connects to R3. Each subinterface is on a different subnet.

To configure subinterfaces on a physical interface, the following steps are required:

Step 1. Remove any network layer address assigned to the physical interface. If the physical interface has an address, frames are not received by the local subinterfaces.

Step 2. Configure Frame Relay encapsulation on the physical interface using the `encapsulation frame-relay` command.

Step 3. For each of the defined PVCs, create a logical subinterface. Specify the port number, followed by a period (.) and the subinterface number. To make troubleshooting easier, it is suggested that the subinterface number matches the DLCI number.

Step 4. Configure an IP address for the interface and set the bandwidth.

Step 5. Configure the local DLCI on the subinterface using the `frame-relay interface-dlci` command. Recall that the Frame Relay service provider assigns the DLCI numbers.

Use the Syntax Checker in Figure 3 to configure router R2's physical interface into point-to-point subinterfaces with the appropriate Frame Relay configuration.

Refer to **Interactive Graphic** in online course.

4.2.2.5 Activity - Identify Frame Relay Bandwidth and Flow Control Terminology

Refer to **Packet Tracer Activity** for this chapter

4.2.2.6 Packet Tracer - Configuring Frame Relay Point-to-Point Subinterfaces

Background/Scenario

In this activity, you will configure Frame Relay with two subinterfaces on each router to reach the other two routers. You will also configure EIGRP and verify end-to-end connectivity.

Refer to **Lab Activity** for this chapter

4.2.2.7 Lab - Configuring Frame Relay and Subinterfaces

In this lab, you will complete the following objectives:

- Part 1: Build the Network and Configure Basic Device Settings
- Part 2: Configure a Frame Relay Switch
- Part 3: Configure Basic Frame Relay
- Part 4: Troubleshoot Frame Relay
- Part 5: Configure a Frame Relay Subinterface

Refer to
Online Course
for Illustration

4.3   Troubleshoot Connectivity

4.3.1   Troubleshoot Frame Relay

4.3.1.1   Verifying Frame Relay Operation: Frame Relay Interface

Frame Relay is generally a very reliable service. Nonetheless, there are times when the network performs at less than expected levels and troubleshooting is necessary. For example, users may report slow and intermittent connections across the circuit, or circuits may go down altogether. Regardless of the reason, network outages are very expensive in terms of lost productivity. A recommended best practice is to verify the configuration before problems appear.

In this topic, you will step though a verification procedure to ensure everything is working correctly before a configuration is launched on a live network.

Verify Frame Relay Interfaces

After configuring a Frame Relay PVC and when troubleshooting an issue, verify that Frame Relay is operating correctly on that interface using the `show interfaces` command.

Recall that with Frame Relay, the router is normally considered a DTE device. However, for testing purposes, a Cisco router can be configured as a DCE device to simulate a Frame Relay switch. In such cases, the router becomes a DCE device when it is configured as a Frame Relay switch.

As shown in the figure, the `show interfaces` command displays how the encapsulation is set up, along with useful Layer 1 and Layer 2 status information, including:

■ LMI DLCI

■ LMI type

■ Frame Relay DTE/DCE type

The first step is always to confirm that the interfaces are properly configured. In the figure, among other things, you can see details about the encapsulation, the DLCI on the Frame Relay-configured serial interface, and the DLCI used for the LMI. Confirm that these values are the expected values; if not, changes may be required.

Refer to
Online Course
for Illustration

4.3.1.2   Verifying Frame Relay Operation: LMI Operations

The next step is to look at some LMI statistics using the `show frame-relay lmi` command. The figure displays a sample output that shows the number of status messages exchanged between the local router and the local Frame Relay switch. Ensure that the counters between status messages being sent and received are incrementing. This validates that there is active communication between the DTE and the DCE.

Also look for any non-zero `Invalid` items. This helps isolate the problem of Frame Relay communications between the carrier's switch and the client router.

Refer to
Online Course
for Illustration

4.3.1.3   Verifying Frame Relay Operation: PVC Status

The figure shows the statistics for the interface.

Use the `show frame-relay pvc [interface` interface] `[dlci]` command to view PVC and traffic statistics. This command is also useful for viewing the number of BECN and FECN packets received by the router. The PVC status can be active, inactive, or deleted.

The `show frame-relay pvc` command displays the status of all the PVCs configured on the router. You can also specify a particular PVC.

After the statistics are gathered, use the `clear counters` command to reset the statistics counters. Wait 5 or 10 minutes after clearing the counters before issuing the `show` commands again. Note any additional errors. If you need to contact the carrier, these statistics help in resolving the issues.

Refer to
Online Course
for Illustration

4.3.1.4   Verifying Frame Relay Operation: Inverse ARP

To clear dynamically created Frame Relay maps that are created using Inverse ARP, use the `clear frame-relay inarp` command, as shown in Figure 1.

A final task is to confirm whether the `frame-relay inverse-arp` command resolved a remote IPv4 address to a local DLCI. Use the `show frame-relay map` command to display the current map entries and information about the connections. Figure 2 shows output from router R3 with a previous Frame Relay configuration on the physical interface, without the use of subinterfaces. Inverse ARP is enabled by default for IPv4. Frame Relay for IPv6 uses Inverse Neighbor Discovery (IND) to obtain a Layer 3 IPv6 address from a Layer 2 DLCI.

The output shows the following information:

- **10.1.1.9** is the IPv4 address of the remote router, dynamically learned via the Inverse ARP process.

- **302** is the decimal value of the local DLCI number.

- **0x12E** is the hex conversion of the DLCI number, 0x12E = 302 decimal.

- **0x48E0** is the value as it would appear on the wire because of the way the DLCI bits are spread out in the address field of the Frame Relay frame.

- **Broadcast/multicast** is enabled on the PVC.

- LMI type is **cisco.**

- PVC status is **active.**

When an Inverse ARP request is made, the router updates its map table with three possible LMI connection states. These states are:

- **ACTIVE**- Indicates a successful end-to-end (DTE to DTE) circuit.

- **INACTIVE**- Indicates a successful connection to the switch (DTE to DCE) without a DTE detected on the other end of the PVC. This can occur due to incorrect configuration on the switch.

- **DELETED**- Indicates that the DTE is configured for a DLCI that the switch does not recognize as valid for that interface.

4.3.1.5   Troubleshooting Frame Relay Operation

If the verification procedure indicates that your Frame Relay configuration is not working properly, the next step is to troubleshoot the configuration.

Use the **debug frame-relay lmi** command to determine whether the router and the Frame Relay switch are sending and receiving LMI packets properly.

Look at the figure to examine the output of an LMI exchange.

- **out** is an LMI status message sent by the router.
- **in** is a message received from the Frame Relay switch.
- A full LMI status message is a **type 0**.
- An LMI exchange is a **type 1**.
- **dlci 102, status 0x2** means that the status of DLCI 102 is active.

The possible values of the status field are as follows:

- **0x0**- The switch has this DLCI programmed, but for some reason it is not usable. The reason could possibly be the other end of the PVC is down.
- **0x2**- The Frame Relay switch has the DLCI and everything is operational.
- **0x4**- The Frame Relay switch does not have this DLCI programmed for the router, but that it was programmed at some point in the past. This could also be caused by the DLCIs being reversed on the router, or by the PVC being deleted by the service provider in the Frame Relay cloud.

4.3.1.6   Lab - Troubleshooting Basic Frame Relay

In this lab, you will complete the following objectives:

- Part 1: Build the Network and Load Device Configurations
- Part 2: Troubleshoot Layer 3 Connectivity
- Part 3: Troubleshoot Frame Relay

4.4   Summary

4.4.1.1   Class Activity - Frame Relay Budget Proposal

Frame Relay Budget Proposal

It has been decided that your company will use Frame Relay technology to provide video connectivity between your main office location and two branch offices. The company will also use the new network for redundancy in case their current ISP network connectivity is interrupted for any reason.

As usual, with any kind of network upgrade, you must develop a cost proposal for your administrator.

After doing some research, you decide to use this Frame Relay web site for your cost analysis. Costs listed on the site are representative of real ISP costs – they are referenced only to help you create your cost analysis design.

Refer to **Packet
Tracer Activity**
for this chapter

4.4.1.2   Packet Tracer - Skills Integration Challenge

Background/Scenario

This activity allows you to practice a variety of skills, including configuring Frame Relay, PPP with CHAP, EIGRP, static, and default routing.

Refer to
Online Course
for Illustration

4.4.1.3   Summary

Frame Relay is a reliable, packet switching, connection-oriented technology that is widely used to interconnect remote sites. This is more cost effective than leased lines, because the bandwidth in the service provider's network is shared, and an endpoint only needs one physical circuit to the circuit provider to support multiple VCs. Each VC is identified by a DLCI.

Layer 3 data is encapsulated into a Frame Relay frame that has both a Frame Relay header and trailer. It is then passed to the physical layer, which is typically EIA/TIA-232, 449 or 530, V.35, or X.21.

Typical Frame Relay topologies include the star topology (hub-and-spoke), a full mesh, and a partial mesh topology.

Mapping between Layer 2 DLCI addresses and Layer 3 addresses can be achieved dynamically by using Inverse ARP or by manually configuring static maps.

LMI is a protocol for messages sent between the DCE and DTE devices to maintain the status information of the Frame Relay between these devices. The LMI type configured on the router must match that of the service provider.

The Frame Relay circuit cost includes the access rate, the number of PVCs, and the CIR. Some bursting above the CIR is normally allowed without an additional cost. A Bc rate can be negotiated to provide some dependable bursting ability for short-term conditions.

Frame Relay uses BECN and FECN bits in the Frame Relay header for congestion control.

The use of subinterfaces in Frame Relay configurations helps to alleviate routing protocol split horizon issues.

Go to the online course to take the quiz and exam.

Chapter 4 Quiz

This quiz is designed to provide an additional opportunity to practice the skills and knowledge presented in the chapter and to prepare for the chapter exam. You will be allowed multiple attempts and the grade does not appear in the gradebook.

Chapter 4 Exam

The chapter exam assesses your knowledge of the chapter content.

Your Chapter Notes

Network Address Translation for IPv4

5.0 Introduction

5.0.1.1 Introduction

All public IPv4 addresses that transverse the Internet must be registered with a Regional Internet Registry (RIR). Organizations can lease public addresses from an SP, but only the registered holder of a public Internet address can assign that address to a network device. However, with a theoretical maximum of 4.3 billion addresses, IPv4 address space is severely limited. When Bob Kahn and Vint Cerf first developed the suite of TCP/IP protocols including IPv4 in 1981, they never envisioned what the Internet would become. At the time, the personal computer was mostly a curiosity for hobbyists and the World Wide Web was still more than a decade away.

With the proliferation of personal computing and the advent of the World Wide Web, it soon became obvious that 4.3 billion IPv4 addresses would not be enough. The long term solution was IPv6, but more immediate solutions to address exhaustion were required. For the short term, several solutions were implemented by the IETF including Network Address Translation (NAT) and RFC 1918 private IPv4 addresses. The chapter discusses how NAT, combined with the use of private address space, is used to both conserve and more efficiently use IPv4 addresses to provide networks of all sizes access to the Internet. This chapter covers:

- NAT characteristics, terminology, and general operations

- The different types of NAT, including static NAT, dynamic NAT, and NAT with overloading

- The benefits and disadvantages of NAT

- The configuration, verification, and analysis of static NAT, dynamic NAT, and NAT with overloading

- How port forwarding can be used to access an internal devices from the Internet

- Troubleshooting NAT using **show** and **debug** commands

- How NAT for IPv6 is used to translate between IPv6 addresses and IPv4 addresses

Refer to **Lab Activity** for this chapter

5.0.1.2 Class Activity - Conceptual NAT

Conceptual NAT

You work for a large university or school system.

Because you are the network administrator, many professors, administrative workers, and other network administrators need your assistance with their networks on a daily basis. They call you at all working hours of the day and, because of the number of telephone calls, you cannot complete your regular network administration tasks.

You need to find a way to limit when you take calls and from whom. You also need to mask your telephone number so that when you call someone, another number is displayed to the recipient.

This scenario describes a very common problem for most small- to medium-sized businesses. Visit, "How Network Address Translation Works", located here, to view more information about how the digital world handles these types of workday interruptions.

Refer to
Interactive Graphic
in online course.

5.1 NAT Operation

5.1.1 NAT Characteristics

5.1.1.1 IPv4 Private Address Space

There are not enough public IPv4 addresses to assign a unique address to each device connected to the Internet. Networks are commonly implemented using private IPv4 addresses, as defined in RFC 1918. Figure 1 shows the range of addresses included in RFC 1918. It is very likely that the computer that you use to view this course is assigned a private address.

These private addresses are used within an organization or site to allow devices to communicate locally. However, because these addresses do not identify any single company or organization, private IPv4 addresses cannot be routed over the Internet. To allow a device with a private IPv4 address to access devices and resources outside of the local network, the private address must first be translated to a public address.

As shown in Figure 2, NAT provides the translation of private addresses to public addresses. This allows a device with a private IPv4 address to access resources outside of their private network, such as those found on the Internet. NAT combined with private IPv4 addresses, has proven to be a useful method of preserving public IPv4 addresses. A single, public IPv4 address can be shared by hundreds, even thousands of devices, each configured with a unique private IPv4 address.

Without NAT, the exhaustion of the IPv4 address space would have occurred well before the year 2000. However, NAT has certain limitations, which will be explored later in this chapter. The solution to the exhaustion of IPv4 address space and the limitations of NAT is the eventual transition to IPv6.

Refer to
Online Course
for Illustration

5.1.1.2 What is NAT?

NAT has many uses, but its primary use is to conserve public IPv4 addresses. It does this by allowing networks to use private IPv4 addresses internally and providing translation to a public address only when needed. NAT has an added benefit of adding a degree of privacy and security to a network, because it hides internal IPv4 addresses from outside networks.

NAT-enabled routers can be configured with one or more valid public IPv4 addresses. These public addresses are known as the NAT pool. When an internal device sends traffic out of the network, the NAT-enabled router translates the internal IPv4 address of the device to a public address from the NAT pool. To outside devices, all traffic entering and exiting the network appears to have a public IPv4 address from the provided pool of addresses.

A NAT router typically operates at the border of a stub network. A stub network is a network that has a single connection to its neighboring network, one way in and one way out of the network. In the example in the figure, R2 is a border router. As seen from the ISP, R2 forms a stub network.

When a device inside the stub network wants to communicate with a device outside of its network, the packet is forwarded to the border router. The border router performs the NAT process, translating the internal private address of the device to a public, outside, routable address.

Note   The connection to the ISP may use a private address or a public address that is shared among customers. For the purposes of this chapter, a public address is shown.

Refer to
Online Course
for Illustration

5.1.1.3   NAT Terminology

In NAT terminology, the inside network is the set of networks that is subject to translation. The outside network refers to all other networks.

When using NAT, IPv4 addresses have different designations based on whether they are on the private network, or on the public network (Internet), and whether the traffic is incoming or outgoing.

NAT includes four types of addresses:

■ Inside local address

■ Inside global address

■ Outside local address

■ Outside global address

When determining which type of address is used, it is important to remember that NAT terminology is always applied from the perspective of the device with the translated address:

■ **Inside address**- The address of the device which is being translated by NAT.

■ **Outside address**- The address of the destination device.

NAT also uses the concept of local or global with respect to addresses:

■ **Local address**- A local address is any address that appears on the inside portion of the network.

■ **Global address**- A global address is any address that appears on the outside portion of the network.

In the figure, PC1 has an inside local address of 192.168.10.10. From the perspective of PC1, the web server has an outside address of 209.165.201.1. When packets are sent from PC1 to the global address of the web server, the inside local address of PC1 is translated to 209.165.200.226 (inside global address). The address of the outside device is not typically translated, because that address is usually a public IPv4 address.

Notice that PC1 has different local and global addresses, whereas the web server has the same public IPv4 address for both. From the perspective of the web server, traffic originating from PC1 appears to have come from 209.165.200.226, the inside global address.

The NAT router, R2 in the figure, is the demarcation point between the inside and outside networks and as between local and global addresses.

Refer to
Online Course
for Illustration

5.1.1.4   NAT Terminology (Cont.)

The terms, inside and outside, are combined with the terms local and global to refer to specific addresses. In the figure, router R2 has been configured to provide NAT. It has a pool of public addresses to assign to inside hosts.

- **Inside local address**- The address of the source as seen from inside the network. In the figure, the IPv4 address 192.168.10.10 is assigned to PC1. This is the inside local address of PC1.

- **Inside global address**- The address of source as seen from the outside network. In the figure, when traffic from PC1 is sent to the web server at 209.165.201.1, R2 translates the inside local address to an inside global address. In this case, R2 changes the IPv4 source address from 192.168.10.10 to 209.165.200.226. In NAT terminology, the inside local address of 192.168.10.10 is translated to the inside global address of 209.165.200.226.

- **Outside global address**- The address of the destination as seen from the outside network. It is a globally routable IPv4 address assigned to a host on the Internet. For example, the web server is reachable at IPv4 address 209.165.201.1. Most often the outside local and outside global addresses are the same.

- **Outside local address**- The address of the destination as seen from the inside network. In this example, PC1 sends traffic to the web server at the IPv4 address 209.165.201.1. While uncommon, this address could be different than the globally routable address of the destination.

The figure shows how traffic is addressed that is sent from an internal PC to an external web server, across the NAT-enabled router. It also shows how return traffic is initially addressed and translated.

Note   The use of the outside local address is outside the scope of this course.

Refer to
Online Course
for Illustration

5.1.1.5   How NAT Works

In this example, PC1 with private address 192.168.10.10 wants to communicate with an outside web server with public address 209.165.201.1.

Click the Play button in the figure to start the animation.

PC1 sends a packet addressed to the web server. The packet is forwarded by R1 to R2.

When the packet arrives at R2, the NAT-enabled router for the network, R2 reads the source IPv4 address of the packet to determine if the packet matches the criteria specified for translation.

In this case, the source IPv4 address does match the criteria and is translated from 192.168.10.10 (inside local address) to 209.165.200.226 (inside global address). R2 adds this mapping of the local to global address to the NAT table.

R2 sends the packet with the translated source address toward the destination.

The web server responds with a packet addressed to the inside global address of PC1 (209.165.200.226).

R2 receives the packet with destination address 209.165.200.226. R2 checks the NAT table and finds an entry for this mapping. R2 uses this information and translates the inside global address (209.165.200.226) to the inside local address (192.168.10.10), and the packet is forwarded toward PC1.

Refer to **Interactive Graphic** in online course.

5.1.1.6   Activity - Identify the NAT Terminology

Refer to **Online Course** for Illustration

5.1.2   Types of NAT

5.1.2.1   Static NAT

There are three types of NAT translation:

- **Static address translation (static NAT)**- One-to-one address mapping between local and global addresses.

- **Dynamic address translation (dynamic NAT)**- Many-to-many address mapping between local and global addresses.

- **Port Address Translation (PAT)**- Many-to-one address mapping between local and global addresses. This method is also known as overloading (NAT overloading).

Static NAT

Static NAT uses a one-to-one mapping of local and global addresses. These mappings are configured by the network administrator and remain constant.

In the figure, R2 is configured with static mappings for the inside local addresses of Svr1, PC2, and PC3. When these devices send traffic to the Internet, their inside local addresses are translated to the configured inside global addresses. To outside networks, these devices have public IPv4 addresses.

Static NAT is particularly useful for web servers or devices that must have a consistent address that is accessible from the Internet, such as a company web server. It is also useful for devices that must be accessible by authorized personnel when offsite, but not by the general public on the Internet. For example, a network administrator from PC4 can SSH to Svr1's inside global address (209.165.200.226). R2 translates this inside global address to the inside local address and connects the administrator's session to Svr1.

Static NAT requires that enough public addresses are available to satisfy the total number of simultaneous user sessions.

Refer to
Online Course
for Illustration

5.1.2.2   Dynamic NAT

Dynamic NAT uses a pool of public addresses and assigns them on a first-come, first-served basis. When an inside device requests access to an outside network, dynamic NAT assigns an available public IPv4 address from the pool.

In the figure, PC3 has accessed the Internet using the first available address in the dynamic NAT pool. The other addresses are still available for use. Similar to static NAT, dynamic NAT requires that enough public addresses are available to satisfy the total number of simultaneous user sessions.

Refer to
Online Course
for Illustration

5.1.2.3   Port Address Translation (PAT)

Port Address Translation (PAT), also known as NAT overload, maps multiple private IPv4 addresses to a single public IPv4 address or a few addresses. This is what most home routers do. The ISP assigns one address to the router, yet several members of the household can simultaneously access the Internet. This is the most common form of NAT.

With PAT, multiple addresses can be mapped to one or to a few addresses, because each private address is also tracked by a port number. When a device initiates a TCP/IP session, it generates a TCP or UDP source port value to uniquely identify the session. When the NAT router receives a packet from the client, it uses its source port number to uniquely identify the specific NAT translation.

PAT ensures that devices use a different TCP port number for each session with a server on the Internet. When a response comes back from the server, the source port number, which becomes the destination port number on the return trip, determines to which device the router forwards the packets. The PAT process also validates that the incoming packets were requested, thus adding a degree of security to the session.

Click the Play and Pause buttons in the figure to control the animation.

The animation illustrates the PAT process. PAT adds unique source port numbers to the inside global address to distinguish between translations.

As R2 processes each packet, it uses a port number (1331 and 1555, in this example) to identify the device from which the packet originated. The source address (SA) is the inside local address with the TCP/IP assigned port number added. The destination address (DA) is the outside local address with the service port number added. In this example, the service port is 80, which is HTTP.

For the source address, R2 translates the inside local address to an inside global address with the port number added. The destination address is not changed, but is now referred to as the outside global IP address. When the web server replies, the path is reversed.

Refer to
Online Course
for Illustration

5.1.2.4   Next Available Port

In the previous example, the client port numbers, 1331 and 1555, did not change at the NAT-enabled router. This is not a very likely scenario, because there is a good chance that these port numbers may have already been attached to other active sessions.

PAT attempts to preserve the original source port. However, if the original source port is already used, PAT assigns the first available port number starting from the beginning of the appropriate port group 0–511, 512–1,023, or 1,024–65,535. When there are no more ports available and there is more than one external address in the address pool, PAT moves to the next address to try to allocate the original source port. This process continues until there are no more available ports or external IP addresses.

Click the Play button in the figure to view PAT operation.

In the animation, the hosts have chosen the same port number 1444. This is acceptable for the inside address, because the hosts have unique private IP addresses. However, at the NAT router, the port numbers must be changed; otherwise, packets from two different hosts would exit R2 with the same source address. In this example, PAT has assigned the next available port (1445) to the second host address.

Refer to
Online Course
for Illustration

5.1.2.5   Comparing NAT and PAT

Summarizing the differences between NAT and PAT helps your understanding of each.

As the figure shows, NAT translates IPv4 addresses on a 1:1 basis between private IPv4 addresses and public IPv4 addresses. However, PAT modifies both the address and the port number.

NAT forwards incoming packets to their inside destination by referring to the incoming source IPv4 address given by the host on the public network. With PAT, there is generally only one or a very few publicly exposed IPv4 addresses. Incoming packets from the public network are routed to their destinations on the private network by referring to a table in the NAT router. This table tracks public and private port pairs. This is called connection tracking.

Packets without a Layer 4 Segment

What about IPv4 packets carrying data other than a TCP or UDP segment? These packets do not contain a Layer 4 port number. PAT translates most common protocols carried by IPv4 that do not use TCP or UDP as a transport layer protocol. The most common of these is ICMPv4. Each of these types of protocols is handled differently by PAT. For example, ICMPv4 query messages, echo requests, and echo replies include a Query ID. ICMPv4 uses the Query ID to identify an echo request with its corresponding echo reply. The Query ID is incremented with each echo request sent. PAT uses the Query ID instead of a Layer 4 port number.

Note   Other ICMPv4 messages do not use the Query ID. These messages and other protocols that do not use TCP or UDP port numbers vary and are beyond the scope of this curriculum.

Refer to **Packet
Tracer Activity**
for this chapter

5.1.2.6   Packet Tracer - Investigating NAT Operation

Background/Scenario

As a frame travels across a network, the MAC addresses may change. IP addresses can also change when a packet is forwarded by a device configured with NAT. In this activity, we will investigate what happens to IP addresses during the NAT process.

Refer to
Online Course
for Illustration

5.1.3   Benefits of NAT

5.1.3.1   Benefits of NAT

As highlighted by the figure, NAT provides many benefits, including:

- NAT conserves the legally registered addressing scheme by allowing the privatization of intranets. NAT conserves addresses through application port-level multiplexing. With NAT overload, internal hosts can share a single public IPv4 address for all external communications. In this type of configuration, very few external addresses are required to support many internal hosts.

- NAT increases the flexibility of connections to the public network. Multiple pools, backup pools, and load-balancing pools can be implemented to ensure reliable public network connections.

- NAT provides consistency for internal network addressing schemes. On a network not using private IPv4 addresses and NAT, changing the public IPv4 address scheme requires the readdressing of all hosts on the existing network. The costs of readdressing hosts can be significant. NAT allows the existing private IPv4 address scheme to remain while allowing for easy change to a new public addressing scheme. This means an organization could change ISPs and not need to change any of its inside clients.

- NAT provides network security. Because private networks do not advertise their addresses or internal topology, they remain reasonably secure when used in conjunction with NAT to gain controlled external access. However, NAT does not replace firewalls.

Refer to
Online Course
for Illustration

5.1.3.2   Disadvantages of NAT

As highlighted by the figure, NAT does have some drawbacks. The fact that hosts on the Internet appear to communicate directly with the NAT-enabled device, rather than with the actual host inside the private network, creates a number of issues.

One disadvantage of using NAT is related to network performance, particularly for real time protocols such as VoIP. NAT increases switching delays because the translation of each IPv4 address within the packet headers takes time. The first packet is always process-switched going through the slower path. The router must look at every packet to decide whether it needs translation. The router must alter the IPv4 header, and possibly alter the TCP or UDP header. The IPv4 header checksum, along with the TCP or UDP checksum must be recalculated each time a translation is made. Remaining packets go through the fast-switched path if a cache entry exists; otherwise, they too are delayed.

Another disadvantage of using NAT is that end-to-end addressing is lost. Many Internet protocols and applications depend on end-to-end addressing from the source to the destination. Some applications do not work with NAT. For example, some security applications, such as digital signatures, fail because the source IPv4 address changes before reaching the destination. Applications that use physical addresses, instead of a qualified domain name, do not reach destinations that are translated across the NAT router. Sometimes, this problem can be avoided by implementing static NAT mappings.

End-to-end IPv4 traceability is also lost. It becomes much more difficult to trace packets that undergo numerous packet address changes over multiple NAT hops, making troubleshooting challenging.

Using NAT also complicates tunneling protocols, such as IPsec, because NAT modifies values in the headers that interfere with the integrity checks done by IPsec and other tunneling protocols.

Services that require the initiation of TCP connections from the outside network, or stateless protocols, such as those using UDP, can be disrupted. Unless the NAT router has been configured to support such protocols, incoming packets cannot reach their destination. Some protocols can accommodate one instance of NAT between participating hosts (passive mode FTP, for example), but fail when both systems are separated from the Internet by NAT.

Refer to
Online Course
for Illustration

5.2   Configuring NAT

5.2.1   Configuring Static NAT

5.2.1.1   Configuring Static NAT

Static NAT is a one-to-one mapping between an inside address and an outside address. Static NAT allows external devices to initiate connections to internal devices using the statically assigned public address. For instance, an internal web server may be mapped to a specific inside global address so that it is accessible from outside networks.

Figure 1 shows an inside network containing a web server with a private IPv4 address. Router R2 is configured with static NAT to allow devices on the outside network (Internet) to access the web server. The client on the outside network accesses the web server using a public IPv4 address. Static NAT translates the public IPv4 address to the private IPv4 address.

There are two basic tasks when configuring static NAT translations.

Step 1. The first task is to create a mapping between the inside local address and the inside global addresses. For example, the 192.168.10.254 inside local address and the 209.165.201.5 inside global address in Figure 1 are configured as a static NAT translation.

Step 2. After the mapping is configured, the interfaces participating in the translation are configured as inside or outside relative to NAT. In the example, the Serial 0/0/0 interface of R2 is an inside interface and Serial 0/1/0 is an outside interface.

Packets arriving on the inside interface of R2 (Serial 0/0/0) from the configured inside local IPv4 address (192.168.10.254) are translated and then forwarded towards the outside network. Packets arriving on the outside interface of R2 (Serial 0/1/0), that are addressed to the configured inside global IPv4 address (209.165.201.5), are translated to the inside local address (192.168.10.254) and then forwarded to the inside network.

Figure 2 outlines the commands needed to configure static NAT.

Figure 3 shows the commands needed on R2 to create a static NAT mapping to the web server in the example topology. With the configuration shown, R2 translates packets from the web server with address 192.168.10.254 to public IPv4 address 209.165.201.5. The Internet client directs web requests to the public IPv4 address 209.165.201.5. R2 forwards that traffic to the web server at 192.168.10.254.

Use the Syntax Checker in Figure 4 to configure an additional static NAT entry on R2.

Refer to
Online Course
for Illustration

5.2.1.2   Analyzing Static NAT

Using the previous configuration, the figure illustrates the static NAT translation process between the client and the web server. Usually static translations are used when clients on the outside network (Internet) need to reach servers on the inside (internal) network.

1. The client wants to open a connection to the web server. The client sends a packet to the web server using the public IPv4 destination address of 209.165.201.5. This is the inside global address of the web server.

2. The first packet that R2 receives from the client on its NAT outside interface causes R2 to check its NAT table. The destination IPv4 address is located in the NAT table and is translated.

3. R2 replaces the inside global address of 209.165.201.5 with the inside local address of 192.168.10.254. R2 then forwards the packet towards the web server.

4. The web server receives the packet and responds to the client using the inside local address, 192.168.10.254.

   5a. R2 receives the packet from the web server on its NAT inside interface with source address of the inside local address of the web server, 192.168.10.254.

   5b. R2 checks the NAT table for a translation for the inside local address. The address is found in the NAT table. R2 translates the source address to the inside global address of 209.165.201.5 and forwards the packet out of its serial 0/1/0 interface toward the client.

5. The client receives the packet and continues the conversation. The NAT router performs Steps 2 to 5b for each packet. Step 6 is not shown in the figure.

Refer to
Online Course
for Illustration

5.2.1.3   Verifying Static NAT

A useful command to verify NAT operation is show `ip nat translations`. This command shows active NAT translations. Static translations, unlike dynamic translations, are always in the NAT table. Figure 1 shows the output from this command using the previous configuration example. Because the example is a static NAT configuration, the translation is always present in the NAT table regardless of any active communications. If the command is issued during an active session, the output also indicates the address of the outside device as shown in Figure 1.

Another useful command is `show ip nat statistics`. As shown in Figure 2, the `show ip nat statistics` command displays information about the total number of active translations, NAT configuration parameters, the number of addresses in the pool, and the number of addresses that have been allocated.

To verify that the NAT translation is working, it is best to clear statistics from any past translations using the `clear ip nat statistics` command before testing.

Prior to any communications with the web server, the `show ip nat statistics` command shows no current hits. After the client establishes a session with the web server, the `show ip nat statistics` command has been incremented to five hits. This verifies that the static NAT translation is taking place on R2.

Refer to **Packet Tracer Activity** for this chapter

5.2.1.4   Packet Tracer - Configuring Static NAT

Background/Scenario

In IPv4 configured networks, clients and servers use private addressing. Before packets with private addressing can cross then Internet, they need to be translated to public addressing. Servers that are accessed from outside the organization are usually assigned both a public and a private static IP address. In this activity, you will configure static NAT so that outside devices can access and inside server at its public address.

Refer to **Online Course** for Illustration

5.2.2   Configuring Dynamic NAT

5.2.2.1   Dynamic NAT Operation

While static NAT provides a permanent mapping between an inside local address and an inside global address, dynamic NAT allows the automatic mapping of inside local addresses to inside global addresses. These inside global addresses are typically public IPv4 addresses. Dynamic NAT uses a group, or pool of public IPv4 addresses for translation.

Dynamic NAT, like static NAT, requires the configuration of the inside and outside interfaces participating in NAT. However, where static NAT creates a permanent mapping to a single address, dynamic NAT uses a pool of addresses.

Note   Translating between public and private IPv4 addresses is by far the most common use of NAT. However, NAT translations can occur between any pair of addresses.

The example topology shown in the figure has an inside network using addresses from the RFC 1918 private address space. Attached to router R1 are two LANs, 192.168.10.0/24 and 192.168.11.0/24. Router R2, the border router, is configured for dynamic NAT using a pool of public IPv4 addresses 209.165.200.226 through 209.165.200.240.

The pool of public IPv4 addresses (inside global address pool) is available to any device on the inside network on a first-come first-served basis. With dynamic NAT, a single inside address is translated to a single outside address. With this type of translation there must be enough addresses in the pool to accommodate all the inside devices needing access to the outside network at the same time. If all of the addresses in the pool have been used, a device must wait for an available address before it can access the outside network.

Refer to **Online Course** for Illustration

5.2.2.2   Configuring Dynamic NAT

Figure 1 shows the steps and the commands used to configure dynamic NAT.

Step 1.   Define the pool of addresses that will be used for translation using the `ip nat pool` command. This pool of addresses is typically a group of public addresses. The addresses are defined by indicating the starting IP address and the ending IP address of the pool. The `netmask` or `prefix-length` keyword indicates which address bits belong to the network and which bits belong to the host for the range of addresses.

Step 2. Configure a standard ACL to identify (permit) only those addresses that are to be translated. An ACL that is too permissive can lead to unpredictable results. Remember there is an implicit **deny all** statement at the end of each ACL.

Step 3. Bind the ACL to the pool. The `ip nat inside source list` access-list-number `number pool` pool name command is used to bind the ACL to the pool. This configuration is used by the router to identify which devices (`list`) receive which addresses (`pool`).

Step 4. Identify which interfaces are inside, in relation to NAT; that is, any interface that connects to the inside network.

Step 5. Identify which interfaces are outside, in relation to NAT; that is, any interface that connects to the outside network.

Figure 2 shows an example topology and configuration. This configuration allows translation for all hosts on the 192.168.0.0/16 network, which includes the 192.168.10.0 and 192.168.11.0 LANs, when they generate traffic that enters S0/0/0 and exits S0/1/0. These hosts are translated to an available address in the pool in the range 209.165.200.226 - 209.165.200.240.

Figure 3 shows the topology used for the Syntax Checker configuration. Use the Syntax Checker in Figure 4 to configure dynamic NAT on R2.

Refer to
Online Course
for Illustration

5.2.2.3   Analyzing Dynamic NAT

Using the previous configuration, the figures illustrate the dynamic NAT translation process between two clients and the web server:

In Figure 1, the traffic flow from inside to outside is shown:

1. The hosts with the source IPv4 addresses (192.168.10.10 (PC1) and 192.168.11.10 (PC2)) send packets requesting a connection to the server at the public IPv4 address (209.165.200.254).

2. R2 receives the first packet from host 192.168.10.10. Because this packet was received on an interface configured as an inside NAT interface, R2 checks the NAT configuration to determine if this packet should be translated. The ACL permits this packet, so R2 will translate the packet. R2 checks its NAT table. Because there is no translation entry for this IP address, R2 determines that the source address 192.168.10.10 must be translated dynamically. R2 selects an available global address from the dynamic address pool and creates a translation entry, 209.165.200.226. The original source IPv4 address (192.168.10.10) is the inside local address and the translated address is the inside global address (209.165.200.226) in the NAT table.

   For the second host, 192.168.11.10, R2 repeats the procedure, selects the next available global address from the dynamic address pool, and creates a second translation entry, 209.165.200.227.

3. R2 replaces the inside local source address of PC1, 192.168.10.10, with the translated inside global address of 209.165.200.226 and forwards the packet. The same process occurs for the packet from PC2 using the translated address for PC2 (209.165.200.227).

In Figure 2, the traffic flow from outside to inside is shown:

4. The server receives the packet from PC1 and responds using the IPv4 destination address of 209.165.200.226. When the server receives the second packet, it responds to PC2 using the IPv4 destination address of 209.165.200.227.

   5a. When R2 receives the packet with the destination IPv4 address of 209.165.200.226; it performs a NAT table lookup. Using the mapping from the table, R2 translates the address back to the inside local address (192.168.10.10) and forwards the packet toward PC1.

   5b. When R2 receives the packet with the destination IPv4 address of 209.165.200.227; it performs a NAT table lookup. Using the mapping from the table, R2 translates the address back to the inside local address (192.168.11.10) and forwards the packet toward PC2.

5. PC1 at 192.168.10.10 and PC2 at 192.168.11.10 receive the packets and continue the conversation. The router performs Steps 2 to 5 for each packet. (Step 6 is not shown in the figures.)

5.2.2.4 Verifying Dynamic NAT

Refer to
Online Course
for Illustration

The output of the `show ip nat translations` command shown in Figure 1 displays the details of the two previous NAT assignments. The command displays all static translations that have been configured and any dynamic translations that have been created by traffic.

Adding the `verbose` keyword displays additional information about each translation, including how long ago the entry was created and used.

By default, translation entries time out after 24 hours, unless the timers have been reconfigured with the `ip nat translation timeout` timeout-seconds command in global configuration mode.

To clear dynamic entries before the timeout has expired, use the `clear ip nat translation` global configuration mode command (Figure 2). It is useful to clear the dynamic entries when testing the NAT configuration. As shown in the table, this command can be used with keywords and variables to control which entries are cleared. Specific entries can be cleared to avoid disrupting active sessions. Use the `clear ip nat translation *` global configuration command to clear all translations from the table.

Note Only the dynamic translations are cleared from the table. Static translations cannot be cleared from the translation table.

In Figure 3, the `show ip nat statistics` command displays information about the total number of active translations, NAT configuration parameters, the number of addresses in the pool, and how many of the addresses have been allocated.

Alternatively, use the `show running-config` command and look for NAT, ACL, interface, or pool commands with the required values. Examine these carefully and correct any errors discovered.

Refer to **Packet Tracer Activity** for this chapter

5.2.2.5   Packet Tracer - Configuring Dynamic NAT

In this Packet Tracer, you will complete the following objectives:

■ Part 1: Configure Dynamic NAT

■ Part 2: Verify NAT Implementation

Refer to **Lab Activity** for this chapter

5.2.2.6   Lab - Configuring Dynamic and Static NAT

In this lab, you will complete the following objectives:

■ Part 1: Build the Network and Verify Connectivity

■ Part 2: Configure and Verify Static NAT

■ Part 3: Configure and Verify Dynamic NAT

Refer to **Online Course** for Illustration

5.2.3   Configuring Port Address Translation (PAT)

5.2.3.1   Configuring PAT: Address Pool

PAT (also called NAT overload) conserves addresses in the inside global address pool by allowing the router to use one inside global address for many inside local addresses. In other words, a single public IPv4 address can be used for hundreds, even thousands of internal private IPv4 addresses. When this type of translation is configured, the router maintains enough information from higher-level protocols, TCP or UDP port numbers, for example, to translate the inside global address back into the correct inside local address. When multiple inside local addresses map to one inside global address, the TCP or UDP port numbers of each inside host distinguish between the local addresses.

Note   The total number of internal addresses that can be translated to one external address could theoretically be as high as 65,536 per IP address. However, the number of internal addresses that can be assigned a single IP address is around 4,000.

There are two ways to configure PAT, depending on how the ISP allocates public IPv4 addresses. In the first instance, the ISP allocates more than one public IPv4 address to the organization, and in the other, it allocates a single public IPv4 address that is required for the organization to connect to the ISP.

Configuring PAT for a Pool of Public IP Addresses

If a site has been issued more than one public IPv4 address, these addresses can be part of a pool that is used by PAT. This is similar to dynamic NAT, except that there are not enough public addresses for a one-to-one mapping of inside to outside addresses. The small pool of addresses is shared among a larger number of devices.

Figure 1 shows the steps to configure PAT to use a pool of addresses. The primary difference between this configuration and the configuration for dynamic, one-to-one NAT is that the `overload` keyword is used. The `overload` keyword enables PAT.

The example configuration shown in Figure 2 establishes overload translation for the NAT pool named NAT-POOL2. NAT-POOL2 contains addresses 209.165.200.226 to

209.165.200.240. Hosts in the 192.168.0.0/16 network are subject to translation. The S0/0/0 interface is identified as an inside interface and the S0/1/0 interface is identified as an outside interface.

Use the Syntax Checker in Figure 3 to configure PAT using an address pool on R2.

Refer to **Online Course** for Illustration

5.2.3.2   Configuring PAT: Single Address
Configuring PAT for a Single Public IPv4 Address

Figure 1 shows the topology of a PAT implementation for a single public IPv4 address translation. In the example, all hosts from network 192.168.0.0/16 (matching ACL 1) that send traffic through router R2 to the Internet will be translated to IPv4 address 209.165.200.225 (IPv4 address of interface S0/1/0). The traffic flows will be identified by port numbers in the NAT table because the `overload` keyword was used.

Figure 2 shows the steps to follow to configure PAT with a single IPv4 address. If only a single public IPv4 address is available, the overload configuration typically assigns the public address to the outside interface that connects to the ISP. All inside addresses are translated to the single IPv4 address when leaving the outside interface.

Step 1.   Define an ACL to permit the traffic to be translated.

Step 2.   Configure source translation using the `interface` and `overload` keywords. The `interface` keyword identifies which interface IP address to use when translating inside addresses. The `overload` keyword directs the router to track port numbers with each NAT entry.

Step 3.   Identify which interfaces are inside in relation to NAT. That is any interface that connects to the inside network.

Step 4.   Identify which interface is outside in relation to NAT. This should be the same interface identified in the source translation statement from Step 2.

The configuration is similar to dynamic NAT, except that instead of a pool of addresses, the `interface` keyword is used to identify the outside IPv4 address. Therefore, no NAT pool is defined.

Use the Syntax Checker in Figure 3 to configure PAT using a single address on R2.

Refer to **Online Course** for Illustration

5.2.3.3   Analyzing PAT

The process of NAT overload is the same whether a pool of addresses is used or a single address is used. Continuing with the previous PAT example, using a single public IPv4 address, PC1 wants to communicate with the web server, Svr1. At the same time another client, PC2, wants to establish a similar session with the web server Svr2. Both PC1 and PC2 are configured with private IPv4 addresses, with R2 enabled for PAT.

PC to Server Process

1. Figure 1 shows both PC1 and PC2 sending packets to Svr1 and Svr2, respectively. PC1 has the source IPv4 address 192.168.10.10 and is using TCP source port 1444. PC2 has the source IPv4 address 192.168.10.11 and is coincidentally assigned the same source port of 1444.

2. The packet from PC1 reaches R2 first. Using PAT, R2 modifies the source IPv4 address to 209.165.200.225 (inside global address). There are no other devices in the NAT table using port 1444, so PAT maintains the same port number. The packet is then forwarded towards Svr1 at 209.165.201.1.

3. Next, the packet from PC2 arrives at R2. PAT is configured to use a single inside global IPv4 address for all translations, 209.165.200.225. Similar to the translation process for PC1, PAT changes PC2's source IPv4 address to the inside global address 209.165.200.225. However, PC2 has the same source port number as a current PAT entry, the translation for PC1. PAT increments the source port number until it is a unique value in its table. In this instance, the source port entry in the NAT table and the packet for PC2 receives 1445.

Although PC1 and PC2 are using the same translated address, the inside global address of 209.165.200.225, and the same source port number of 1444; the modified port number for PC2 (1445) makes each entry in the NAT table unique. This will become evident with the packets sent from the servers back to the clients.

Server to PC Process

4. As shown in Figure 2, in a typical client-server exchange, Svr1 and Svr2 respond to the requests received from PC1 and PC2, respectively. The servers use the source port from the received packet as the destination port, and the source address as the destination address for the return traffic. The servers seem as if they are communicating with the same host at 209.165.200.225; however, this is not the case.

5. As the packets arrive, R2 locates the unique entry in its NAT table using the destination address and the destination port of each packet. In the case of the packet from Svr1, the destination IPv4 address of 209.165.200.225 has multiple entries but only one with the destination port 1444. Using the entry in its table, R2 changes the destination IPv4 address of the packet to 192.168.10.10, with no change required for the destination port. The packet is then forwarded toward PC1.

6. When the packet from Svr2 arrives R2 performs a similar translation. The destination IPv4 address of 209.165.200.225 is located, again with multiple entries. However, using the destination port of 1445, R2 is able to uniquely identify the translation entry. The destination IPv4 address is changed to 192.168.10.11. In this case, the destination port must also be modified back to its original value of 1444, which is stored in the NAT table. The packet is then forwarded toward PC2.

Refer to
Online Course
for Illustration

5.2.3.4 Verifying PAT

Router R2 has been configured to provide PAT to the 192.168.0.0/16 clients. When the internal hosts exit router R2 to the Internet, they are translated to an IPv4 address from the PAT pool with a unique source port number.

The same commands used to verify static and dynamic NAT are used to verify PAT, as shown in Figure 1. The `show ip nat translations` command displays the translations from two different hosts to different web servers. Notice that two different inside hosts are allocated the same IPv4 address of 209.165.200.226 (inside global address). The source port numbers in the NAT table differentiate the two transactions.

As shown in Figure 2, the `show ip nat statistics` command verifies that NAT-POOL2 has allocated a single address for both translations. Included in the output is information about the number and type of active translations, NAT configuration parameters, the number of addresses in the pool, and how many have been allocated.

Refer to
Interactive Graphic
in online course.

5.2.3.5 Activity - Identify the Address Information at Each Hop

Refer to **Packet Tracer Activity**
for this chapter

5.2.3.6 Packet Tracer - Implementing Static and Dynamic NAT

In this Packet Tracer, you will complete the following objectives:

- Part 1: Configure Dynamic NAT with PAT

- Part 2: Configure Static NAT

- Part 3: Verify NAT Implementation

Refer to
Lab Activity
for this chapter

5.2.3.7 Lab - Configuring Port Address Translation (PAT)

In this lab, you will complete the following objectives:

- Part 1: Build the Network and Verify Connectivity

- Part 2: Configure and Verify NAT Pool Overload

- Part 3: Configure and Verify PAT

Refer to
Online Course
for Illustration

5.2.4 Port Forwarding

5.2.4.1 Port Forwarding

Port forwarding (sometimes referred to as tunneling) is the act of forwarding traffic addressed to a specific a network port from one network node to another. This technique allows an external user to reach a port on a private IPv4 address (inside a LAN) from the outside, through a NAT-enabled router.

Typically, peer-to-peer file-sharing programs and operations, such as web serving and outgoing FTP, require that router ports be forwarded or opened to allow these applications to work, as shown in Figure 1. Because NAT hides internal addresses, peer-to-peer only works from the inside out where NAT can map outgoing requests against incoming replies.

The problem is that NAT does not allow requests initiated from the outside. This situation can be resolved with manual intervention. Port forwarding can be configured to identify specific ports that can be forwarded to inside hosts.

Recall that Internet software applications interact with user ports that need to be open or available to those applications. Different applications use different ports. This makes it predictable for applications and routers to identify network services. For example, HTTP operates through the well-known port 80. When someone enters the http://cisco.com address, the browser displays the Cisco Systems, Inc. website. Notice that they do not have to specify the HTTP port number for the page request, because the application assumes port 80.

If a different port number is required, it can be appended to the URL separated by a colon (:). For example, if the web server is listening on port 8080, the user would type http://www.example.com:8080.

Port forwarding allows users on the Internet to access internal servers by using the WAN port address of the router and the matched external port number. The internal servers are typically configured with RFC 1918 private IPv4 addresses. When a request is sent to the IPv4 address of the WAN port via the Internet, the router forwards the request to the appropriate server on the LAN. For security reasons, broadband routers do not by default permit any external network request to be forwarded to an inside host.

Figure 2 shows a small business owner using a point of sale (PoS) server to track sales and inventories at the store. The server can be accessed within the store, but because it has a private IPv4 address, it is not publically accessible from the Internet. Enabling the local router for port forwarding allows the owner to access the point of sale server from anywhere on the Internet. Port forwarding on the router is configured using the destination port number and the private IPv4 address of the point of sale server. To access the server, the client software would use the public IPv4 address of the router and the destination port of the server.

Refer to
Online Course
for Illustration

5.2.4.2   SOHO Example

The figure shows the Single Port Forwarding configuration window of a Linksys EA6500 SOHO router. By default, port forwarding is not enabled on the router.

Port forwarding can be enabled for applications by specifying the inside local address that requests should be forwarded to. In the figure, HTTP service requests, coming into this Linksys router, are forwarded to the web server with the inside local address of 192.168.1.254. If the external WAN IPv4 address of the SOHO router is 209.165.200.225, the external user can enter http://www.example.com and the Linksys router redirects the HTTP request to the internal web server at IPv4 address 192.168.1.254, using the default port number 80.

A port other than the default port 80 can be specified. However, the external user would have to know the specific port number to use. To specify a different port, the value of the External Port in the Single Port Forwarding window would be modified.

The approach taken to configure port forwarding depends on the brand and model of the broadband router in the network. However, there are some generic steps to follow. If the instructions supplied by the ISP, or those that came with the router, do not provide adequate guidance, the website http://www.portforward.com provides guides for several broadband routers. You can follow the instructions to add or delete ports as required to meet the needs of any applications you want to allow or deny.

Refer to
Online Course
for Illustration

5.2.4.3   Configuring Port Forwarding with IOS

Implementing port forwarding with IOS commands is similar to the commands used to configure static NAT. Port forwarding is essentially a static NAT translation with a specified TCP or UDP port number.

Figure 1 shows the static NAT command used to configure port forwarding using IOS.

Figure 2 shows an example of configuring port forwarding using IOS commands on router R2. 192.168.10.254 is the inside local IPv4 address of the web server listening on port 80. Users will access this internal web server using the global IP address 209.165.200.225, a globally unique public IPv4 address. In this case, it is the address of the Serial 0/1/0 interface of R2. The global port is configured as 8080. This will be the destination port used, along with the global IPv4 address of 209.165.200.225 to access the internal web server.

Notice within the NAT configuration, the following command parameters:

- local-ip = 192.168.10.254
- local-port = 80
- global-ip = 209.165.200.225
- global-port = 8080

When a well-known port number is not being used, the client must specify the port number in the application.

Like other types of NAT, port forwarding requires the configuration of both the inside and outside NAT interfaces.

Similar to static NAT, the `show ip nat translations` command can be used to verify the port forwarding, as shown in Figure 3.

In the example, when the router receives the packet with the inside global IPv4 address of 209.165.200.225 and a TCP destination port 8080, the router performs a NAT table lookup using the destination IPv4 address and destination port as the key. The router then translates the address to the inside local address of host 192.168.10.254 and destination port 80. R2 then forwards the packet to the web server. For return packets from the web server back to the client, this process is reversed.

Refer to **Packet Tracer Activity** for this chapter

5.2.4.4   Packet Tracer - Configuring Port Forwarding on a Linksys Router

Background/Scenario

Your friend wants to play a game with you on your server. Both of you are at your respective homes, connected to the Internet. You need to configure your SOHO (Small Office, Home Office) router to port forward HTTP requests to your server so that your friend can access the game lobby web page.

Refer to **Online Course** for Illustration

5.2.5   Configuring NAT and IPv6

5.2.5.1   NAT for IPv6?

Since the early 1990s, the concern about the depletion of IPv4 address space has been a priority of the IETF. The combination of RFC 1918 private IPv4 addresses and NAT has been instrumental in slowing this depletion. NAT has significant disadvantages, and in January of 2011, IANA allocated the last of its IPv4 addresses to RIRs.

One of the unintentional benefits of NAT for IPv4 is that it hides the private network from the public Internet, as shown in the figure. NAT has the advantage of providing a perceived level of security by denying computers in the public Internet from accessing internal hosts. However, it should not be considered a substitute for proper network security, such as that provided by a firewall.

In RFC 5902, the Internet Architecture Board (IAB) included the following quote concerning IPv6 network address translation:

"It is commonly perceived that a NAT box provides one level of protection because external hosts cannot directly initiate communication with hosts behind a NAT. However, one should not confuse NAT boxes with firewalls. As discussed Section 2.2 in RFC4864, the act of translation does not provide security in itself. The stateful filtering function can provide the same level of protection without requiring a translation function."

IPv6, with a 128-bit address, provides 340 undecillion addresses. Therefore, address space is not an issue. IPv6 was developed with the intention of making NAT for IPv4 with its translation between public and private IPv4 addresses unnecessary. However, IPv6 does implement a form of NAT. IPv6 includes both its own IPv6 private address space and NAT, which are implemented differently than they are for IPv4.

Refer to
Online Course
for Illustration

5.2.5.2   IPv6 Unique Local Addresses

IPv6 unique local addresses (ULA) are similar to RFC 1918 private addresses in IPv4, but there are significant differences as well. The intent of ULA is to provide IPv6 address space for communications within a local site; it is not meant to provide additional IPv6 address space, nor is it meant to provide a level of security.

As shown in the figure, ULA have the prefix FC00::/7, which results in a first hextet range of FC00 to FDFF. The next 1 bit is set to 1 if the prefix is locally assigned. Set to 0 may be defined in the future. The next 40 bits is a global ID followed by a 16-bit Subnet ID. These first 64 bits combine to make the ULA prefix. This leaves the remaining 64 bits for the interface ID, or in IPv4 terms, the host portion of the address.

Unique local addresses are defined in RFC 4193. ULAs are also known as local IPv6 addresses (not to be confused with IPv6 link-local addresses) and have several characteristics including:

- Allows sites to be combined or privately interconnected, without creating any address conflicts or requiring renumbering of interfaces that use these prefixes.

- Independent of any ISP and can be used for communications within a site without having any Internet connectivity.

- Not routable across the Internet, however, if accidentally leaked by routing or DNS, there is not conflict with other addresses.

ULA is not quite as straight-forward as RFC 1918 addresses. Unlike private IPv4 addresses, it has not been the intention of the IETF to use a form of NAT to translate between unique local addresses and IPv6 global unicast addresses.

The implementation and potential uses for IPv6 unique local addresses are still being examined by the Internet community. For example, the IETF is considering allowing the option to have the ULA prefix created locally using FC00::/8, or to have it assigned automatically by a third-party beginning with FD00::/8.

Note   The original IPv6 specification allocated address space for site-local addresses, defined in RFC 3513. Site-local addresses have been deprecated by the IETF in RFC 3879 because the term "site" was somewhat ambiguous. Site-local addresses had the prefix range of FEC0::/10 and may still be found in some older IPv6 documentation.

Refer to
Online Course
for Illustration

5.2.5.3   NAT for IPv6

NAT for IPv6 is used in a much different context than NAT for IPv4, as shown in the figure. The varieties of NAT for IPv6 are used to transparently provide access between IPv6-only and IPv4-only networks. It is not used as a form of private IPv6 to global IPv6 translation.

Ideally, IPv6 should be run natively wherever possible. This means IPv6 devices communicating with each other over IPv6 networks. However, to aid in the move from IPv4 to IPv6, the IETF has developed several transition techniques to accommodate a variety of IPv4-to-IPv6 scenarios, including dual-stack, tunneling, and translation.

Dual-stack is when the devices are running protocols associated with both the IPv4 and IPv6. Tunneling for IPV6 is the process of encapsulating an IPv6 packet inside an IPv4 packet. This allows the IPv6 packet to be transmitted over an IPv4-only network.

NAT for IPv6 should not be used as a long term strategy, but as a temporary mechanism to assist in the migration from IPv4 to IPv6. Over the years, there have been several types of NAT for IPv6 including Network Address Translation-Protocol Translation (NAT-PT). NAT-PT has been deprecated by IETF in favor of its replacement, NAT64. NAT64 is beyond the scope of this curriculum.

Refer to
Online Course
for Illustration

5.3   Troubleshooting NAT

5.3.1   Troubleshooting NAT

5.3.1.1   Troubleshooting NAT: show commands

Figure 1 shows R2 enabled for PAT, using the range of addresses 209.165.200.226 to 209.165.200.240.

When there are IPv4 connectivity problems in a NAT environment, it is often difficult to determine the cause of the problem. The first step in solving the problem is to rule out NAT as the cause. Follow these steps to verify that NAT is operating as expected:

Step 1.   Based on the configuration, clearly define what NAT is supposed to achieve. This may reveal a problem with the configuration.

Step 2.   Verify that correct translations exist in the translation table using the `show ip nat translations` command.

Step 3.   Use the `clear` and `debug` commands to verify that NAT is operating as expected. Check to see if dynamic entries are recreated after they are cleared.

Step 4.   Review in detail what is happening to the packet, and verify that routers have the correct routing information to move the packet.

Figure 2 shows the output of the `show ip nat statistics` and `show ip nat translations` commands. Prior to using the `show` commands, the NAT statistics and entries in the NAT table are cleared with the `clear ip nat statistics` and `clear ip nat translation *` commands. After the host at 192.168.10.10 telnets to the server at 209.165.201.1, the NAT statistics and NAT table are displayed to verify NAT is working as expected.

In a simple network environment, it is useful to monitor NAT statistics with the `show ip nat statistics` command. The `show ip nat statistics` command displays information about the total number of active translations, NAT configuration parameters, the number of addresses in the pool, and the number that have been allocated. However, in a more complex NAT environment, with several translations taking place, this command may not clearly identify the issue. It may be necessary to run `debug` commands on the router.

5.3.1.2   Troubleshooting NAT: debug command

Use the `debug ip nat` command to verify the operation of the NAT feature by displaying information about every packet that is translated by the router. The `debug ip nat detailed` command generates a description of each packet considered for translation. This command also provides information about certain errors or exception conditions, such as the failure to allocate a global address. The `debug ip nat detailed` command generates more overhead than the `debug ip nat` command, but it can provide the detail that may be needed to troubleshoot the NAT problem. Always turn off debugging when finished.

Figure 1 shows a sample `debug ip nat` output. The output shows that the inside host (192.168.10.10) initiated traffic to the outside host (209.165.201.1) and the source address was translated to address 209.165.200.226.

When decoding the debug output, note what the following symbols and values indicate:

- *** (asterisk)**- The asterisk next to NAT indicates that the translation is occurring in the fast-switched path. The first packet in a conversation is always process-switched, which is slower. The remaining packets go through the fast-switched path if a cache entry exists.

- **s=**- This symbol refers to the source IP address.

- **a.b.c.d--->w.x.y.z** - This value indicates that source address a.b.c.d is translated to w.x.y.z.

- **d=**- This symbol refers to the destination IP address.

- **[xxxx]**- The value in brackets is the IP identification number. This information may be useful for debugging in that it enables correlation with other packet traces from protocol analyzers.

Note   Verify that the ACL referenced in the NAT command reference is permitting all of the necessary networks. In Figure 2, only 192.168.0.0/16 addresses are eligible to be translated. Packets from the inside network destined for the Internet with source addresses that are not explicitly permitted by ACL 1 are not translated by R2.

5.3.1.3   Case Study

Case Study

Figure 1 shows that hosts from the 192.168.0.0/16 LANs, PC1, and PC2 cannot ping servers on the outside network, Svr1, and Svr2.

To begin troubleshooting the problem, use the `show ip nat translations` command to see if any translations are currently in the NAT table. The output in Figure 1 shows that no translations are in the table.

The `show ip nat statistics` command is used to determine whether any translations have taken place. It also identifies the interfaces that translation should be occurring between. As shown in the output of Figure 2, the NAT counters are at 0, verifying that no translation has occurred. By comparing the output with the topology shown in Figure 1, notice that the router interfaces are incorrectly defined as NAT inside or NAT outside. The incorrect configuration can also be verified using the `show running-config` command.

The current NAT interface configuration must be deleted from the interfaces before applying the correct configuration.

After correctly defining the NAT inside and outside interfaces, another ping from PC1 to Svr1 fails. Using the `show ip nat translations` and `show ip nat statistics` commands again verifies that translations are still not occurring.

As shown in Figure 3, the `show access-lists` command is used to determine whether the ACL that the NAT command references is permitting all of the necessary networks. Examining the output indicates that an incorrect wildcard bit mask has been used in the ACL that defines the addresses which need to be translated. The wildcard mask is only permitting the 192.168.0.0/24 subnet. The access list is first removed and then reconfigured using the correct wildcard mask.

After configurations are corrected, another ping is generated from PC1 to Svr1, and this time the ping succeeds. As shown in Figure 4, the `show ip nat translations` and `show ip nat statistics` commands are used to verify that the NAT translation is occurring.

Refer to **Packet Tracer Activity** for this chapter

5.3.1.4   Packet Tracer - Verifying and Troubleshooting NAT Configurations

Background/Scenario

A contractor restored an old configuration to a new router running NAT. But the network has changed, and a new subnet was added after the old configuration was backed up. It is your job to get the network working again.

Refer to **Lab Activity** for this chapter

5.3.1.5   Lab - Troubleshooting NAT Configurations

In this lab, you will complete the following objectives:

■ Part 1: Build the Network and Configure Basic Device Settings

■ Part 2: Troubleshoot Static NAT

■ Part 3: Troubleshoot Dynamic NAT

Refer to **Online Course** for Illustration

5.4   Summary

Refer to **Lab Activity** for this chapter

5.4.1.1   Class Activity - NAT Check

NAT Check

Network address translation is not currently included in your company's network design. It has been decided to configure some devices to use NAT services for connecting to the mail server.

Before deploying NAT live on the network, you prototype it using a network simulation program.

Refer to **Packet Tracer Activity** for this chapter

5.4.1.2   Packet Tracer - Skills Integration Challenge

Background/Scenario

This culminating activity includes many of the skills that you have acquired during this course. First, you will complete the documentation for the network. So make sure you have a printed version of the instructions. During implementation, you will configure VLANs, trunking, port security, and SSH remote access on a switch. Then, you will implement inter-VLAN routing and NAT on a router. Finally, you will use your documentation to verify your implementation by testing end-to-end connectivity.

Refer to **Online Course** for Illustration

5.4.1.3   Summary

This chapter has outlined how NAT is used to help alleviate the depletion of IPv4 address space. NAT for IPv4 allows network administrators to use RFC 1918 private address space while providing connectivity to the Internet, using a single or limited number of public addresses.

NAT conserves public address space and saves considerable administrative overhead in managing adds, moves, and changes. NAT and PAT can be implemented to conserve public address space and build private secure intranets without affecting the ISP connection. However, NAT has drawbacks in terms of its negative effects on device performance, security, mobility, and end-to-end connectivity and should be considered a short term implementation for address exhaustion with the long term solution being IPv6.

This chapter discussed NAT for IPv4, including:

- NAT characteristics, terminology, and general operations
- The different types of NAT including static NAT, dynamic NAT, and PAT
- The benefits and disadvantages of NAT
- The configuration, verification, and analysis of static NAT, dynamic NAT, and PAT
- How port forwarding can be used to access an internal devices from the Internet
- Troubleshooting NAT using `show` and `debug` commands

Go to the online course to take the quiz and exam.

Chapter 5 Quiz

This quiz is designed to provide an additional opportunity to practice the skills and knowledge presented in the chapter and to prepare for the chapter exam. You will be allowed multiple attempts and the grade does not appear in the gradebook.

Chapter 5 Exam

The chapter exam assesses your knowledge of the chapter content.

Your Chapter Notes

Broadband Solutions

6.0 Broadband Solutions

6.0.1.1 Introduction

Teleworking, or working from a non-traditional workplace such as at home, offers many benefits to the worker and to the business. Broadband solutions provide these workers with high-speed connection options to business locations and to the Internet. Small branch offices can also connect using these same technologies.

This chapter covers commonly used broadband solutions, such as cable, DSL, and wireless. VPN technology provides security options for data running over these connections. This chapter also discusses the factors to consider if more than one broadband solution is available to service a particular location.

Refer to
Lab Activity
for this chapter

6.0.1.2 Class Activity - Broadband Varieties

Broadband Varieties

Telework employment opportunities are expanding in your local area every day. You have been offered employment as a teleworker for a major corporation. The new employer requires teleworkers to have access the Internet to fulfill their job responsibilities.

Research the following broadband Internet connection types that are available in your geographic area:

- DSL
- Cable
- Satellite

Consider the advantages and disadvantages of each broadband variation as you notate your research, which may include cost, speed, security, and ease of implementation or installation.

Refer to
Interactive Graphic
in online course.

6.1 Teleworking

6.1.1 Benefits of Teleworking

6.1.1.1 Introducing Teleworking

Teleworking is working away from the traditional workplace, such as working from a home office. The reasons for choosing teleworking are varied and include everything from personal convenience to allowing sick or disabled employees the opportunity to continue working.

Teleworking is a broad term referring to conducting work by connecting to a workplace from a remote location, with the assistance of telecommunications. Efficient teleworking is possible because of broadband Internet connections, Virtual Private Networks (VPNs), Voice over IP (VoIP), and videoconferencing.

Many modern enterprises are offering employment opportunities for people who cannot commute to work every day, or for whom working out of a home office is more practical. These people, called teleworkers, must connect to the company network so that they can work and share information from their home offices.

Broadband solutions are integral to successful teleworking. This chapter details the benefits of teleworking and how broadband solutions enable teleworking as a smarter way to do business.

Refer to
Online Course
for Illustration

6.1.1.2   Employer Benefits of Teleworking

For organizations, there are many benefits of offering a teleworking environment. Some of the most cited benefits include:

- **Improved employee productivity**- In general, teleworking allows employees to do more and maintain better quality work, than those workers confined exclusively to an office space. According to a British Telecom Study by the Gartner Group, the average telecommuter works 11 percent more hours than an office counterpart. The Bell Atlantic Corporation (now Verizon) cited that 25 hours spent working at home is the equivalent of 40 office hours.

- **Reduced costs and expenses**- A major expense in many organizations is the cost of real estate. Teleworking means reduced requirements for office space. Savings in real estate cost have the potential of equaling anywhere from 10 to 80 percent. Even a 10 percent saving in real estate costs may be the difference between profit and loss. Additional savings include: heating, air-conditioning, car parks, lighting, office equipment and supplies, as all these costs, and more, drop as staff take up telework.

- **Easier recruitment and retention**- Being able to offer flexibility can reduce staff turnover by up to 20 percent. With staff replacement costing 75 percent or more of salary, this is a significant saving, even before training and retention costs are considered. Some observers have calculated that the cost of turnover and replacing staff is as high as 250 percent of salary.

- **Reduced absenteeism**- Telework can reduce absenteeism by as much as 80 percent.

- **Improved morale**- Improvements that offer the option of telework are often seen as family-friendly employers.

- **Improved corporate citizenship**- Allowing employees to work from home, and reducing the commuting emissions of a company's employees can be an important part of an organization's plan to become carbon neutral and environmentally responsible. This can have many benefits, including: creating marketing opportunities, adding value to products and services, addressing concerns expressed by customers, and responding to supply chain requirements.

- **Improved customer service**- With staff able to start their working day without first commuting to the office, clients and customers will experience improved contact and response times leading to large improvements in client retention and value. Clients and customers report quicker response and better service.

With better response times, better customer service, lower costs, and increased employee productivity, enterprises are better able to compete in rapidly changing markets. Teleworking really is a smart way to do business.

Refer to **Online Course** for Illustration

6.1.1.3   Community and Government Benefits

Teleworking can benefit organizations of all sizes, from small businesses to large corporations. However, those benefits actually expand beyond the organizational level, offering unique advantages to public entities such as communities, and even local and national governments.

Public entities such as communities and governments are businesses that must manage income and expenses. They should be as efficient, accountable, and as transparent as possible because taxpayer money is at stake. For this reason, from the business perspective, all of the employee and cost saving benefits of teleworking apply to these public entities. In addition, public entities benefit from teleworking in the following ways:

- **Helps reduce traffic and infrastructure requirements**- Telework eliminates many contemporary problems at the source. Traffic is only one example. According to a 2004 Washington Post article, traffic delays in the Washington, D.C. region drop 10 percent for every 3 percent of commuters who work from home. In addition, teleworking reduces infrastructure and service delivery costs.

- **Helps reduce urban drift**- Urban drift refers to the movement of individuals from rural locations to city centers and towns in search of better conditions and employment opportunities. Urban drift results in overcrowding and congestion. Teleworking allows individuals to work regardless of physical location, reducing the need for individuals to relocate due to employment.

- **Improved rural and suburban amenities**- More people working in rural or suburban region could mean better mass transit services and changes to local retail facilities. The post office, doctor, bank, or gas station might be less likely to close up and move somewhere else. With more flexible response, more productive enterprises, and the ability of all individuals to contribute, the regions or nation becomes more competitive and attracts more employment and development.

Refer to **Online Course** for Illustration

6.1.1.4   Individual Benefits of Teleworking

Individuals also gain significant benefits from being able to work remotely, including:

- **Productivity**- Over 70 percent of teleworkers claim they are significantly more productive, which means they do more in less time; thus, saving time or earning more in the same time.

- **Flexibility**- Teleworkers can better manage when and where work is performed. They have more flexibility to handle many other details of modern life, like getting the car serviced, avoiding the traffic at holiday weekends, and taking children to the doctor.

- **Cost savings**- Employees that must commute to an office spend a significant amount of money adding up vehicle fuel and maintenance, lunches, work clothes, eating out, and all the other costs of traditional work that one can reduce by teleworking.

- **Home and family**- For many people, spending more time with the family or caring for dependent relatives is a major reason for teleworking.

Refer to
Online Course
for Illustration

6.1.1.5   Detriments to Telework

While there are many benefits to teleworking, there are some detriments that must also be considered:

From an employer perspective:

■ **Tracking of employee progress**- It may be difficult for some managers to track the work accomplishments of employees that telework. It is necessary to arrange checkpoints and validate task progress in a different manner with employees who work from home.

■ **Necessary to implement a new management style**- Managers that oversee employees within an office have the capability to maintain in-person contact with all employees. This means if a problem arises, or there is a misunderstanding of assigned tasks, an unscheduled face-to-face meeting can often resolve the issue quickly. In telework environment, managers should establish processes for validating understanding and remain flexible to the various needs of the teleworking employee.

From the employee perspective:

■ **Feeling of isolation**- For many people, working on their own becomes lonely.

■ **Slower connections**- Residential and rural areas do not generally get the kind of technology support and services that inner city offices can receive, and they can be expensive. If the work requires high bandwidth, think carefully about whether a home office is the right choice.

■ **Distractions**- Whether it is a neighbor, a spouse, a child, lawn mowing, the laundry, the TV or the refrigerator, there are distractions in the home office. Additionally, many individuals think that telework negates the need for childcare, but this is not necessarily true. With young children especially, it is important to plan for childcare at times when it is necessary to completely focus on work.

Refer to
Interactive Graphic
in online course.

6.1.1.6   Activity – Benefits of Teleworking

Refer to
Online Course
for Illustration

6.1.2   Business Requirements for Teleworker Services

6.1.2.1   Teleworker Solution

Organizations need secure, reliable, and cost-effective networks to connect corporate headquarters, branch offices, and suppliers. With the growing number of teleworkers, enterprises increasingly need secure, reliable, and cost-effective ways to connect teleworkers with the organizational resources on corporate LAN sites.

The figure illustrates the remote connection topologies that modern networks use to connect remote locations. In some cases, the remote locations only connect to the headquarters location, while in other cases, remote locations connect to multiple sites. The branch office in the figure connects to the headquarters and partner sites, while the teleworker has a single connection to the headquarters.

There are three primary remote connection technologies available to organizations supporting teleworker services:

- **Broadband connections**- The broadband term refers to advanced communications systems capable of providing high-speed transmission of services, such as data, voice, and video, over the Internet and other networks. Transmission is provided by a wide range of technologies, including DSL, fiber-to-the-home, coaxial cable systems, wireless, and satellite. The broadband service data transmission speeds typically exceed 200 kb/s in at least one direction between the ISP and the user.

- **IPsec VPNs**- This is the most common option for teleworkers, combined with remote access over broadband, to establish a secure VPN over the public Internet. This type of WAN connection offers flexible and scalable connectivity. Site-to-site connections can provide a secure, fast, and reliable remote connection to teleworkers.

- **Traditional private WAN Layer 2 technologies**- These types of connections provide many remote connection solutions and include technologies, such as Frame Relay, ATM, and leased lines. The security of these connections is dependent upon the service provider providing them.

6.1.2.2   Teleworker Connectivity Requirements

Refer to **Online Course** for Illustration

Regardless of the remote connection technology used to connect effectively to an organization's networks, teleworkers require both home office components and corporate components:

- **Home office components**- The required home office components are a laptop or desktop computer, broadband access (cable, DSL, or wireless), and a VPN router or VPN client software installed on the computer. Additional components might include a wireless access point. When traveling, teleworkers need an Internet connection and a VPN client to connect to the corporate network over any available dialup, network, or broadband connection.

- **Corporate components**- Corporate components are VPN-capable routers, VPN concentrators, multifunction security appliances, authentication, and central management devices for resilient aggregation and termination of the VPN connections.

Quality of service (QoS)-supported VoIP and videoconferencing components is becoming an integral component of the teleworkers toolkit. QoS refers to the capability of a network to provide better service to selected network traffic, as required by voice and video applications. Providing support for VoIP and videoconferencing requires upgrades routers and devices that support QoS functionality.

The figure shows an encrypted VPN tunnel connecting the teleworker to the corporate network. This is the primary basis of secure and reliable teleworker connections. A VPN is a private data network that uses the public telecommunication infrastructure. VPN security maintains privacy using a tunneling protocol and security procedures. This course presents the IP Security (IPsec) protocol as the favored approach to building secure VPN tunnels. Unlike earlier security approaches that apply security at the application layer of the OSI model, IPsec works at the network layer where packet processing occurs.

As stated, a secure VPN tunnel is used over a public telecommunication infrastructure. This means that prior to initiating a VPN, home users must first be able to connect to Internet services using some form of high-speed, broadband access. The three most common forms of broadband access include:

- Cable

- DSL

- Broadband wireless

Refer to
Interactive Graphic
in online course.

6.1.2.3   Activity - Classify Requirements for Teleworker Connectivity

Refer to
Online Course
for Illustration

6.2   Comparing Broadband Solutions

6.2.1   Cable

6.2.1.1   What is a Cable System?

Accessing the Internet through a cable network is a popular option used by teleworkers to access their enterprise network. The cable system uses a coaxial cable that carries radio frequency (RF) signals across the network. Coaxial cable is the primary medium used to build cable TV systems.

Cable television first began in Pennsylvania in 1948. John Walson, the owner of an appliance store in a small mountain town, needed to solve poor over-the-air reception problems experienced by customers trying to receive TV signals from Philadelphia through the mountains. Walson erected an antenna on a utility pole on a local mountaintop that enabled him to demonstrate the televisions in his store with strong broadcasts coming from the three Philadelphia stations. He connected the antenna to his appliance store via a cable and modified signal boosters. He then connected several of his customers who were located along the cable path. This was the first Community Antenna Television (CATV) system in the United States.

Walson's company grew over the years, and he is recognized as the founder of the cable television industry. He was also the first cable operator to use microwave to import distant television stations, and the first to use coaxial cable to improve picture quality.

Most cable operators use satellite dishes to gather TV signals. Early systems were one-way, with cascading amplifiers placed in series along the network to compensate for signal loss. These systems used taps to couple video signals from the main trunks to subscriber homes via drop cables.

Modern cable systems provide two-way communication between subscribers and the cable operator. Cable operators now offer customers advanced telecommunications services, including high-speed Internet access, digital cable television, and residential telephone service. Cable operators typically deploy hybrid fiber-coaxial (HFC) networks to enable high-speed transmission of data to cable modems located in a SOHO.

Click the highlighted areas in the figure to see more information about the components of a typical modern cable system.

Refer to
Online Course
for Illustration

6.2.1.2   Cable and the Electromagnetic Spectrum

The electromagnetic spectrum encompasses a broad range of frequencies.

Frequency is the rate at which current, or voltage, cycles occur. Frequency is computed as the number of waves per second. Wavelength is the distance from the peak of one wave to the peak of the next wave. Wavelength is calculated as the speed of propagation of the electromagnetic signal divided by its frequency in cycles per second.

Radio waves, often called RF, constitute a portion of the electromagnetic spectrum between approximately 1 kHz and 1 THz, as indicated in the figure. When users tune a radio or television to find different radio stations or television channels, they are tuning to different electromagnetic frequencies across that RF spectrum. The same principle applies to the cable system.

The cable TV industry uses a portion of the RF electromagnetic spectrum. Within the cable, different frequencies carry TV channels and data. At the subscriber end, equipment such as TVs, Blu-ray players, DVRs, and HDTV set-top boxes tune to certain frequencies that allow the user to view the channel or use a cable modem to receive high-speed Internet access.

A cable network is capable of transmitting signals on the cable in either direction at the same time. The following frequency scopes are used:

- **Downstream**- The direction of an RF signal transmission, such as TV channels and data, from the source, or headend, to the destination, or subscribers. Transmission from source to destination is called the forward path. Downstream frequencies are in the range of 50 to 860 MHz.

- **Upstream**- The direction of the RF signal transmission from subscribers to the headend. Upstream frequencies are in the range of 5 to 42 MHz.

Refer to
Online Course
for Illustration

6.2.1.3   DOCSIS

The Data-over-Cable Service Interface Specification (DOCSIS) is an international standard developed by CableLabs, a non-profit research and development consortium for cable-related technologies. CableLabs tests and certifies cable equipment vendor devices, such as cable modems and cable modem termination systems, and grants DOCSIS-certified or qualified status.

DOCSIS defines the communications and operation support interface requirements for a data-over-cable system, and permits the addition of high-speed data transfer to an existing CATV system. Cable operators employ DOCSIS to provide Internet access over their existing HFC infrastructure

DOCSIS specifies the OSI Layer 1 and Layer 2 requirements:

- **Physical layer**- For data signals that the cable operator can use, DOCSIS specifies the channel widths, or bandwidths of each channel, as 200 kHz, 400 kHz, 800 kHz, 1.6 MHz, 3.2 MHz, and 6.4 MHz. DOCSIS also specifies modulation technique, which is how to use the RF signal to convey digital data.

- **MAC layer**- Defines a deterministic access method, Time-Division Multiple Access (TDMA), or Synchronous Code Division Multiple Access method (S-CDMA).

To understand the MAC layer requirements for DOCSIS, an explanation of how various communication technologies divide channel access is helpful. TDMA divides access by time. Frequency-Division Multiple Access (FDMA) divides access by frequency. Code Division Multiple Access (CDMA) employs spread-spectrum technology and a special coding scheme in which each transmitter is assigned a specific code.

An analogy that illustrates these concepts starts with a room representing a channel. The room is full of people needing to speak to one another. In other words, each person needs channel access. One solution is for the people to take turns speaking (time division). Another is for each person to speak at different pitches (frequency division). In CDMA, they would speak different languages. People speaking the same language can understand each other, but not other people. In radio CDMA used by many North American cell phone networks, each group of users has a shared code. Many codes occupy the same channel, but only users associated with a particular code can understand each other. S-CDMA is a proprietary version of CDMA developed by Terayon Corporation for data transmission across coaxial cable networks. S-CDMA scatters digital data up and down a wide frequency band and allows multiple subscribers connected to the network to transmit and receive concurrently. S-CDMA is secure and extremely resistant to noise.

Plans for frequency allocation bands differ between North American and European cable systems. Euro-DOCSIS is adapted for use in Europe. The main differences between DOCSIS and Euro-DOCSIS relate to channel bandwidths. TV technical standards vary across the world, which affects the way DOCSIS variants develop. International TV standards include NTSC in North American and parts of Japan; PAL in most of Europe, Asia, Africa, Australia, Brazil, and Argentina; and SECAM in France and some Eastern European countries.

6.2.1.4   Cable Components

Refer to **Online Course** for Illustration

Delivering services over a cable network requires different radio frequencies. Downstream frequencies are in the 50 to 860 MHz range, and the upstream frequencies are in the 5 to 42 MHz range.

Two types of equipment are required to send digital modem signals upstream and downstream on a cable system:

- Cable Modem Termination System (CMTS) at the headend of the cable operator
- Cable Modem (CM) on the subscriber end

Click the highlighted components in the figure for more information about how each device contributes to communication.

A headend CMTS communicates with CMs located in subscriber homes. The headend is actually a router with databases for providing Internet services to cable subscribers. The architecture is relatively simple, using a mixed optical-coaxial network in which optical fiber replaces the lower bandwidth coaxial cable.

A web of fiber trunk cables connects the headend to the nodes where optical-to-RF signal conversion takes place. The fiber carries the same broadband content for Internet connections, telephone service, and streaming video as the coaxial cable carries. Coaxial feeder cables originate connect the node to the subscribers and carries RF signals.

In a modern HFC network, typically 500 to 2,000 active data subscribers are connected to a cable network segment, all sharing the upstream and downstream bandwidth. The actual bandwidth for Internet service over a CATV line can be up to 160 Mb/s downstream with the latest iteration of DOCSIS, and up to 120 Mb/s upstream.

When high usage causes congestion, the cable operator can add additional bandwidth for data services by allocating an additional TV channel for high-speed data. This addition may effectively double the downstream bandwidth that is available to subscribers. Another option is to reduce the number of subscribers served by each network segment. To reduce the number of subscribers, the cable operator further subdivides the network by laying the fiber-optic connections deeper into the neighborhoods.

Refer to **Interactive Graphic** in online course.

6.2.1.5   Activity - Identify Cable Terminology

Refer to **Online Course** for Illustration

6.2.2   DSL

6.2.2.1   What is DSL?

DSL is a means of providing high-speed connections over installed copper wires. DSL is one of the key teleworker solutions available.

Several years ago, Bell Labs identified that a typical voice conversation over a local loop only required bandwidth of 300 Hz to 3 kHz. For many years, the telephone networks did not use the bandwidth above 3 kHz. Advances in technology allowed DSL to use the additional bandwidth from 3 kHz up to 1 MHz to deliver high-speed data services over ordinary copper lines.

As an example, asymmetric DSL (ADSL) uses a frequency range from approximately 20 kHz to 1 MHz. Fortunately, only relatively small changes to existing telephone company infrastructure are required to deliver high-bandwidth data rates to subscribers. The figure shows a representation of bandwidth space allocation on a copper wire for ADSL. The area labeled POTS identifies the frequency range used by the voice-grade telephone service. The area labeled ADSL represents the frequency space used by the upstream and down-stream DSL signals. The area that encompasses both the POTS area and the ADSL area represents the entire frequency range supported by the copper wire pair.

Another form of DSL technology is symmetric DSL (SDSL). All forms of DSL service are categorized as ADSL or SDSL, and there are several varieties of each type. ADSL provides higher downstream bandwidth to the user than upload bandwidth. SDSL provides the same capacity in both directions.

The different varieties of DSL provide different bandwidths, some with capabilities exceeding 40 Mb/s. The transfer rates are dependent on the actual length of the local loop (connecting the subscriber to the central office), and the type and condition of the cabling. For satisfactory ADSL service, the loop must be less than 3.39 miles (5.46 km).

Refer to **Online Course** for Illustration

6.2.2.2   DSL Connections

Service providers deploy DSL connections in the last step of a local telephone network, called the local loop or last mile. The connection is set up between a pair of modems on either end of a copper wire that extends between the customer premises equipment (CPE) and the DSL access multiplexer (DSLAM). A DSLAM is the device located at the Central

Office (CO) of the provider and concentrates connections from multiple DSL subscribers. A DSLAM is often built into an aggregation router.

Figure 1 shows the equipment needed to provide a DSL connection to a SOHO. The two components are the DSL transceiver and the DSLAM:

- **Transceiver**- Connects the computer of the teleworker to the DSL. Usually the transceiver is a DSL modem connected to the computer using a USB or Ethernet cable. Newer DSL transceivers can be built into small routers with multiple 10/100 switch ports suitable for home office use.

- **DSLAM**- Located at the CO of the carrier, the DSLAM combines individual DSL connections from users into one high-capacity link to an ISP, and therefore, to the Internet.

Figure 2 depicts modern DSL routers and broadband aggregation routers. The advantage that DSL has over cable technology is that DSL is not a shared medium. Each user has a separate direct connection to the DSLAM. Adding users does not impede performance, unless the DSLAM Internet connection to the ISP, or the Internet, becomes saturated.

Refer to **Online Course** for Illustration

6.2.2.3   Separating Voice and Data in ADSL

The major benefit of ADSL is the ability to provide data services along with POTS voice services. Transmissions of voice and data signals are propagated along the same wire pair, as shown in Figure 1. Data circuits are offloaded from the voice switch.

When the service provider puts analog voice and ADSL on the same wire pair, ADSL signals can distort voice transmission. For this reason, the provider splits the POTS channel from the ADSL modem at the customer premises using filters or splitters. This setup guarantees uninterrupted regular phone service even if ADSL fails. When filters or splitters are in place, the user can use the phone line and the ADSL connection simultaneously without adverse effects on either service.

Figure 1 shows the local loop terminating on the customer premises at the demarcation point. The demarcation point is the point where the phone line enters the customer premises. The actual device that marks the demarcation point is the Network Interface Device (NID). At this point, a splitter can be attached to the phone line. The splitter forks the phone line; one branch provides the original house telephone wiring for telephones, and the other branch connects to the ADSL modem. The splitter acts as a low-pass filter, allowing only the 0 to 4 kHz frequencies to pass to or from the telephone.

There are two ways to separate ADSL from voice at the customer premises: using a microfilter or using a splitter.

A microfilter is a passive low-pass filter with two ends, as shown in Figure 2. One end connects to the telephone, and the other end connects to the telephone wall jack. Click the highlight in Figure 2 to see an image of a microfilter. This solution allows the user to use any jack in the house for voice or ADSL service.

A POTS splitter, shown in Figure 3, separates the DSL traffic from the POTS traffic. The POTS splitter is a passive device. Click the highlight in Figure 3 to see a diagram of a splitter. In the event of a power failure, the voice traffic still travels to the voice switch in the CO of the carrier. Splitters are located at the CO and, in some deployments, at the customer premises. At the CO, the POTS splitter separates the voice traffic, destined for POTS connections, and the data traffic destined for the DSLAM. Installing the POTS splitter at the NID usually means that a technician must go to the customer site.

Refer to
Interactive Graphic
in online course.

6.2.2.4   Activity - Identify DSL Terminology

Refer to
Online Course
for Illustration

6.2.3   Broadband Wireless

6.2.3.1   Types of Broadband Wireless Technologies

In place of cable connectivity and DSL, many users are now opting for wireless connectivity.

The reach of wireless connections now includes personal area networks, LANs, and WANs. The number of hotspots has increased access to wireless connections across the world. A hotspot is the area covered by one or more interconnected access points. Public gathering places, like coffee shops, cafes, and libraries, have Wi-Fi hotspots. By overlapping access points, hotspots can cover many square miles.

Developments in broadband wireless technology are increasing wireless availability. These broadband types are explained in Figure 1 and include:

- Municipal Wi-Fi (Mesh)
- WiMAX (Worldwide Interoperability for Microwave Access)
- Cellular/mobile
- Satellite Internet

Municipal Wi-Fi

Many municipal governments, often working with service providers, are deploying wireless networks. Some of these networks provide high-speed Internet access at no cost or for substantially less than the price of other broadband services. Other cities reserve their Wi-Fi networks for official use, providing police, fire fighters, and city workers remote access to the Internet and municipal networks.

Most municipal wireless networks use a mesh topology rather than a hub-and-spoke model. A mesh is a series of interconnected access points as shown in Figure 2. Each access point is in range and can communicate with at least two other access points. The mesh blankets its area with radio signals. Signals travel from access point to access point through this cloud.

A meshed network has several advantages over a singular wireless router hotspot. Installation is easier and can be less expensive because there are fewer wires. Deployment over a large urban area is faster and more reliable. If a node fails, others in the mesh compensate for it.

WiMAX

WiMAX, as shown in Figure 3, is a telecommunications technology aimed at providing wireless data over long distances in a variety of ways, from point-to-point links to full mobile cellular type access. WiMAX operates at higher speeds, over greater distances, and for a greater number of users than Wi-Fi. Because of its higher speed (bandwidth) and falling component prices, it is predicted that WiMAX will soon supplant municipal mesh networks for wireless deployments.

A WiMAX network consists of two main components:

■ A tower that is similar in concept to a cellular telephone tower. A single WiMAX tower can provide coverage to an area as large as 3,000 square miles (7,500 square km).

■ A WiMAX receiver that is connected to a USB port or is built into a laptop or other wireless device.

A WiMAX tower station connects directly to the Internet using a high-bandwidth connection, such as a T3 line. A tower can also connect to other WiMAX towers using line-of-sight microwave links. WiMAX is thus able to provide coverage to rural areas out of reach of last mile cable and DSL technologies.

Refer to **Online Course** for Illustration

6.2.3.2   Types of Broadband Wireless Technologies, Cont.

Cellular/Mobile Implementations

Mobile broadband refers to wireless Internet access delivered through mobile phone towers to computers, mobile phones, and other digital devices using portable modems. Figure 1 shows a cell tower used in a mobile broadband network.

Mobile phones use radio waves to communicate through a nearby mobile phone tower. The mobile phone has a small radio antenna. The provider has a much larger antenna that sits at the top of a tower, as shown in the figure.

Cellular/mobile broadband access consists of various standards supporting speeds of up to 5 Mb/s. Variations include 2G using GSM, CDMA, or TDMA; 3G using UMTS, CDMA2000, EDGE, or HSPA+; and 4G, using WiMAX or LTE. A mobile phone subscription does not necessarily include a mobile broadband subscription.

Three common terms that are used when discussing cellular/mobile networks include:

■ **Wireless Internet**- A general term for Internet services from a mobile phone or from any device that uses the same technology.

■ **2G/3G/4G Wireless**- Major changes to the mobile phone companies' wireless networks through the evolution of the second, third, and fourth generations of wireless mobile technologies.

■ **Long-Term Evolution (LTE)**- A newer and faster technology considered to be part of 4G technology.

Satellite Implementations

Satellite Internet services are used in locations where land-based Internet access is not available, or for temporary installations that are mobile. Internet access using satellites is available worldwide, including for providing Internet access to vessels at sea, airplanes in flight, and vehicles moving on land.

There are three ways to connect to the Internet using satellites:

■ **One-way multicast**- Satellite Internet systems are used for IP multicast-based data, audio, and video distribution. Even though most IP protocols require two-way communication for Internet content including web pages, one-way satellite-based Internet services can be used to push pages to local storage at end-user sites. Two-way interactivity is impossible.

- **One-way terrestrial return**- Satellite Internet systems use traditional dialup access to send outbound data through a modem and receive downloads from the satellite.

- **Two-way satellite Internet**- Sends data from remote sites via satellite to a hub, which then sends the data to the Internet. The satellite dish at each location needs precise positioning to avoid interference with other satellites.

Figure 2 illustrates a two-way satellite Internet system. Upload speeds are about one-tenth of the download speed, which is in the range of 500 kb/s.

The primary installation requirement is for the antenna to have a clear view toward the equator, where most orbiting satellites are stationed. Trees and heavy rains can affect reception of the signals.

Two-way satellite Internet uses IP multicasting technology that allows one satellite to serve up to 5,000 communication channels simultaneously. IP multicast sends data from one point to many points at the same time by sending data in a compressed format. Compression reduces the size of the data and the bandwidth requirements.

A company can create a private WAN using satellite communications and Very Small Aperture Terminals (VSAT). A VSAT is a type of satellite dish similar to the ones used for satellite TV from the home and is usually about 1 meter in width. The VSAT dish sits outside, pointed at a specific satellite, and is cabled to a special router interface, with the router inside the building. Using VSATs creates a private WAN.

Refer to **Interactive Graphic** in online course.

6.2.3.3 Activity - Identify Broadband Wireless Terminology

Refer to **Online Course** for Illustration

6.2.4 Selecting Broadband Solutions

6.2.4.1 Comparing Broadband Solutions

Each broadband solution has advantages and disadvantages. The ideal is to have a fiber optic cable directly connected to the SOHO network. Some locations have only one option, such as cable or DSL. Some locations only have broadband wireless options for Internet connectivity.

If there are multiple broadband solutions available, a cost-versus-benefit analysis should be performed to determine the best solution.

Some factors to consider in making a decision include:

- **Cable**- Bandwidth is shared by many users, upstream data rates are often slow.

- **DSL**- Limited bandwidth that is distance sensitive, upstream rate is proportionally quite small compared to downstream rate.

- **Fiber-to-the-Home**- Requires fiber installation directly to the home (shown in the figure).

- **Cellular/Mobile**- Coverage is often an issue, even within a SOHO, bandwidth is relatively limited.

- **Wi-Fi Mesh**- Most municipalities do not have a mesh network deployed; if it is available and the SOHO is in range, then it is a viable option.

- **WiMAX**- Bit rate is limited to 2 Mb/s per subscriber, cell size is 1 to 2 km (1.25 mi).

- **Satellite**- Expensive, limited capacity per subscriber; often provides access where no other access is possible.

Refer to
Lab Activity
for this chapter

6.2.4.2   Lab - Researching Broadband Internet Access Technologies
In this lab, you will complete the following objectives:

- Part 1: Investigate Broadband Distribution

- Part 2: Research Broadband Access Options for Specific Scenarios

Refer to
Online Course
for Illustration

6.3   Configuring xDSL Connectivity

6.3.1   PPPoE Overview

6.3.1.1   PPPoE Motivation

In addition to understanding the various technologies available for broadband Internet access, it is also important to understand the underlying data link layer protocol used by the ISP to form a connection.

A commonly used data link layer protocol by ISPs is the Point-to-Point Protocol (PPP). PPP can be used on all serial links including those links created with dial-up analog and ISDN modems. To this day, the link from a dialup user to an ISP, using analog modems, likely uses PPP. Figure 1 shows a basic representation of that analog dial connection with PPP.

Additionally, ISPs often use PPP as the data link protocol over broadband connections. There are several reasons for this. First, PPP supports the ability to assign IP addresses to remote ends of a PPP link. With PPP enabled, ISPs can use PPP to assign each customer one public IPv4 address. More importantly, PPP supports CHAP authentication. ISPs often want to use CHAP to authenticate customers because during authentication, ISPs can check accounting records to determine whether the customer's bill is paid, prior to letting the customer connect to the Internet.

These technologies came to market in the following order, with varying support for PPP:

1. Analog modems for dialup that could use PPP and CHAP

2. ISDN for dialup that could use PPP and CHAP

3. DSL, which did not create a point-to-point link and could not support PPP and CHAP

ISPs value PPP because of the authentication, accounting, and link management features. Customers appreciate the ease and availability of the Ethernet connection. However, Ethernet links do not natively support PPP. A solution to this problem was created, PPP over Ethernet (PPPoE). As shown in Figure 2, PPPoE allows the sending of PPP frames encapsulated inside Ethernet frames.

Refer to
Online Course
for Illustration

6.3.1.2   PPPoE Concepts

As shown in the figure, the customer's router is usually connected to a DSL modem using an Ethernet cable. PPPoE creates a PPP tunnel over an Ethernet connection. This allows PPP frames to be sent across the Ethernet cable to the ISP from the customer's router. The modem converts the Ethernet frames to PPP frames by stripping the Ethernet headers. The modem then transmits these PPP frames on the ISP's DSL network.

Refer to
Online Course
for Illustration

6.3.2   Configuring PPPoE

6.3.2.1   PPPoE Configuration

With the ability to send and receive PPP frames between the routers, the ISP could continue to use the same authentication model as with analog and ISDN. To make it all work, the client and ISP routers need additional configuration, including PPP configuration. To understand the configuration, consider the following:

1. To create a PPP tunnel, the configuration uses a dialer interface. A dialer interface is a virtual interface. The PPP configuration is placed on the dialer interface, not the physical interface. The dialer interface is created using the **interface dialer** number command. The client can configure a static IP address, but will more likely be automatically assigned a public IP address by the ISP.

2. The PPP CHAP configuration usually defines one-way authentication; therefore, the ISP authenticates the customer. The hostname and password configured on the customer router must match the hostname and password configured on the ISP router. Notice in the figure that the CHAP username and password match the settings on the ISP router.

3. The physical Ethernet interface that connects to the DSL modem is then enabled with the command **pppoe enable** that enables PPPoE and links the physical interface to the dialer interface. The dialer interface is linked to the Ethernet interface with the **dialer pool** and **pppoe-client** commands, using the same number. The dialer interface number does not have to match the dialer pool number.

4. The maximum transmission unit (MTU) should be set down to 1492, versus the default of 1500, to accommodate the PPPoE headers.

Refer to
Interactive Graphic
in online course.

6.3.2.2   Syntax Checker - Configuring PPPoE

Refer to
Lab Activity
for this chapter

6.3.2.3   Lab - Configuring a Router as a PPPoE Client for DSL Connectivity

In this lab, you will complete the following objectives:

■ Part 1: Build the Network

■ Part 2: Configure the ISP Router

■ Part 3: Configure the Cust1 Router

Refer to
Online Course
for Illustration

Refer to
Lab Activity
for this chapter

6.4   Summary

6.4.1.1   Class Activity - Telework Proposal

Telework Proposal

Your small- to medium-sized business has just been awarded a large marketing design contract. Because your office space is limited, it has been decided that it would be a good idea to hire teleworkers to help with the contract.

Therefore, a very general teleworking program must be designed for your company due to anticipation of company growth. As more contracts are awarded, you will revise and expand the program to fit your company's needs.

Develop a basic telework proposal outline for your company to consider as groundwork for a telework program.

Refer to
Online Course
for Illustration

6.4.1.2   Summary

Broadband transmission is provided by a wide range of technologies, including digital subscriber line (DSL), fiber-to-the-home, coaxial cable systems, wireless, and satellite. This transmission requires additional components at the home end and at the corporate end.

DOCSIS is a CableLabs standard that permits the addition of high-speed data transfer to an existing CATV system. The bandwidth for Internet service over a CATV line can be up to 160 Mb/s downstream with the latest iteration of DOCSIS, and up to 120 Mb/s upstream, simultaneously. It requires the use of a Cable Modem Termination System (CMTS) at the head-end of the cable operator, and a Cable Modem (CM) on the subscriber end

The two basic types of DSL technologies are ADSL and Symmetric (SDSL). ADSL provides higher downstream bandwidth to the user than upload bandwidth. SDSL provides the same capacity in both directions. DSL can provide bandwidth exceeding 40 Mbps. DSL requires the use of a DSLAM at the carrier CO and a transceiver, often built into a home router, at the customer end.

Broadband wireless solutions include municipal Wi-Fi, WiMAX, cellular/mobile, and satellite Internet. Municipal Wi-Fi mesh networks are not widely deployed. The WiMAX bit rate is limited to 2 Mbps per subscriber. Cellular/mobile coverage can be limited and bandwidth can be an issue. Satellite Internet is relatively expensive and limited, but it may be the only method to provide access.

If multiple broadband connections are available to a particular location, a cost-benefit analysis should be performed to determine the best solution. The best solution may be to connect to multiple service providers to provide redundancy and reliability.

Go to the online course to take the quiz and exam.

Chapter 6 Quiz

This quiz is designed to provide an additional opportunity to practice the skills and knowledge presented in the chapter and to prepare for the chapter exam. You will be allowed multiple attempts and the grade does not appear in the gradebook.

Chapter 6 Exam

The chapter exam assesses your knowledge of the chapter content.

Your Chapter Notes

Securing Site-to-Site Connectivity

7.0 Introduction

7.0.1.1 Introduction

Security is a concern when using the public Internet to conduct business. Virtual Private Networks (VPNs) are used to ensure the security of data across the Internet. A VPN is used to create a private tunnel over a public network. Data can be secured by using encryption in this tunnel through the Internet and by using authentication to protect data from unauthorized access.

This chapter explains the concepts and processes related to VPNs, as well as the benefits of VPN implementations and the underlying protocols required to configure VPNs.

Refer to
Lab Activity
for this chapter

7.0.1.2 Class Activity - VPNs at a Glance

VPNs at a Glance

A small- to medium-sized business is growing and needs customers, teleworkers, and wired/wireless employees to be able to access the main network from any location. As the network administrator for the business, you have decided to implement VPNs for security, network access ease, and cost savings.

It is your job to ensure that all of the network administrators start the VPN planning process with the same knowledge set.

Four basic VPN informational areas need to be researched and presented to the network administrative team:

- Concise definition of VPNs
- Some general VPN facts
- IPsec as a VPN security option
- Ways VPNs use tunneling

Refer to **Interactive Graphic** in online course.

7.1 VPNs

7.1.1 Fundamentals of VPNs

7.1.1.1 Introducing VPNs

Organizations need secure, reliable, and cost-effective ways to interconnect multiple networks, such as allowing branch offices and suppliers to connect to a corporation's headquarter network. Additionally, with the growing number of teleworkers, enterprises have an increasing need for secure, reliable, and cost-effective ways to connect employees working in small office/home office (SOHO) and other remote locations, with resources on corporate sites.

The figure illustrates the topologies that modern networks use to connect remote locations. In some cases, the remote locations connect only to the headquarters location, while in other cases, remote locations connect to additional sites.

Organizations use VPNs to create an end-to-end private network connection over third-party networks such as the Internet or extranets. The tunnel eliminates the distance barrier and enables remote users to access central site network resources. A VPN is a private network created via tunneling over a public network, usually the Internet. A VPN is a communications environment in which access is strictly controlled to permit peer connections within a defined community of interest.

The first VPNs were strictly IP tunnels that did not include authentication or encryption of the data. For example, Generic Routing Encapsulation (GRE) is a tunneling protocol developed by Cisco that can encapsulate a wide variety of network layer protocol packet types inside IP tunnels. This creates a virtual point-to-point link to Cisco routers at remote points over an IP internetwork.

Today, a secure implementation of VPN with encryption, such as IPsec VPNs, is what is usually meant by virtual private networking.

To implement VPNs, a VPN gateway is necessary. The VPN gateway could be a router, a firewall, or a Cisco Adaptive Security Appliance (ASA). An ASA is a standalone firewall device that combines firewall, VPN concentrator, and intrusion prevention functionality into one software image.

Refer to **Online Course** for Illustration

7.1.1.2 Benefits of VPNs

As shown in the figure, a VPN uses virtual connections that are routed through the Internet from the private network of an organization to the remote site or employee host. The information from a private network is securely transported over the public network, to form a virtual network.

The benefits of a VPN include the following:

- **Cost savings**- VPNs enable organizations to use cost-effective, third-party Internet transport to connect remote offices and remote users to the main site; therefore, eliminating expensive, dedicated WAN links and modem banks. Furthermore, with the advent of cost-effective, high-bandwidth technologies, such as DSL, organizations can use VPNs to reduce their connectivity costs while simultaneously increasing remote connection bandwidth.

■ **Scalability**- VPNs enable organizations to use the Internet infrastructure within ISPs and devices, which makes it easy to add new users. Therefore, organizations are able to add large amounts of capacity without adding significant infrastructure.

■ **Compatibility with broadband technology**- VPNs allow mobile workers and telecommuters to take advantage of high-speed, broadband connectivity, such as DSL and cable, to access to their organizations' networks. Broadband connectivity provides flexibility and efficiency. High-speed, broadband connections also provide a cost-effective solution for connecting remote offices.

■ **Security**- VPNs can include security mechanisms that provide the highest level of security by using advanced encryption and authentication protocols that protect data from unauthorized access.

Refer to
Interactive Graphic
in online course.

7.1.1.3   Activity - Identify the Benefits of VPNs

Refer to
Online Course
for Illustration

7.1.2   Types of VPNs

7.1.2.1   Site-to-Site VPNs

There are two types of VPN networks:

■ Site-to-site

■ Remote access

Site-to-Site VPN

A site-to-site VPN is created when devices on both sides of the VPN connection are aware of the VPN configuration in advance, as shown in the figure. The VPN remains static, and internal hosts have no knowledge that a VPN exists. In a site-to-site VPN, end hosts send and receive normal TCP/IP traffic through a VPN "gateway". The VPN gateway is responsible for encapsulating and encrypting outbound traffic for all traffic from a particular site. The VPN gateway then sends it through a VPN tunnel over the Internet to a peer VPN gateway at the target site. Upon receipt, the peer VPN gateway strips the headers, decrypts the content, and relays the packet toward the target host inside its private network.

A site-to-site VPN is an extension of a classic WAN network. Site-to-site VPNs connect entire networks to each other, for example, they can connect a branch office network to a company headquarters network. In the past, a leased line or Frame Relay connection was required to connect sites, but because most corporations now have Internet access, these connections can be replaced with site-to-site VPNs.

Refer to
Online Course
for Illustration

7.1.2.2   Remote-access VPNs

Remote-access VPNs

Where a site-to-site VPN is used to connect entire networks, a remote-access VPN supports the needs of telecommuters, mobile users, and extranet, consumer-to-business traffic. A remote-access VPN is created when VPN information is not statically set up, but instead allows for dynamically changing information, and can be enabled and disabled.

Remote-access VPNs support a client/server architecture, where the VPN client (remote host) gains secure access to the enterprise network via a VPN server device at the network edge.

Remote-access VPNs are used to connect individual hosts that must access their company network securely over the Internet. Internet connectivity used by telecommuters is typically a broadband, DSL, wireless, or cable connection, as indicated in the figure.

VPN client software may need to be installed on the mobile user's end device; for example, each host may have Cisco AnyConnect Secure Mobility Client software installed. When the host tries to send any traffic, the Cisco AnyConnect VPN Client software encapsulates and encrypts this traffic. The encrypted data is then sent over the Internet to the VPN gateway at the edge of the target network. Upon receipt, the VPN gateway behaves as it does for site-to-site VPNs.

Note   The Cisco AnyConnect Secure Mobility Client software builds on prior Cisco AnyConnect VPN Client and Cisco VPN Client offerings to improve the always-on VPN experience across more laptop and smart phone-based mobile devices. This client supports IPv6.

Refer to
Interactive Graphic
in online course.

7.1.2.3   Activity - Compare Types of VPNs

Refer to **Packet Tracer Activity** for this chapter

7.1.2.4   Packet Tracer - Configuring VPNs (Optional)
Background/Scenario

In this activity, you will configure two routers to support a site-to-site IPsec VPN for traffic flowing from their respective LANs. The IPsec VPN traffic will pass through another router that has no knowledge of the VPN. IPsec provides secure transmission of sensitive information over unprotected networks such as the Internet. IPsec acts at the network layer, protecting and authenticating IP packets between participating IPsec devices (peers), such as Cisco routers.

Refer to
Online Course
for Illustration

7.2   Site-to-Site GRE Tunnels

7.2.1   Fundamentals of Generic Routing Encapsulation

7.2.1.1   Introduction to GRE

Generic Routing Encapsulation (GRE) is one example of a basic, non-secure, site-to-site VPN tunneling protocol. GRE is a tunneling protocol developed by Cisco that can encapsulate a wide variety of protocol packet types inside IP tunnels. GRE creates a virtual point-to-point link to Cisco routers at remote points, over an IP internetwork.

GRE is designed to manage the transportation of multiprotocol and IP multicast traffic between two or more sites, that may only have IP connectivity. It can encapsulate multiple protocol packet types inside an IP tunnel.

As shown in the figure, a tunnel interface supports a header for each of the following:

- An encapsulated protocol (or passenger protocol), such as IPv4, IPv6, AppleTalk, DECnet, or IPX

- An encapsulation protocol (or carrier), such as GRE

- A transport delivery protocol, such as IP, which is the protocol that carries the encapsulated protocol

Refer to
Online Course
for Illustration

7.2.1.2   Characteristics of GRE

GRE is a tunneling protocol developed by Cisco that can encapsulate a wide variety of protocol packet types inside IP tunnels, creating a virtual point-to-point link to Cisco routers at remote points over an IP internetwork. IP tunneling using GRE enables network expansion across a single-protocol backbone environment. It does this by connecting multiprotocol subnetworks in a single-protocol backbone environment.

GRE has these characteristics:

- GRE is defined as an IETF standard (RFC 2784).

- In the outer IP header, 47 is used in the protocol field to indicate that a GRE header will follow.

- GRE encapsulation uses a protocol type field in the GRE header to support the encapsulation of any OSI Layer 3 protocol. Protocol Types are defined in RFC 1700 as "EtherTypes".

- GRE itself is stateless; by default it does not include any flow-control mechanisms.

- GRE does not include any strong security mechanisms to protect its payload.

- The GRE header, together with the tunneling IP header indicated in the figure, creates at least 24 bytes of additional overhead for tunneled packets.

Refer to
Interactive Graphic
in online course.

7.2.1.3   Activity - Identify GRE Characteristics

Refer to
Online Course
for Illustration

7.2.2   Configuring GRE Tunnels

7.2.2.1   GRE Tunnel Configuration

GRE is used to create a VPN tunnel between two sites, as shown in Figure 1. To implement a GRE tunnel, the network administrator must first learn the IP addresses of the endpoints. After that, there are five steps to configuring a GRE tunnel:

Step 1.   Create a tunnel interface using the `interface tunnel number` command.

Step 2.   Specify the tunnel source IP address.

Step 3.   Specify the tunnel destination IP address.

Step 4.   Configure an IP address for the tunnel interface.

Step 5.   (Optional) Specify GRE tunnel mode as the tunnel interface mode. GRE tunnel mode is the default tunnel interface mode for Cisco IOS software.

The sample configuration in Figure 2 illustrates a basic GRE tunnel configuration for router R1.

The configuration of R2 in Figure 3 mirrors the configuration of R1.

The minimum configuration requires specification of the tunnel source and destination addresses. The IP subnet must also be configured to provide IP connectivity across the tunnel link. Both tunnel interfaces have the tunnel source set as the local serial S0/0/0 interface and the tunnel destination set as the peer router serial S0/0/0 interface. The IP address is assigned to the tunnel interfaces on both routers. OSPF has also been configured to exchange routes over the GRE tunnel.

The individual GRE tunnel command descriptions are displayed in Figure 4.

Note   When configuring GRE tunnels, it can be difficult to remember which IP networks are associated with the physical interfaces and which IP networks are associated with the tunnel interfaces. Remember that before a GRE tunnel is created, the physical interfaces have already been configured. The `tunnel source` and `tunnel destination` commands reference the IP addresses of the preconfigured physical interfaces. The `ip address` command on the tunnel interfaces refers to an IP network specifically manufactured for the purposes of the GRE tunnel.

Refer to
Online Course
for Illustration

7.2.2.2   GRE Tunnel Verification

There are several commands that can be used to monitor and troubleshoot GRE tunnels. To determine whether the tunnel interface is up or down, use the `show ip interface brief` command, as shown in Figure 1.

To verify the state of a GRE tunnel, use the `show interface tunnel` command. The line protocol on a GRE tunnel interface is up as long as there is a route to the tunnel destination. Before implementing a GRE tunnel, IP connectivity must already be in effect between the IP addresses of the physical interfaces on opposite ends of the potential GRE tunnel. The tunnel transport protocol is displayed in the output, also shown in Figure 1.

If OSPF has also been configured to exchange routes over the GRE tunnel, verify that an OSPF adjacency has been established over the tunnel interface using the `show ip ospf neighbor` command. In Figure 2, note that the peering address for the OSPF neighbor is on the IP network created for the GRE tunnel.

In Figure 3, use the Syntax Checker to configure and verify a GRE tunnel on R2 followed by R1.

GRE is considered a VPN because it is a private network that is created by tunneling over a public network. Using encapsulation, a GRE tunnel creates a virtual point-to-point link to Cisco routers at remote points over an IP internetwork. The advantages of GRE are that it can be used to tunnel non-IP traffic over an IP network, allowing for network expansion by connecting multiprotocol subnetworks across a single-protocol backbone environment. GRE also supports IP multicast tunneling. This means that routing protocols can be used across the tunnel, enabling dynamic exchange of routing information in the virtual network. Finally, it is common practice to create IPv6 over IPv4 GRE tunnels, where IPv6 is the encapsulated protocol and IPv4 is the transport protocol. In the future, these roles will likely be reversed as IPv6 takes over as the standard IP protocol.

However, GRE does not provide encryption or any other security mechanisms. Therefore, data sent across a GRE tunnel is not secure. If secure data communication is needed, IPsec or SSL VPNs should be configured.

Refer to **Packet Tracer Activity** for this chapter

7.2.2.3   Packet Tracer - Configuring GRE

Background/Scenario

You are the network administrator for a company which wants to set up a GRE tunnel to a remote office. Both networks are locally configured, and need only the tunnel configured.

Refer to **Packet Tracer Activity** for this chapter

7.2.2.4   Packet Tracer - Troubleshooting GRE

Background/Scenario

A junior network administrator was hired to set up a GRE tunnel between two sites and was unable to complete the task. You have been asked to correct configuration errors in the company network.

Refer to **Lab Activity** for this chapter

7.2.2.5   Lab - Configuring a Point-to-Point GRE VPN Tunnel

In this lab, you will complete the following objectives:

- Part 1: Configure Basic Device Settings
- Part 2: Configure a GRE Tunnel
- Part 3: Enable Routing over the GRE Tunnel

Refer to **Online Course** for Illustration

7.3   Introducing IPsec

7.3.1   Internet Protocol Security

7.3.1.1   IPsec

IPsec VPNs offer flexible and scalable connectivity. Site-to-site connections can provide a secure, fast, and reliable remote connection. With an IPsec VPN, the information from a private network is securely transported over a public network. This forms a virtual network instead of using a dedicated Layer 2 connection, as shown in the figure. To remain private, the traffic is encrypted to keep the data confidential.

IPsec is an IETF standard that defines how a VPN can be configured in a secure manner using the Internet Protocol.

IPsec is a framework of open standards that spells out the rules for secure communications. IPsec is not bound to any specific encryption, authentication, security algorithms, or keying technology. Rather, IPsec relies on existing algorithms to implement secure communications. IPsec allows newer and better algorithms to be implemented without amending the existing IPsec standards.

IPsec works at the network layer, protecting and authenticating IP packets between participating IPsec devices, also known as peers. IPsec secures a path between a pair of gateways, a pair of hosts, or a gateway and host. As a result, IPsec can protect virtually all application traffic because the protection can be implemented from Layer 4 to Layer 7.

All implementations of IPsec have a plaintext Layer 3 header, so there are no issues with routing. IPsec functions over all Layer 2 protocols, such as Ethernet, ATM, or Frame Relay.

IPsec characteristics can be summarized as follows:

- IPsec is a framework of open standards that is algorithm-independent.
- IPsec provides data confidentiality, data integrity, and origin authentication.
- IPsec acts at the network layer, protecting and authenticating IP packets.

Refer to
Online Course
for Illustration

7.3.1.2   IPsec Security Services

IPsec security services provide four critical functions, as shown in the figure:

- **Confidentiality (encryption)**- In a VPN implementation, private data travels over a public network. For this reason, data confidentiality is vital. It can be attained by encrypting the data before transmitting it across the network. This is the process of taking all the data that one computer is sending to another and encoding it into a form that only the other computer will be able to decode. If the communication is intercepted, it cannot be read by a hacker. IPsec provides enhanced security features, such as strong encryption algorithms.

- **Data Integrity**- The receiver can verify that the data was transmitted through the Internet without being changed or altered in any way. While it is important that data is encrypted over a public network, it is just as important to verify that it has not been changed while in transit. IPsec has a mechanism to ensure that the encrypted portion of the packet, or the entire header and data portion of the packet, has not been changed. IPsec ensures data integrity by using checksums, which is a simple redundancy check. If tampering is detected, the packet is dropped.

- **Authentication**- Verify the identity of the source of the data that is sent. This is necessary to guard against a number of attacks that depend on spoofing the identity of the sender. Authentication ensures that the connection is made with the desired communication partner. The receiver can authenticate the source of the packet by certifying the source of the information. IPsec uses Internet Key Exchange (IKE) to authenticate users and devices that can carry out communication independently. IKE uses several types of authentication, including username and password, one-time password, biometrics, pre-shared key (PSK), and digital certificates.

- **Anti-Replay Protection**- This is the ability to detect and reject replayed packets and helps prevent spoofing. Anti-replay protection verifies that each packet is unique and not duplicated. IPsec packets are protected by comparing the sequence number of the received packets with a sliding window on the destination host or security gateway. A packet that has a sequence number that is before the sliding window is considered to be late or a duplicate packet. Late and duplicate packets are dropped.

The acronym CIA is often used to help remember the first three of these functions: confidentiality, integrity, and authentication.

Refer to
Online Course
for Illustration

7.3.2   IPsec Framework

7.3.2.1   Confidentiality with Encryption

Confidentiality

VPN traffic is kept confidential with encryption. Plaintext data that is transported over the Internet can be intercepted and read. Encrypt the date to keep it private. Digitally encrypting the data renders it unreadable until it is unencrypted by the authorized receiver.

For encrypted communication to work, both the sender and the receiver must know the rules that are used to transform the original message into its coded form. Rules are based on algorithms and associated keys. In the context of encryption, an algorithm is a mathematical sequence of steps that combines a message, text, digits, or all three with a string of digits that are called a key. The output is an unreadable cipher string. The encryption algorithm also specifies how an encrypted message is decrypted. Decryption is extremely difficult or impossible without the correct key.

In the figure, Gail wants to send an electronic funds transfer (EFT) across the Internet to Jeremy. At the local end, the document is combined with a key and run through an encryption algorithm. The output is encrypted ciphertext. The ciphertext is then sent through the Internet. At the remote end, the message is recombined with a key and sent back through the encryption algorithm. The output is the original financial document.

Confidentiality is achieved through the encryption of traffic as it travels through a VPN. The degree of security depends on the key length of the encryption algorithm and the sophistication of the algorithm. If a hacker tries to hack the key through a brute-force attack, the number of possibilities to try is a function of the key length. The time to process all of the possibilities is a function of the computer power of the attacking device. The shorter the key, the easier it is to break. For example, where a relatively sophisticated computer may take approximately one year to break a 64-bit long key, the same computer may take anywhere from 10 to 19 years to decrypt a 128-bit long key.

Refer to
Online Course
for Illustration

7.3.2.2   Encryption Algorithms

The degree of security depends on the key length of the encryption algorithm. As key length increases, it becomes more difficult to break the encryption. However, a longer key requires more processor resources when encrypting and decrypting data.

DES and 3DES are no longer considered secure; therefore, it is recommended that AES be used for IPsec encryption. The greatest security for IPsec encryption of VPNs between Cisco devices is provided by the 256-bit option of AES. In addition, 512-bit and 768-bit Rivest-Shamir-Adleman (RSA) keys have been cracked and Cisco recommends using 2048-bit keys with the RSA option, if used during the authentication phase of IKE.

Symmetric Encryption

Encryption algorithms, such as AES, require a shared secret key to perform encryption and decryption. Each of the two networking devices must know the key to decode the information. With symmetric key encryption, also called secret-key encryption, each device encrypts the information before sending it over the network to the other device. Symmetric key encryption requires knowledge of which devices talk to each other so that the same key can be configured on each device, as depicted in Figure 1.

For example, a sender creates a coded message where each letter is substituted with the letter that is two letters down in the alphabet; A becomes C, B becomes D, and so on. In this case, the word SECRET becomes UGETGV. The sender has already told the recipient that the secret key is shift by 2. When the recipient receives the message UGETGV, the recipient computer decodes the message by shifting back two letters and calculating SECRET. Anyone else who sees the message sees only the encrypted message, which looks like nonsense, unless the person knows the secret key.

Here is a synopsis for symmetric algorithms:

- Uses symmetric key cryptography

- Encryption and decryption use the same key

- Typically used to encrypt the content of the message

- Examples: DES, 3DES, and AES

How do the encrypting and decrypting devices both have a shared secret key? One could use email, courier, or overnight express to send the shared secret keys to the administrators of the devices. Another, more secure method is asymmetric encryption.

Asymmetric Encryption

Asymmetric encryption uses different keys for encryption and decryption. Knowing one of the keys does not allow a hacker to deduce the second key and decode the information. One key encrypts the message, while a second key decrypts the message, as depicted in Figure 2. It is not possible to encrypt and decrypt with the same key.

Public key encryption is a variant of asymmetric encryption that uses a combination of a private key and a public key. The recipient gives a public key to any sender with whom the recipient wants to communicate. The sender uses a private key that is combined with the public key of the recipient to encrypt the message. Also, the sender must share its public key with the recipient. To decrypt a message, the recipient will use the public key of the sender with its own private key.

Here is a synopsis for asymmetric algorithms:

- Uses public key cryptography

- Encryption and decryption use a different key

- Typically used in digital certification and key management

- Examples: RSA

Refer to
Online Course
for Illustration

7.3.2.3   Diffie-Hellman Key Exchange

Data Integrity

Diffie-Hellman (DH) is not an encryption mechanism and is not typically used to encrypt data. Instead, it is a method to securely exchange the keys that encrypt data. (DH) algorithms allow two parties to establish a shared secret key that is used by encryption and hash algorithms.

Introduced by Whitfield Diffie and Martin Hellman in 1976, DH was the first system to utilize public key or asymmetric cryptographic keys. Today, DH is part of the IPsec standard. Also, a protocol known as OAKLEY uses a DH algorithm. OAKLEY is used by the

IKE protocol, which is part of the overall framework called Internet Security Association and Key Management Protocol.

Encryption algorithms such as DES, 3DES, and AES, as well as the MD5 and SHA-1 hashing algorithms require a symmetric, shared secret key to perform encryption and decryption. How do the encrypting and decrypting devices get the shared secret key? The easiest key exchange method is a public key exchange method between the encrypting and decrypting devices.

The DH algorithm specifies a public key exchange method that provides a way for two peers to establish a shared secret key that only they know, although they are communicating over an insecure channel. Like all cryptographic algorithms, DH key exchange is based on a mathematical sequence of steps.

Refer to
Online Course
for Illustration

7.3.2.4   Integrity with Hash Algorithms

The integrity and authentication of VPN traffic is handled by hash algorithms. Hashes provide data integrity and authentication by ensuring that unauthorized persons do not tamper with transmitted messages. A hash, also called a message digest, is a number that is generated from a string of text. The hash is smaller than the text itself. It is generated by using a formula in such a way that it is extremely unlikely that some other text will produce the same hash value.

The original sender generates a hash of the message and sends it with the message itself. The recipient parses the message and the hash, produces another hash from the received message, and compares the two hashes. If they are the same, the recipient can be reasonably sure of the integrity of the original message.

In the figure, Gail sent Alex an EFT of $100. Jeremy has intercepted and altered this EFT to show himself as the recipient and the amount as $1000. In this case, if a data integrity algorithm were used, the hashes would not match, and the transaction would be invalid.

VPN data is transported over the public Internet. As shown, there is potential for this data to be intercepted and modified. To guard against this threat, hosts can add a hash to the message. If the transmitted hash matches the received hash, the integrity of the message has been preserved. However, if there is no match, the message was altered.

VPNs use a message authentication code to verify the integrity and the authenticity of a message, without using any additional mechanisms.

Hash-based Message Authentication Code (HMAC) is a mechanism for message authentication using hash functions. A keyed HMAC is a data integrity algorithm that guarantees the integrity of a message. An HMAC has two parameters, a message input and a secret key that is known only to the message originator and intended receivers. The message sender uses an HMAC function to produce a value (the message authentication code) that is formed by condensing the secret key and the message input. The message authentication code is sent along with the message. The receiver computes the message authentication code on the received message using the same key and HMAC function as the sender used. Then the receiver compares the result that is computed with the received message authentication code. If the two values match, the message has been correctly received and the receiver is assured that the sender is a member of the community of users that share the key. The cryptographic strength of the HMAC depends upon the cryptographic strength of the underlying hash function, on the size and quality of the key, and on the size of the hash output length in bits.

There are two common HMAC algorithms:

- **MD5**- Uses a 128-bit shared secret key. The variable-length message and 128-bit shared secret key are combined and run through the HMAC-MD5 hash algorithm. The output is a 128-bit hash. The hash is appended to the original message and forwarded to the remote end.

- **SHA**- SHA-1 uses a 160-bit secret key. The variable-length message and the 160-bit shared secret key are combined and run through the HMAC-SHA1 hash algorithm. The output is a 160-bit hash. The hash is appended to the original message and forwarded to the remote end.

Note   Cisco IOS also supports, 256-bit, 384-bit, and 512-bit SHA implementations.

Refer to **Online Course** for Illustration

7.3.2.5   IPsec Authentication

Authentication

IPsec VPNs support authentication. When conducting business long distance, it is necessary to know who is at the other end of the phone, email, or fax. The same is true of VPN networks. The device on the other end of the VPN tunnel must be authenticated before the communication path is considered secure, as indicated in the figure. There are two peer authentication methods:

- **PSK**- A secret key that is shared between the two parties using a secure channel before it needs to be used. Pre-shared keys (PSKs) use symmetric key cryptographic algorithms. A PSK is entered into each peer manually and is used to authenticate the peer. At each end, the PSK is combined with other information to form the authentication key.

- **RSA signatures**- Digital certificates are exchanged to authenticate peers. The local device derives a hash and encrypts it with its private key. The encrypted hash, or digital signature, is attached to the message and forwarded to the remote end. At the remote end, the encrypted hash is decrypted using the public key of the local end. If the decrypted hash matches the recomputed hash, the signature is genuine.

IPsec uses RSA (public-key cryptosystem) for authentication in the context of IKE. The RSA signature method uses a digital signature setup in which each device digitally signs a set of data and sends it to the other party. RSA signatures use a certificate authority (CA) to generate a unique-identity digital certificate that is assigned to each peer for authentication. The identity digital certificate is similar in function to a PSK, but provides much stronger security. Each initiator and responder to an IKE session using RSA signatures sends its own ID value, its identity digital certificate, and an RSA signature value consisting of a variety of IKE values, all encrypted by the negotiated IKE encryption method (such as AES).

The Digital Signature Algorithm (DSA) is another option for authentication.

Refer to **Online Course** for Illustration

7.3.2.6   IPsec Protocol Framework

As stated earlier, the IPsec protocol framework describes the messaging to secure the communications, but it relies on existing algorithms.

There are two main IPsec protocols depicted in Figure 1:

- **Authentication Header (AH)-** AH is the appropriate protocol to use when confidentiality is not required or permitted. It provides data authentication and integrity for IP packets that are passed between two systems. However, AH does not provide data confidentiality (encryption) of packets. All text is transported in plaintext. Used alone, the AH protocol provides weak protection.

- **Encapsulating Security Payload (ESP)-** A security protocol that provides confidentiality and authentication by encrypting the IP packet. IP packet encryption conceals the data and the identities of the source and destination. ESP authenticates the inner IP packet and ESP header. Authentication provides data origin authentication and data integrity. Although both encryption and authentication are optional in ESP, at a minimum, one of them must be selected.

Figure 2 illustrates the components of IPsec configuration. There are four basic building blocks of the IPsec framework that must be selected.

- **IPsec framework protocol-** When configuring an IPsec gateway to provide security services, an IPsec protocol must be selected. The choices are some combination of ESP and AH. Realistically, the ESP or ESP+AH options are almost always selected because AH itself does not provide encryption, as shown in Figure 3.

- **Confidentiality (If IPsec is implemented with ESP)-** The encryption algorithm chosen should best meet the desired level of security: DES, 3DES, or AES. AES is strongly recommended, with AES-GCM providing the greatest security.

- **Integrity-** Guarantees that the content has not been altered in transit. Implemented through the use of hash algorithms. Choices include MD5 and SHA.

- **Authentication-** Represents how devices on either end of the VPN tunnel are authenticated. The two methods are PSK or RSA.

- **DH algorithm group-** Represents how a shared secret key is established between peers. There are several options, but DH24 provides the greatest security.

It is the combination of these building blocks that provides the confidentiality, integrity, and authentication options for IPsec VPNs.

Note   This section introduced IPsec to provide an understanding of how IPsec secures VPN tunnels. Configuring IPsec VPNs are beyond the scope of this course.

Refer to **Interactive Graphic** in online course.

7.3.2.7   Activity - Identify IPsec Terminology and Concepts

Refer to **Packet Tracer Activity** for this chapter

7.3.2.8   Packet Tracer - Configuring. GRE over IPsec (Optional)

Background/Scenario

You are the network administrator for a company which wants to set up a GRE tunnel over IPsec to remote offices. All networks are locally configured, and need only the tunnel and the encryption configured.

Refer to
Online Course
for Illustration

7.4   Remote Access

7.4.1   Remote-access VPN Solutions

7.4.1.1   Types of Remote-access VPNs

VPNs have become the logical solution for remote access connectivity for many reasons. VPNs provide secure communications with access rights tailored to individual users, such as employees, contractors, and partners. They also enhance productivity by extending the corporate network and applications securely while reducing communication costs and increasing flexibility.

Using VPN technology, employees can essentially take their office with them, including access to emails and network applications. VPNs can also allow contractors and partners to have limited access to the specific servers, web pages, or files required. This network access allows them to contribute to business productivity without compromising network security.

There are two primary methods for deploying remote-access VPNs:

■ Secure Sockets Layer (SSL)

■ IP Security (IPsec)

The type of VPN method implemented is based on the access requirements of the users and the organization's IT processes.

Both IPsec and SSL VPN technologies offer access to virtually any network application or resource. SSL VPNs offer such features as easy connectivity from non-company-managed desktops, little or no desktop software maintenance, and user-customized web portals upon login.

Refer to
Online Course
for Illustration

7.4.1.2   Cisco SSL VPN

Cisco IOS SSL VPN is the industry's first router-based SSL VPN solution. It offers "any-where" connectivity not only from company-managed resource, but also from employee-owned PCs, contractor or business partner desktops, and Internet kiosks.

The SSL protocol supports various cryptographic algorithms for operations, such as authenticating the server and client to each other, transmitting certificates, and establishing session keys. Cisco SSL VPN solutions can be customized for businesses of any size. These solutions deliver many remote-access connectivity features and benefits, including:

■ Web-based, clientless access and complete network access without preinstalled desktop software. This facilitates customized remote access based on user and security requirements, and it minimizes desktop support costs.

■ Protection against viruses, worms, spyware, and hackers on a VPN connection by integrating network and endpoint security in the Cisco SSL VPN platform. This reduces cost and management complexity by eliminating the need for additional security equipment and management infrastructure.

■ Use of a single device for both SSL VPN and IPsec VPN. This reduces cost and management complexity by facilitating robust remote access and site-to-site VPN services from a single platform with unified management.

Cisco IOS SSL VPN is a technology that provides remote access by using a web browser and the web browser's native SSL encryption. Alternatively, it can provide remote access using the Cisco AnyConnect Secure Mobility Client software.

The Cisco ASA provides two main deployment modes that are found in Cisco SSL VPN solutions, as shown in the figure:

■ **Cisco AnyConnect Secure Mobility Client with SSL-** Requires the Cisco AnyConnect Client

■ **Cisco Secure Mobility Clientless SSL VPN-** Requires an internet browser

The Cisco ASA must be configured to support the SSL VPN connection.

Refer to
Online Course
for Illustration

7.4.1.3   Cisco SSL VPN Solutions

Cisco AnyConnect Secure Mobility Client with SSL

Client-Based SSL VPNs provide authenticated users with LAN-like, full network access to corporate resources. However, the remote devices require a client application, such as the Cisco VPN Client or the newer AnyConnect client to be installed on the end-user device.

In a basic Cisco ASA configured for full tunneling and a remote access SSL VPN solution, remote users use the Cisco AnyConnect Secure Mobility Client, shown in Figure 1, to establish an SSL tunnel with the Cisco ASA. After the Cisco ASA establishes the VPN with the remote user, the remote user can forward IP traffic into the SSL tunnel. The Cisco AnyConnect Secure Mobility Client creates a virtual network interface to provide this functionality. The client can use any application to access any resource, subject to access rules, behind the Cisco ASA VPN gateway.

Cisco Secure Mobility Clientless SSL VPN

The clientless SSL VPN deployment model enables corporations to provide access to corporate resources even when the remote device is not corporately-managed. In this deployment model, the Cisco ASA is used as a proxy device to network resources. It provides a web portal interface for remote devices to navigate the network using port-forwarding capabilities.

In a basic Cisco ASA clientless SSL VPN solution, remote users employ a standard web browser to establish an SSL session with the Cisco ASA, as shown in Figure 2. The Cisco ASA presents the user with a web portal over which the user can access internal resources. In the basic clientless solution, the user can access only some services, such as internal web applications, and browser-based, file-sharing resources, as shown in Figure 3.

Refer to
Interactive Graphic
in online course.

7.4.1.4   Activity – Compare Cisco SSL VPN Solutions

Refer to
Online Course
for Illustration

7.4.2   IPsec Remote-access VPNs

7.4.2.1   IPsec Remote Access

Many applications require the security of an IPsec remote-access VPN connection for authentication and encryption of data. When deploying VPNs for telecommuters and small branch offices, ease of deployment is critical if technical resources are not available for VPN configuration on a remote site router.

The Cisco Easy VPN solution feature offers flexibility, scalability, and ease of use for both site-to-site and remote access IPsec VPNs. The Cisco Easy VPN solution consists of three components:

- **Cisco Easy VPN Server**- A Cisco IOS router or Cisco ASA Firewall acting as the VPN head-end device in site-to-site or remote-access VPNs.

- **Cisco Easy VPN Remote**- A Cisco IOS router or Cisco ASA Firewall acting as a remote VPN client.

- **Cisco VPN Client**- An application supported on a PC used to access a Cisco VPN server.

Using the Cisco Easy VPN server makes it possible for mobile and remote workers using a VPN Client on their PCs, or using Cisco Easy VPN Remote on an edge router, to create secure IPsec tunnels to access their headquarters' intranet, as shown in the figure.

Refer to
Online Course
for Illustration

7.4.2.2   Cisco Easy VPN Server and Remote

Cisco Easy VPN Server

The Cisco Easy VPN Server makes it possible for mobile and remote workers using VPN Client software on their PCs to create secure IPsec tunnels to access their headquarters' intranet where critical data and applications exist. It enables Cisco IOS routers and Cisco ASA Firewalls to act as VPN head-end devices in site-to-site or remote-access VPNs. Remote office devices use the Cisco Easy VPN Remote feature or the Cisco VPN Client application to connect to the server, which then pushes defined security policies to the remote VPN device. This ensures that those connections have up-to-date policies in place before the connection is established.

Cisco Easy VPN Remote

The Cisco Easy VPN Remote enables Cisco IOS routers or software clients to act as remote VPN clients. These devices can receive security policies from a Cisco Easy VPN Server, minimizing VPN configuration requirements at the remote location. This cost-effective solution is ideal for remote offices with little IT support or for large customer premises equipment (CPE) deployments where it is impractical to individually configure multiple remote devices.

The figure shows three network devices with Easy VPN Remote enabled, all connecting to an Easy VPN server for configuration parameters.

7.4.2.3   Cisco Easy VPN Client

Cisco VPN Client

The Cisco VPN Client is simple to deploy and operate. It allows organizations to establish end-to-end, encrypted VPN tunnels for secure connectivity for mobile employees or telecommuters.

To initiate an IPsec connection using the Cisco VPN client, all the user must do is open the Cisco VPN client window, as shown in Figure 1. The Cisco VPN client application lists the available preconfigured sites. The user double-clicks a site to select it and the VPN client initiates the IPsec connection. In the user authentication dialog box, the user is authenticated with a username and password, as shown in Figure 2. After authentication, the Cisco VPN Client displays a connected status.

Most of the VPN parameters are defined on the Cisco IOS Easy VPN Server to simplify deployment. After a remote client initiates a VPN tunnel connection, the Cisco Easy VPN Server pushes the IPsec policies to the client, minimizing configuration requirements at the remote location.

This simple and highly scalable solution is ideal for large remote access deployments where it is impractical to configure policies individually for multiple remote PCs. This architecture also ensures that those connections are using up-to-date security policies and eliminates the operational costs associated with maintaining a consistent policy and key management method.

Note   Configuring the Cisco VPN client is beyond the scope of this course. Check www. cisco.com for more information.

7.4.2.4   Comparing IPsec and SSL

Both IPsec and SSL VPN technologies offer access to virtually any network application or resource, as shown in the figure. SSL VPNs offer such features as easy connectivity from non-company-managed desktops, little or no desktop software maintenance, and user-customized web portals upon login.

IPsec exceeds SSL in many significant ways:

- Number of applications that are supported

- Strength of encryption

- Strength of authentication

- Overall security

When security is an issue, IPsec is the superior choice. If support and ease of deployment are the primary issues, consider SSL.

IPsec and SSL VPN are complementary because they solve different problems. Depending on its needs, an organization can implement one or both. This complementary approach allows a single device such as an ISR router or an ASA firewall appliance to address all remote-access user requirements. While many solutions offer either IPsec or SSL, Cisco remote-access VPN solutions offer both technologies integrated on a single platform with unified management. Offering both IPsec and SSL technologies enables organizations to customize their remote-access VPN without any additional hardware or management complexity.

Refer to
Interactive Graphic
in online course.

7.4.2.5   Activity - Identify Remote-Access Characteristics

Refer to
Online Course
for Illustration

Refer to
Lab Activity
for this chapter

7.5   Summary

7.5.1.1   Class Activity - VPN Planning Design

VPN Planning Design

Your small- to medium-sized business has received quite a few new contracts lately. This has increased the need for teleworkers and workload outsourcing. The new contract vendors and clients will also need access to your network as the projects progress.

As network administrator for the business, you recognize that VPNs must be incorporated as a part of your network strategy to support secure access by the teleworkers, employees, and vendors or clients.

To prepare for implementation of VPNs on the network, you devise a planning checklist to bring to the next department meeting for discussion.

Refer to Packet
Tracer Activity
for this chapter

7.5.1.2   Packet Tracer - Skills Integration Challenge

Backgroud/Scenario

This activity allows you to practice a variety of skills, including configuring Frame Relay, PPP with CHAP, NAT overloading (PAT), and GRE tunnels. The routers are partially configured for you.

Refer to
Online Course
for Illustration

7.5.1.3   Summary

VPNs are used to create a secure end-to-end private network connection over a third party network, such as the Internet. A site-to-site VPN uses a VPN gateway device at the edge of both sites. The end hosts are unaware of the VPN and have no additional supporting software.

A remote-access VPN requires software to be installed on the individual host device that accesses the network from a remote location. The two types of remote-access VPNs are SSL and IPsec. SSL technology can provide remote access using a client's web browser and the browser's native SSL encryption. Using Cisco AnyConnect software on the client, users can have LAN-like, full network access using SSL.

GRE is a basic, non-secure site-to-site VPN tunneling protocol that can encapsulate a wide variety of protocol packet types inside IP tunnels, thus allowing an organization to deliver other protocols through an IP-based WAN. Today it is primarily used to deliver IP multicast traffic or IPv6 traffic over an IPv4 unicast-only connection.

IPsec, an IETF standard, is a secure tunnel operating at Layer 3 of the OSI model that can protect and authenticate IP packets between IPsec peers. It can provide confidentiality by using encryption, data integrity, authentication, and anti-replay protection. Data integrity is provided by using a hash algorithm, such as MD5 or SHA. Authentication is provided by the PSK or RSA peer authentication method.

The level of confidentiality provided by encryption depends on the algorithm used and the key length. Encryption can be symmetrical or asymmetrical. DH is a method used to securely exchange the keys to encrypt data.

Go to the online
course to take the
quiz and exam.

Chapter 7 Quiz

This quiz is designed to provide an additional opportunity to practice the skills and knowledge presented in the chapter and to prepare for the chapter exam. You will be allowed multiple attempts and the grade does not appear in the gradebook.

Chapter 7 Exam

The chapter exam assesses your knowledge of the chapter content.

Your Chapter Notes

Monitoring the Network

8.0 Monitoring the Network

8.0.1.1 Introduction

Monitoring an operational network can provide a network administrator with information to proactively manage the network and to report network usage statistics to others. Link activity, error rates, and link status are a few of the factors that help a network administrator determine the health and usage of a network. Collecting and reviewing this information over time enables a network administrator to see and project growth, and may enable the administrator to detect and replace a failing part before it completely fails.

This chapter covers three protocols that a network administrator can use to monitor the network. Syslog, SNMP, and NetFlow are popular protocols with different strengths and weaknesses. Together, they provide a good toolset for understanding what is happening on a network. The Network Time Protocol (NTP) is used to synchronize time across devices, which is especially important when trying to compare log files from different devices.

Refer to **Lab Activity** for this chapter

8.0.1.2 Class Activity - Network Maintenance Development

Network Maintenance Development

Currently, there are no formal policies or procedures for recording problems experienced on your company's network. Furthermore, when network problems occur, you must try many methods to find the causes and this approach takes time.

You know there must be a better way to resolve these issues. You decide to create a network maintenance plan to keep repair records and pinpoint the causes of errors on the network.

Refer to **Interactive Graphic** in online course.

8.1 Syslog

8.1.1 Syslog Operation

8.1.1.1 Introduction to Syslog

When certain events occur on a network, networking devices have trusted mechanisms to notify the administrator with detailed system messages. These messages can be either non-critical or significant. Network administrators have a variety of options for storing, interpreting, and displaying these messages, and for being alerted to those messages that could have the greatest impact on the network infrastructure.

The most common method of accessing system messages that networking devices provide is to use a protocol called syslog.

Syslog is a term used to describe a standard. It is also used to describe the protocol developed for that standard. The syslog protocol was developed for UNIX systems in the 1980s, but was first documented as RFC 3164 by IETF in 2001. Syslog uses UDP port 514 to send event notification messages across IP networks to event message collectors, as illustrated in the figure.

Many networking devices support syslog, including: routers, switches, application servers, firewalls, and other network appliances. The syslog protocol allows networking devices to send their system messages across the network to syslog servers. It is possible to build a special out-of-band (OOB) network for this purpose.

There are several different syslog server software packages for Windows and UNIX. Many of them are freeware.

The syslog logging service provides three primary functions:

- The ability to gather logging information for monitoring and troubleshooting
- The ability to select the type of logging information that is captured
- The ability to specify the destinations of captured syslog messages

Refer to
Online Course
for Illustration

8.1.1.2   Syslog Operation

On Cisco network devices, the syslog protocol starts by sending system messages and `debug` output to a local logging process internal to the device. How the logging process manages these messages and outputs is based on device configurations. For example, syslog messages may be sent across the network to an external syslog server. These messages can be retrieved without the need of accessing the actual device. Log messages and outputs stored on the external server can be pulled into various reports for easier reading.

Alternatively, syslog messages may be sent to an internal buffer. Messages sent to the internal buffer are only viewable through the CLI of the device.

Finally, the network administrator may specify that only certain types of system messages are sent to various destinations. For example, the device may be configured to forward all system messages to an external syslog server. However, debug-level messages are forwarded to the internal buffer and are only accessible by the administrator from the CLI.

As shown in the figure, popular destinations for syslog messages include:

- Logging buffer (RAM inside a router or switch)
- Console line
- Terminal line
- Syslog server

It is possible to remotely monitor system messages by viewing the logs on a syslog server, or by accessing the device through Telnet, SSH, or through the console port.

Refer to
Online Course
for Illustration

8.1.1.3   Syslog Message Format

Cisco devices produce syslog messages as a result of network events. Every syslog message contains a severity level and a facility.

The smaller numerical levels are the more critical syslog alarms. The severity level of the messages can be set to control where each type of message is displayed (i.e. on the console or the other destinations). The complete list of syslog levels is shown in Figure 1.

Each syslog level has its own meaning:

■ **Warning Level - Emergency Level**- These messages are error messages about software or hardware malfunctions; these types of messages mean that the functionality of the device is affected. The severity of the issue determines the actual syslog level applied.

■ **Debugging Level**- This level indicates that the messages are output generated from issuing various `debug` commands.

■ **Notification Level**- The notifications level is only for information, device functionality is not affected. Interface up or down transitions, and system restart messages are displayed at the notifications level.

In addition to specifying the severity, syslog messages also contain information on the facility. Syslog facilities are service identifiers that identify and categorize system state data for error and event message reporting. The logging facility options that are available are specific to the networking device. For example, Cisco 2960 Series switches running Cisco IOS Release 15.0(2) and Cisco 1941 routers running Cisco IOS Release 15.2(4) support 24 facility options that are categorized into 12 facility types.

Some common syslog message facilities reported on Cisco IOS routers include:

■ IP

■ OSPF protocol

■ SYS operating system

■ IP security (IPsec)

■ Interface IP (IF)

By default, the format of syslog messages on the Cisco IOS Software is as follows:

```
seq no: timestamp: %facility-severity-MNEMONIC: description
```

The fields contained in the Cisco IOS Software syslog message are explained in Figure 2.

For example, sample output on a Cisco switch for an EtherChannel link changing state to up is:

```
00:00:46: %LINK-3-UPDOWN: Interface Port-channel1, changed state to up
```

Here the facility is LINK and the severity level is 3, with a MNEMONIC of UPDOWN.

The most common messages are link up and down messages, and messages that a device produces when it exits from configuration mode. If ACL logging is configured, the device generates syslog messages when packets match a parameter condition.

Refer to
Online Course
for Illustration

8.1.1.4 Service Timestamp

Log messages can be time-stamped and the source address of syslog messages can be set. This enhances real-time debugging and management.

When the `service timestamps log uptime` global configuration mode command is entered, the amount of time since the switch last booted is displayed on logged events. A more useful version of this command applies the `datetime` keyword in place of the `uptime` keyword; this forces each logged event to display the date and time associated with the event.

When using the `datetime` keyword, the clock on the networking device must be set. This can be accomplished in one of two ways:

- Manually set, using the `clock set` command
- Automatically set, using the Network Time Protocol (NTP)

Recall that NTP is a protocol that is used to allow network devices to synchronize their time settings with an NTP server.

To allow the software clock to be synchronized by an NTP time server, use the `ntp server` ip-address command in global configuration mode. A sample configuration is shown in the figure. R1 is configured as an NTP client, while router R2 serves as an authoritative NTP server. A network device can be configured as either an NTP server, thereby allowing other devices to synchronize off of its time, or as an NTP client.

For the remainder of the chapter, it is assumed that the clock has been set and the `service timestamps log datetime` command has been configured on all devices.

Refer to
Interactive Graphic
in online course.

8.1.1.5 Activity - Interpret Syslog Output

8.1.2 Configuring Syslog

8.1.2.1 Syslog Server

To view syslog messages, a syslog server must be installed on a workstation in the network. There are several freeware and shareware versions of syslog, as well as enterprise versions for purchase. In Figure 1, an evaluation version of the Kiwi Syslog Daemon is displayed on a Windows 7 machine.

The syslog server provides a relatively user-friendly interface for viewing syslog output. The server parses the output and places the messages into pre-defined columns for easy interpretation. If timestamps are configured on the networking device sourcing the syslog messages, then the date and time of each message displays in the syslog server output, as shown in Figure 2.

Network administrators can easily navigate the large amount of data compiled on a syslog server. One advantage of viewing syslog messages on a syslog server is the ability to perform granular searches through the data. Also, a network administrator can quickly delete unimportant syslog messages from the database.

Refer to
Online Course
for Illustration

8.1.2.2   Default Logging

By default, Cisco routers and switches send log messages for all severity levels to the console. On some IOS versions, the device also buffers log messages by default. To enable these two settings, use the `logging console` and `logging buffered` global configuration commands, respectively.

The `show logging` command displays the default logging service settings on a Cisco router, as shown in the figure. The first lines of output list information about the logging process, with the end of the output listing log messages.

The first highlighted line states that this router logs to the console and includes debug messages. This actually means that all debug level messages, as well as any lower level messages (such as notification level messages), are logged to the console. The output also notes that 32 such messages have been logged.

The second highlighted line states that this router logs to an internal buffer. Because this router has enabled logging to an internal buffer, the `show logging` command also lists the messages in that buffer. You can view some of the system messages that have been logged at the end of the output.

Refer to
Online Course
for Illustration

8.1.2.3   Router and Switch Commands for Syslog Clients

There are three steps to configuring the router to send system messages to a syslog server where they can be stored, filtered, and analyzed:

Step 1.   Configure the destination hostname or IP address of the syslog server in global configuration mode:

```
R1(config)# logging 192.168.1.3
```

Step 2.   Control the messages that will be sent to the syslog server with the `logging trap` level global configuration mode command. For example, to limit the messages to levels 4 and lower (0 to 4), use one of the two equivalent commands:

```
R1(config)# logging trap 4
R1(config)# logging trap warning
```

Step 3.   Optionally, configure the source interface with the `logging source-interface` interface-type interface number global configuration mode command. This specifies that syslog packets contain the IPv4 or IPv6 address of a specific interface, regardless of which interface the packet uses to exit the router. For example, to set the source interface to g0/0, use the following command:

```
R1(config)# logging source-interface g0/0
```

In Figure 1, R1 is configured to send log messages of levels 4 and lower to the syslog server at 192.168.1.3. The source interface is set as the G0/0 interface. A loopback interface is created, then shut down, and then brought back up. The console output reflects these actions.

Shown in Figure 2, the Tftpd32 syslog server has been set up on a Windows 7 machine with IP address 192.168.1.3. As you can see, the only messages that appear on the syslog server are those with severity level of 4 or lower (more severe). The messages with severity level of 5 or higher (less severe) appear on the router console output, but do not appear on the syslog server output, because the `logging trap` limits the syslog messages sent to the syslog server based on severity.

Refer to
Online Course
for Illustration

8.1.2.4   Verifying Syslog

You can use the `show logging` command to view any messages that are logged. When the logging buffer is large, it is helpful to use the pipe option (|) with the `show logging` command. The pipe option allows the administrator to specifically state which messages should be displayed.

For example, issuing the `show logging | include changed state to up` command, as shown in Figure 1, ensures that only interface notifications stating that the interface has "changed to state up", will be displayed.

Also shown in Figure 1, issuing the `show logging | begin June 12 22:35` command displays the contents of the logging buffer that occurred on or after June 12.

Use the Syntax Checker in Figure 2 to configure and verify the syslog on R1.

Refer to **Packet
Tracer Activity**
for this chapter

8.1.2.5   Packet Tracer - Configuring Syslog and NTP

Background/Scenario

In this activity, you will enable and use the Syslog service and the NTP service so that the network administrator is able to monitor the network more effectively.

Refer to
Lab Activity
for this chapter

8.1.2.6   Lab - Configuring Syslog and NTP

In this lab, you will complete the following objectives:

- Part 1: Configure Basic Device Settings
- Part 2: Configure NTP
- Part 3: Configure Syslog

Refer to
Online Course
for Illustration

8.2   SNMP

8.2.1   SNMP Operation

8.2.1.1   Introduction to SNMP

Simple Network Management (SNMP)

SNMP was developed to allow administrators to manage nodes, such as servers, workstations, routers, switches, and security appliances, on an IP network. It enables network administrators to manage network performance, find and solve network problems, and plan for network growth.

SNMP is an application layer protocol that provides a message format for communication between managers and agents. The SNMP system consists of three elements:

- SNMP manager
- SNMP agents (managed node)
- Management Information Base (MIB)

To configure SNMP on a networking device, it is first necessary to define the relationship between the manager and the agent.

The SNMP manager is part of a network management system (NMS). The SNMP manager runs SNMP management software. As shown in the figure, the SNMP manager can collect information from an SNMP agent using the "get" action and can change configurations on an agent using the "set" action. In addition, SNMP agents can forward information directly to an NMS using "traps".

The SNMP agent and MIB reside on networking device clients. Network devices that must be managed, such as switches, routers, servers, firewalls, and workstations, are equipped with an SMNP agent software module. MIBs store data about the device operation and are meant to be available to authenticated remote users. The SNMP agent is responsible for providing access to the local MIB of objects that reflects resources and activity.

SNMP defines how management information is exchanged between network management applications and management agents. SNMP uses UDP, port number 162, to retrieve and send management information.

Refer to **Online Course** for Illustration

8.2.1.2   SNMP Operation

SNMP agents that reside on managed devices collect and store information about the device and its operation. This information is stored by the agent locally in the MIB. The SNMP manager then uses the SNMP agent to access information within the MIB.

There are two primary SNMP manager requests, get and set. A get request is used by the NMS to query the device for data. A set request is used by the NMS to change configuration variables in the agent device. A set request can also initiate actions within a device. For example, a set can cause a router to reboot, send a configuration file, or receive a configuration file. The SNMP manager uses the get and set actions to perform the operations described in the table in Figure 1.

The SNMP agent responds to SNMP manager requests as follows:

- **Get an MIB variable**- The SNMP agent performs this function in response to a GetRequest-PDU from the NMS. The agent retrieves the value of the requested MIB variable and responds to the NMS with that value.

- **Set an MIB variable**- The SNMP agent performs this function in response to a SetRequest-PDU from the NMS. The SNMP agent changes the value of the MIB variable to the value specified by the NMS. An SNMP agent reply to a set request includes the new settings in the device.

Figure 2 illustrates the use of an SNMP GetRequest to determine if interface G0/0 is up/up.

Refer to **Online Course** for Illustration

8.2.1.3   SNMP Agent Traps

An NMS periodically polls the SNMP agents residing on managed devices, by querying the device for data using the get request. Using this process, a network management application can collect information to monitor traffic loads and to verify device configurations of managed devices. The information can be displayed via GUI on the NMS. Averages, minimums, or maximums can be calculated, the data can be graphed, or thresholds can be set to trigger a notification process when the thresholds are exceeded. For example, an

NMS can monitor CPU utilization of a Cisco router. The SNMP manager samples the value periodically and presents this information in a graph for the network administrator to use in creating a baseline.

Periodic SNMP polling does have disadvantages. First, there is a delay between the time that an event occurs and the time that it is noticed (via polling) by the NMS. Second, there is a trade-off between polling frequency and bandwidth usage.

To mitigate these disadvantages, it is possible for SNMP agents to generate and send traps to inform the NMS immediately of certain events. Traps are unsolicited messages alerting the SNMP manager to a condition or event on the network. Examples of trap conditions include, but are not limited to, improper user authentication, restarts, link status (up or down), MAC address tracking, closing of a TCP connection, loss of connection to a neighbor, or other significant events. Trap-directed notifications reduce network and agent resources, by eliminating the need for some of SNMP polling requests.

Figure 1 illustrates the use of an SNMP trap to alert the network administrator that interface G0/0 has failed. The NMS software can send the network administrator a text message, pop up a window on the NMS software, or turn the router icon red in the NMS GUI.

The exchange of all SNMP messages is illustrated in Figure 2.

Refer to
Online Course
for Illustration

8.2.1.4   SNMP Versions

There are several versions of SNMP, including:

- **SNMPv1**- The Simple Network Management Protocol, a Full Internet Standard, defined in RFC 1157.

- **SNMPv2c**- Defined in RFCs 1901 to 1908; utilizes community-string-based Administrative Framework.

- **SNMPv3**- Interoperable standards-based protocol originally defined in RFCs 2273 to 2275; provides secure access to devices by authenticating and encrypting packets over the network. It includes these security features: message integrity to ensure that a packet was not tampered with in transit; authentication to determine that the message is from a valid source, and encryption to prevent the contents of a message from being read by an unauthorized source.

All versions use SNMP managers, agents, and MIBs. Cisco IOS software supports the above three versions. Version 1 is a legacy solution and not often encountered in networks today; therefore, this course focuses on versions 2c and 3.

Both SNMPv1 and SNMPv2c use a community-based form of security. The community of managers able to access the agent's MIB is defined by an ACL and password.

Unlike SNMPv1, SNMPv2c includes a bulk retrieval mechanism and more detailed error message reporting to management stations. The bulk retrieval mechanism retrieves tables and large quantities of information, minimizing the number of round-trips required. The SNMPv2c improved error-handling includes expanded error codes that distinguish different kinds of error conditions. These conditions are reported through a single error code in SNMPv1. Error return codes in SNMPv2c include the error type.

Note SNMPv1 and SNMPv2c offer minimal security features. Specifically, SNMPv1 and SNMPv2c can neither authenticate the source of a management message nor provide encryption. SNMPv3 is most currently described in RFCs 3410 to 3415. It adds methods to ensure the secure transmission of critical data between managed devices.

SNMPv3 provides for both security models and security levels. A security model is an authentication strategy set up for a user and the group within which the user resides. A security level is the permitted level of security within a security model. A combination of the security level and the security model determine which security mechanism is used when handling an SNMP packet. Available security models are SNMPv1, SNMPv2c, and SNMPv3.

The figure identifies the characteristics of the different combinations of security models and levels.

A network administrator must configure the SNMP agent to use the SNMP version supported by the management station. Because an agent can communicate with multiple SNMP managers, it is possible to configure the software to support communications using SNMPv1, SNMPv2c, or SNMPv3.

Refer to
Online Course
for Illustration

8.2.1.5   Community Strings

For SNMP to operate, the NMS must have access to the MIB. To ensure that access requests are valid, some form of authentication must be in place.

SNMPv1 and SNMPv2c use community strings that control access to the MIB. Community strings are plaintext passwords. SNMP community strings authenticate access to MIB objects.

There are two types of community strings:

- **Read-only (ro)**- Provides access to the MIB variables, but does not allow these variables to be changed, only read. Because security is minimal in version 2c, many organizations use SNMPv2c in read-only mode.

- **Read-write (rw)**- Provides read and write access to all objects in the MIB.

To view or set MIB variables, the user must specify the appropriate community string for read or write access. Play the animation in the figure to view how SNMP operates with the community string.

Note Plaintext passwords are not considered a security mechanism. This is because plaintext passwords are highly vulnerable to man-in-the-middle attacks, in which they are compromised through the capture of packets.

Refer to
Online Course
for Illustration

8.2.1.6   Management Information Base Object ID

The MIB organizes variables hierarchically. MIB variables enable the management software to monitor and control the network device. Formally, the MIB defines each variable as an object ID (OID). OIDs uniquely identify managed objects in the MIB hierarchy. The MIB organizes the OIDs based on RFC standards into a hierarchy of OIDs, usually shown as a tree.

The MIB tree for any given device includes some branches with variables common to many networking devices and some branches with variables specific to that device or vendor.

RFCs define some common public variables. Most devices implement these MIB variables. In addition, networking equipment vendors, like Cisco, can define their own private branches of the tree to accommodate new variables specific to their devices. Figure 1 shows portions of the MIB structure defined by Cisco Systems, Inc. Note how the OID can be described in words or numbers to help locate a particular variable in the tree. OIDs belonging to Cisco, as shown in Figure 1, are numbered as follows: .iso (1).org (3).dod (6). internet (1).private (4).enterprises (1).cisco (9). This is displayed as 1.3.6.1.4.1.9.

Because the CPU is one of the key resources, it should be measured continuously. CPU statistics should be compiled on the NMS and graphed. Observing CPU utilization over an extended time period allows the administrator to establish a baseline estimate for CPU utilization. Threshold values can then be set relative to this baseline. When CPU utilization exceeds this threshold, notifications are sent. An SNMP graphing tool can periodically poll SNMP agents, such as a router, and graph the gathered values. Figure 2 illustrates 5-minute samples of router CPU utilization over the period of a few weeks.

The data is retrieved via the snmpget utility, issued on the NMS. Using the snmpget utility, one can manually obtain values for the average of the CPU busy percentage. The snmpget utility requires that the SNMP version, the correct community, the IP address of the network device to query, and the OID number are set. Figure 3 demonstrates the use of the freeware snmpget utility, which allows quick retrieval of information from the MIB.

Figure 3 shows a rather long command with several parameters, including:

- `-v2c` - version of SNMP
- `-c community` - SNMP password, called a community string
- `10.250.250.14` - IP address of monitored device
- `1.3.6.1.4.1.9.2.1.58.0` - OID of MIB variable

The last line shows the response. The output shows a shortened version of the MIB variable. It then lists the actual value in the MIB location. In this case, the 5-minute exponential moving average of the CPU busy percentage is 11 percent. The utility gives some insight into the basic mechanics of how SNMP works. However, working with long MIB variable names like 1.3.6.1.4.1.9.2.1.58.0 can be problematic for the average user. More commonly, the network operations staff uses a network management product with an easy-to-use GUI, with the entire MIB data variable naming transparent to the user.

The Cisco SNMP Navigator website allows a network administrator to research details about a particular OID. Figure 4 displays an example associated with a configuration change on a Cisco 2960 switch.

Refer to Interactive Graphic in online course.

8.2.1.7   Activity - Identify Characteristics of SNMP Versions

Refer to Lab Activity for this chapter

8.2.1.8   Lab - Researching Network Monitoring Software
In this lab, you will complete the following objectives:

- Part 1: Survey Your Understanding of Network Monitoring
- Part 2: Research Network Monitoring Tools
- Part 3: Select a Network Monitoring Tool

Refer to
Online Course
for Illustration

8.2.2   Configuring SNMP

8.2.2.1   Steps for Configuring SNMP

A network administrator can configure SNMPv2 to obtain network information from network devices. As shown in the figure, the basic steps to configuring SNMP are all in global configuration mode.

Step 1.   (Required) Configure the community string and access level (read-only or read-write) with the `snmp-server community` string `ro` | `rw` command.

Step 2.   (Optional) Document the location of the device using the `snmp-server location` text command.

Step 3.   (Optional) Document the system contact using the `snmp-server contact` text command.

Step 4.   (Optional) Restrict SNMP access to NMS hosts (SNMP managers) that are permitted by an ACL: define the ACL and then reference the ACL with the `snmp-server community` string access-list-number-or-name command. This command can be used both to specify a community string and to restrict SNMP access via ACLs. Step 1 and Step 4 can be combined into one step, if desired; the Cisco networking device combines the two commands into one if they are entered separately.

Step 5.   (Optional) Specify the recipient of the SNMP trap operations with the `snmp-server host` host-id [`version`{`1`| `2c` | `3` [`auth` | `noauth` | `priv`]}] community-string command. By default, no trap manager is defined.

Step 6.   (Optional) Enable traps on an SNMP agent with the `snmp-server enable traps` notification-types command. If no trap notification types are specified in this command, then all trap types are sent. Repeated use of this command is required if a particular subset of trap types is desired.

Note   By default, SNMP does not have any traps set. Without this command, SNMP managers must poll for all relevant information.

Refer to
Online Course
for Illustration

8.2.2.2   Verifying SNMP Configuration

There are several software solutions for viewing SNMP output. For our purposes, the Kiwi Syslog Server displays SNMP messages associated with SNMP traps.

PC1 and R1 are configured to demonstrate output on an SNMP Manager as related to SNMP traps.

As shown in Figure 1, PC1 is assigned the IP address 192.168.1.3/24. The Kiwi Syslog Server is installed on PC1.

After R1 is configured, whenever an event occurs which qualifies as a trap, the SNMP traps are sent to the SNMP manager. For instance, if an interface comes up, a trap is sent to the server. Configuration changes on the router also trigger SNMP traps to be sent to the SNMP manager. A list of over 60 trap notification types can be seen with the `snmp-server enable traps ?` command. In the configuration of R1, no trap notification types are specified in the `snmp-server enable traps` notification-types command, so all traps are sent.

In Figure 2, a check box is checked in the **Setup** menu to indicate that the network administrator wants SNMP manager software to listen for SNMP traps on UDP port 162.

In Figure 3, the top row of the displayed SNMP trap output indicates that interface GigabitEthernet0/0 changed state to up. Also, each time the global configuration mode is entered from privileged EXEC mode, a trap is received by the SNMP manager, as shown in the highlighted row.

To verify the SNMP configuration, use any of the variations of the `show snmp` privileged EXEC mode command. The most useful command is simply the `show snmp` command, as it displays the information that is commonly of interest when examining the SNMP configuration. Unless there is an involved SNMPv3 configuration, for the most part the other command options only display selected portions of the output of the `show snmp` command. Figure 4 provides an example of `show snmp` output.

The `show snmp` command output does not display information relating to the SNMP community string or, if applicable, the associated ACL. Figure 5 displays the SNMP community string and ACL information, using the `show snmp community` command.

Use the Syntax Checker in Figure 6 to configure and verify SNMP on R1.

Refer to
Online Course
for Illustration

8.2.2.3 Security Best Practices

While SNMP is very useful for monitoring and troubleshooting, like the one shown in the figure, it can also create security vulnerabilities. For this reason, prior to implementing SNMP, be mindful of security best practices.

Both SNMPv1 and SNMPv2c rely on SNMP community strings in plaintext to authenticate access to MIB objects. These community strings, as with all passwords, should be carefully chosen to ensure that they are not too easy to crack. Additionally, community strings should be changed at regular intervals and in accordance with network security policies. For example, the strings should be changed when a network administrator changes roles or leaves the company. If SNMP is used only to monitor devices, use read-only communities.

Ensure that SNMP messages do not spread beyond the management consoles. ACLs should be used to prevent SNMP messages from going beyond the required devices. ACL should also be used on the monitored devices to limit access for management systems only.

SNMPv3 is recommended because it provides security authentication and encryption. There are a number of other global configuration mode commands that a network administrator can implement to take advantage of the authentication and encryption support in SNMPv3:

- The `snmp-server group` groupname {`v1` | `v2c` | `v3` {`auth` | `noauth` | `priv`}} command creates a new SNMP group on the device.

- The `snmp-server user` username groupname `v3` [`encrypted`] [`auth` {`md5` | `sha`} auth-password] [priv {`des` | `3des` | `aes` {`128` | `192` | `256`}} priv-password] command is used to add a new user to the SNMP group specified in the `snmp-server group` groupname command.

Note   SNMPv3 configuration is beyond the scope of the CCNA curricula.

Refer to
Lab Activity
for this chapter

8.2.2.4   Lab - Configuring SNMP

In this lab, you will complete the following objectives:

- Part 1: Build the Network and Configure Basic Device Settings
- Part 2: Configure an SNMP Manager and Agents
- Part 3: Convert OID Codes with the Cisco SNMP Object Navigator

Refer to
Online Course
for Illustration

8.3   NetFlow

8.3.1   NetFlow Operation

8.3.1.1   Introducing NetFlow

NetFlow is a Cisco IOS technology that provides statistics on packets flowing through a Cisco router or multilayer switch. NetFlow is the standard for collecting IP operational data from IP networks.

Historically, NetFlow technology was developed because networking professionals needed a simple and efficient method for tracking TCP/IP flows in the network, and SNMP was not sufficient for these purposes. While SNMP attempts to provide a very wide range of network management features and options, NetFlow is focused on providing statistics on IP packets flowing through network devices.

NetFlow provides data to enable network and security monitoring, network planning, traffic analysis to include identification of network bottlenecks, and IP accounting for billing purposes. For example, in the figure, PC 1 connects to PC 2 using an application such as HTTPS. NetFlow can monitor that application connection, tracking byte and packet counts for that individual application flow. It then pushes the statistics over to an external server called a NetFlow collector.

NetFlow has become a monitoring standard, and is now widely supported in the networking industry.

Flexible NetFlow is the latest NetFlow technology. Flexible NetFlow improves on "original NetFlow" by adding the capability to customize the traffic analysis parameters for the specific requirements of a network administrator. Flexible NetFlow facilitates the creation of more complex configurations for traffic analysis and data export through the use of reusable configuration components.

Flexible NetFlow uses the Version 9 export format. The distinguishing feature of the NetFlow Version 9 export format is that it is template-based. Templates provide an extensible design to the record format, a feature that allows future enhancements to NetFlow services without requiring concurrent changes to the basic flow-record format. It is important to note that many useful Flexible NetFlow commands were introduced with Cisco IOS Release 15.1.

Refer to
Online Course
for Illustration

8.3.1.2   Understanding NetFlow

There are many potential uses of the statistics that NetFlow provides; however, most organizations use NetFlow for some or all of the following important data collection purposes:

- Measuring who is using what network resources for what purpose.

- Accounting and charging back according to the resource utilization level.

- Using the measured information to do more effective network planning so that resource allocation and deployment is well-aligned with customer requirements.

- Using the information to better structure and customize the set of available applications and services to meet user needs and customer service requirements.

When comparing the functionality of SNMP to NetFlow, an analogy for SNMP might be remote-control software for an unmanned vehicle; whereas an analogy for NetFlow is a simple, yet detailed phone bill. Phone records provide call-by-call and aggregated statistics that enable the person paying the bill to track long calls, frequent calls, or calls that should not have been made.

In contrast to SNMP, NetFlow uses a "push-based" model. The collector simply listens for NetFlow traffic, and the networking devices are in charge of sending NetFlow data to the collector, based on changes in their flow cache. Another difference between NetFlow and SNMP is that NetFlow only gathers traffic statistics, as shown in the figure, whereas SNMP can also collect many other performance indicators, such as interface errors, CPU usage, and memory usage. On the other hand, the traffic statistics collected using NetFlow have a lot more granularity than the traffic statistics that can be collected using SNMP.

Note   Do not confuse NetFlow's purpose and results with that of packet capture hardware and software. Whereas packet captures record all possible information exiting or entering a network device for later analysis, NetFlow targets specific statistical information.

When Cisco sought out to create NetFlow, two key criteria provided guidance in its creation:

- NetFlow should be completely transparent to the applications and devices in the network.

- NetFlow should not have to be supported and running on all devices in the network to function.

Achieving these design criteria ensured that NetFlow is very easy to implement in the most complex modern networks.

Note   Although NetFlow is simple to implement and transparent to the network, it does consume additional memory on the Cisco device, because NetFlow stores record information in "cache" on the device. The default size of this cache varies based on the platform, and the administrator can adjust this value.

Refer to
Online Course
for Illustration

8.3.1.3   Network Flows

NetFlow breaks down TCP/IP communications for statistical record keeping using the concept of a flow. A flow is a unidirectional stream of packets between a specific source system and a specific destination. The figure demonstrates the flow concept.

For NetFlow, which is built around TCP/IP, the source and destination are defined by their network layer IP addresses and their transport layer source and destination port numbers.

NetFlow technology has seen several generations that provide more sophistication in defining traffic flows, but "original NetFlow" distinguished flows using a combination of seven fields. Should one of these fields vary in value from another packet, the packets could be safely determined to be from different flows:

- Source IP address

- Destination IP address

- Source port number

- Destination port number

- Layer 3 protocol type

- Type of Service (ToS) marking

- Input logical interface

The first four of the fields NetFlow uses to identify a flow should be familiar. The source and destination IP addresses, plus the source and destination ports, identify the connection between source and destination application. The Layer 3 protocol type identifies the type of header that follows the IP header (usually TCP or UDP, but other options include ICMP). The ToS byte in the IPv4 header holds information about how devices should apply quality of service (QoS) rules to the packets in that flow.

Flexible NetFlow supports more options with flow data records. Flexible NetFlow enables an administrator to define records for a Flexible NetFlow flow monitor cache by specifying the user-defined optional and required fields to customize the data collection to suit specific requirements. When defining records for a Flexible NetFlow flow monitor cache, they are referred to as user-defined records. The values in optional fields are added to flows to provide additional information about the traffic in the flows. A change in the value of an optional field does not create a new flow.

Refer to
Interactive Graphic
in online course.

8.3.1.4   Activity - Compare SNMP and NetFlow

Refer to
Online Course
for Illustration

8.3.2   Configuring NetFlow

8.3.2.1   Configuring NetFlow

To implement NetFlow on a router:

Step 1.   **Configure NetFlow data capture** - NetFlow captures data from ingress (incoming) and egress (outgoing) packets.

Step 2.   **Configure NetFlow data export** - The IP address or hostname of the NetFlow collector must be specified and the UDP port to which the NetFlow collector listens.

Step 3.   **Verify NetFlow, its operation and statistics** - After configuring NetFlow, the exported data can be analyzed on a workstation running an application, such as SolarWinds NetFlow Traffic Analyzer, Plixer Scrutinizer, or Cisco NetFlow Collector (NFC). Minimally, one can rely on the output from a number of `show` commands on the router itself.

Some NetFlow configuration considerations include:

- Newer Cisco routers, such as the ISR G2 series, support both NetFlow and Flexible NetFlow.

- Newer Cisco switches, such as the 3560-X series switches, support Flexible NetFlow; however, some Cisco switches, such as Cisco 2960 Series switches, do not support NetFlow or Flexible NetFlow.

- NetFlow consumes additional memory. If a Cisco networking device has memory constraints, the size of the NetFlow cache can be pre-set so that it contains a smaller number of entries. The default cache size depends on the platform.

- NetFlow software requirements for the NetFlow collector vary. For example, the Scrutinizer NetFlow software on a Windows host requires 4 GB of RAM and 50 GB of drive space.

Note   The focus here is on Cisco router configuration of the original NetFlow (referred to simply as NetFlow in the Cisco documentation). The configuration of Flexible Netflow is beyond the scope of this course.

A NetFlow flow is unidirectional. This means that one user connection to an application exists as two NetFlow flows, one for each direction. To define the data to be captured for NetFlow in interface configuration mode:

- Capture NetFlow data for monitoring incoming packets on the interface using the `ip flow ingress` command.

- Capture NetFlow data for monitoring outgoing packets on the interface using the `ip flow egress` command.

To enable the NetFlow data to be sent to the NetFlow collector, there are several items to configure on the router in global configuration mode:

- **NetFlow collector's IP address and UDP port number**- Use the `ip flow-export destination` ip-address udp-port command. The collector has one or more ports, by default, for NetFlow data capture. The software allows the administrator to specify which port or ports to accept for NetFlow capture. Some common UDP ports allocated are 99, 2055, and 9996.

- **(Optional) NetFlow version to follow when formatting the NetFlow records sent to the collector**- Use the `ip flow-export version` version command. NetFlow exports data in UDP in one of five formats (1, 5, 7, 8, and 9). Version 9 is the most versatile export data format, but it is not backward compatible with previous versions. Version 1 is the default version if the version is not specified with Version 5. Version 1 should be used only when it is the only NetFlow data export format version that is supported by the NetFlow collector software.

- **(Optional) Source interface to use as the source of the packets sent to the collector-** Use the `ip flow-export source` typenumber command.

The figure shows a basic NetFlow configuration. Router R1 has IP address 192.168.1.1 on the G0/1 interface. The NetFlow collector has the IP address of 192.168.1.3 and is configured to capture the data on UDP port 2055. Ingress and egress traffic through G0/1 is monitored. NetFlow data is sent in Version 5 format.

Refer to **Online Course** for Illustration

8.3.2.2   Verifying NetFlow

After it is verified that NetFlow is working properly, data collection can begin on the NetFlow collector. Netflow verification is done by examining the information stored on the NetFlow collector. At a minimum, check the local NetFlow cache on a router to ensure that the router is collecting the data.

NetFlow was configured on router R1 as follows:

- IP address 192.168.1.1/24 on G0/1

- Ingress and egress traffic monitored by NetFlow

- NetFlow collector at 192.168.1.3/24

- NetFlow UDP capture port 2055

- NetFlow Version 5 export format

To display a summary of the NetFlow accounting statistics, as well as which protocol uses the highest volume of the traffic, and to see between which hosts this traffic flows, use the `show ip cache flow` command in user EXEC or privileged EXEC mode. This command is entered on R1 to verify the NetFlow configuration, as seen in Figure 1. The command output details which protocol uses the highest volume of the traffic and between which hosts this traffic flows. The table in Figure 1 describes the significant fields shown in the flow switching cache lines of the display.

The output at the top of the display confirms that the router is collecting data. The first highlighted entry lists a count of 178,617 packets monitored by NetFlow. The end of the output shows statistics about three flows, the highlighted one corresponding to an active HTTPS connection between the NetFlow collector and R1. It also shows the source port (SrcP) and destination port (DstP) in hexadecimal.

Note   Hexadecimal 01BB is equal to decimal 443, the well-known TCP port for HTTPS.

Figure 2 describes the significant fields in the flow switching cache lines of the `show ip cache flow` command output.

Figure 3 describes the significant fields in the activity by protocol lines of the `show ip cache flow` command output.

Figure 4 describes the significant fields in the NetFlow record lines of the `show ip cache flow` command output.

Although the output of the `show ip cache flow` command confirms that the router is collecting data, to ensure that NetFlow is configured on the correct interfaces in the correct directions, use the `show ip flow interface` command, as shown in Figure 5.

To check the configuration of the export parameters, use the `show ip flow export` command, shown in Figure 5. The first highlighted line shows that NetFlow is enabled with Version 5 export format. The last highlighted lines in Figure 5 show that 1764 flows have been exported in the form of 532 UDP datagrams to the NetFlow collector at 192.168.1.3 via port 2055.

Use the Syntax Checker in Figure 6 to configure and verify NetFlow on R1.

Refer to
Online Course
for Illustration

8.3.3   Examining Traffic Patterns

8.3.3.1   Identifying NetFlow Collector Functions

A NetFlow collector is a host that is running application software. This software is specialized for handling raw NetFlow data. This collector can be configured to receive NetFlow information from many networking devices. NetFlow collectors aggregate and organize NetFlow data as prescribed by the network administrator within the constraints of the software.

On a NetFlow collector, the NetFlow data is written to a drive, at specified intervals. The administrator may run multiple collection schemes or threads concurrently. For example, different cuts of data can be stored to support planning versus billing; a NetFlow collector can easily produce the appropriate aggregation schemes.

Figure 1 illustrates a NetFlow collector passively listening for exported NetFlow datagrams. A NetFlow collector application provides a high-performance, easy-to-use, scalable solution to accommodate consumption of NetFlow export data from multiple devices. The intended use by an organization varies, but often the purpose is to support critical flows associated with consumer applications. These include accounting, billing, and network planning and monitoring.

There are several NetFlow collectors on the market. These tools enable traffic analysis on the network by showing the top (or most active) hosts, most used applications, and other means of measuring the traffic data, as shown in Figure 2. A NetFlow collector displays the kinds of traffic (web, mail, FTP, peer-to-peer, etc.) on the network, as well as the devices that send and receive most of the traffic. Collecting data provides a network administrator with data on top talkers, top hosts, and top listeners. Because data is preserved over time, after-the-fact network traffic analyses can determine network use trends.

Based on usage of NetFlow analyzers, a network administrator is able to identify:

- Who are the top talkers and to whom are they talking?

- What websites are routinely visited and what is downloaded?

- Who is generating the most traffic?

- Is there enough bandwidth to support mission-critical activity?

- Who is monopolizing the bandwidth?

The amount of information that can be analyzed by a NetFlow collector varies based on the NetFlow version used, because different NetFlow export formats consist of distinct NetFlow record types. A NetFlow record contains the specific information about the actual traffic that makes up a NetFlow flow.

A NetFlow collector provides real-time visualization and analysis of recorded and aggregated flow data. The routers and supported switches can be specified, as well as the aggregation scheme and the time interval to store data prior to the next periodic analysis. One can sort and visualize the data in a manner which makes sense for the users: bar charts, pie charts, or histograms of the sorted reports. The data can then be exported to spreadsheets, such as Microsoft Excel, for more detailed analysis, trending, and reporting.

Refer to
Online Course
for Illustration

8.3.3.2   NetFlow Analysis with a NetFlow Collector

Plixer International developed the Scrutinizer NetFlow Analyzer software. Scrutinizer is one of many options for capturing and analyzing NetFlow data on a NetFlow collector.

Recall the configuration from the previous topic:

- IP address 192.168.1.1/24 on G0/1

- Ingress and egress traffic monitored for NetFlow

- NetFlow collector at 192.168.1.3/24

- NetFlow UDP capture port 2055

- NetFlow Version 5 export format

The Scrutinizer software has been installed on the NetFlow collector at 192.168.1.3/24.

Figure 1 displays the software interface upon opening the Scrutinizer application.

Figure 2 displays the result of clicking the Status tab after the application is running. The software displays a message: `Flows detected, please wait while Scrutinizer prepares the initial reports.`

Figure 3 displays the Status screen after a few minutes. Router R1 has been configured with the cisco.com domain name.

The SNMP configuration from the previous section is still active on R1. The Scrutinizer software was configured with the SNMP community *batonaug* in the **Admin Settings** tab. When the SNMP link under R1.cisco.com in the left panel is clicked, the display in Figure 4 appears. This shows a basic traffic analysis for R1 communicated to the NetFlow collector via SNMPv2c. The Multi Router Traffic Grapher (MRTG) is free software that many network administrators use for basic traffic analysis. The Scrutinizer application integrates MRTG and the graphs in Figure 4 are produced by MRTG. The top graph reflects ingress traffic and the bottom graph reflects egress traffic for interface G0/1 on R1.

Finally, in Figure 5 the **Dashboard** tab displays actual NetFlow data reported for Top Hosts and Top Applications. The Scrutinizer software has dozens of these gadgets available for displaying various categorizations of data. In Figure 5, the top host is R1, with the greatest amount of traffic between R1 and the NetFlow collector. The top application is HTTPS, followed by SNMP, HTTP, SSH, ICMP, and NetBIOS.

Refer to
Lab Activity
for this chapter

8.3.3.3   Lab - Collecting and Analyzing NetFlow Data

In this lab, you will complete the following objectives:

- Part 1: Build the Network and Configure Basic Device Settings

- Part 2: Configure NetFlow on a Router

- Part 3: Analyze NetFlow Using the CLI

- Part 4: Explore NetFlow Collector and Analyzer Software

Refer to
Online Course
for Illustration

8.4   Summary

Refer to
Lab Activity
for this chapter

8.4.1.1   Class Activity - A Network Administrator's Toolbox for Monitoring

A Network Administrator's Toolbox for Monitoring

As the network administrator for a small- to medium-sized business, you have just started using CLI network monitoring on the company routers, switches, and servers.

You decide to create a situational listing explaining when to use each method. Network monitoring methods to include are:

- Syslog

- SNMP

- NetFlow

Refer to
Online Course
for Illustration

8.4.1.2   Summary

The time on Cisco network devices can be synchronized using NTP.

Cisco network devices can log syslog messages to an internal buffer, the console, a terminal line, or an external syslog server. A network administrator can configure the types of messages to be collected and where to send the time-stamped messages.

The SNMP protocol has three elements: the Manager, the Agent, and the MIB. The SNMP manager resides on the NMS, while the Agent and the MIB are on the client devices. The SNMP Manager can poll the client devices for information, or it can use a TRAP message that tells a client to report immediately if the client reaches a particular threshold. SNMP can also be used to change the configuration of a device. SNMPv3 is the recommended version because it provides security. SNMP is a comprehensive and powerful remote management tool. Nearly every item available in a `show` command is available through SNMP.

NetFlow is a Cisco IOS technology that is the standard for collecting IP operational data from IP networks. NetFlow efficiently measures what network resources are being used and for what purposes. NetFlow uses header fields to distinguish between data flows. NetFlow is a "push" technology, where the client device initiates the sending of data to a configured server.

Go to the online course to take the quiz and exam.

Chapter 8 Quiz

This quiz is designed to provide an additional opportunity to practice the skills and knowledge presented in the chapter and to prepare for the chapter exam. You will be allowed multiple attempts and the grade does not appear in the gradebook.

Chapter 8 Exam

The chapter exam assesses your knowledge of the chapter content.

Your Chapter Notes

Troubleshooting the Network

9.0 Troubleshooting the Network

9.0.1.1 Introduction

If a network or a portion of a network goes down, it can have a severe negative impact on the business. Network administrators must use a systematic approach to troubleshooting when network problems occur to bring the network back to full production as quickly as possible.

The ability for a network administrator to be able to resolve network problems quickly and efficiently is one of the most sought after skills in IT. Enterprises need individuals with strong network troubleshooting skills and the only way to gain these skills is through hands-on experience and by using systematic troubleshooting approaches.

This chapter describes the network documentation that should be maintained and general troubleshooting procedures, methods, and tools. Typical symptoms and causes at several layers of the OSI model are also discussed. This chapter also includes some information about troubleshooting path and ACL issues.

Refer to **Lab Activity** for this chapter

9.0.1.2 Class Activity - Network Breakdown

Network Breakdown

You have just moved in to your new office, and your network is very small. After a long weekend of setting up the new network, you discover that it is not working correctly.

Some of the devices cannot access each other and some cannot access the router which connects to the ISP.

It is your responsibility to troubleshoot and fix the problems. You decide to start with basic commands to identify possible troubleshooting areas.

Refer to **Interactive Graphic** in online course.

9.1 Troubleshooting with a Systematic Approach

9.1.1 Network Documentation

9.1.1.1 Documenting the Network

For network administrators to be able to monitor and troubleshoot a network, they must have a complete set of accurate and current network documentation. This documentation includes:

- Configuration files, including network configuration files and end-system configuration files

- Physical and logical topology diagrams

- A baseline performance level

Network documentation allows network administrators to efficiently diagnose and correct network problems, based on the network design and the expected performance of the network under normal operating conditions. All network documentation information should be kept in a single location, either as hard copy, or on the network on a protected server. Backup documentation should be maintained and kept in a separate location.

Network Configuration Files

Network configuration files contain accurate, up-to-date records of the hardware and software used in a network. Within the network configuration files a table should exist for each network device used on the network, containing all relevant information about that device. Figure 1 shows sample network configuration tables for two routers. Figure 2 is a similar table for a LAN switch.

Information that could be captured within a device table includes:

- Type of device, model designation

- IOS image name

- Device network hostname

- Location of the device (building, floor, room, rack, panel)

- If it is a modular device, include all module types and in which module slot they are located

- Data link layer addresses

- Network layer addresses

- Any additional important information about physical aspects of the device

End-system Configuration Files

End-system configuration files focus on the hardware and software used in end-system devices, such as servers, network management consoles, and user workstations. An incorrectly configured end system can have a negative impact on the overall performance of a network. For this reason, having a sample baseline record of the hardware and software used on devices, and recorded in end-system documentation as shown in Figure 3 can be very useful when troubleshooting.

For troubleshooting purposes, the following information could be documented within the end-system configuration table:

- Device name (purpose)

- Operating system and version

- IPv4 and IPv6 addresses

- Subnet mask and prefix length

- Default gateway, DNS server, and WINS server addresses

- Any high-bandwidth network applications that the end system runs

Refer to
Online Course
for Illustration

9.1.1.2   Network Topology Diagrams

Network Topology Diagrams

Network topology diagrams keep track of the location, function, and status of devices on the network. There are two types of network topology diagrams: the physical topology and the logical topology.

Physical Topology

A physical network topology shows the physical layout of the devices connected to the network. It is necessary to know how devices are physically connected to troubleshoot physical layer problems. Information recorded on the diagram typically includes:

■ Device type

■ Model and manufacturer

■ Operating system version

■ Cable type and identifier

■ Cable specification

■ Connector type

■ Cabling endpoints

Figure 1 shows a sample physical network topology diagram.

Logical Topology

A logical network topology illustrates how devices are logically connected to the network, meaning how devices actually transfer data across the network when communicating with other devices. Symbols are used to represent network elements, such as routers, servers, hosts, VPN concentrators, and security devices. Additionally, connections between multiple sites may be shown, but do not represent actual physical locations. Information recorded on a logical network diagram may include:

■ Device identifiers

■ IP address and prefix lengths

■ Interface identifiers

■ Connection type

■ DLCI for virtual circuits

■ Site-to-site VPNs

■ Routing protocols

■ Static routes

■ Data-link protocols

■ WAN technologies used

Figure 2 shows a sample logical IPv4 network topology. Although IPv6 addresses could also be displayed in the same topology, it may be clearer to create a separate logical IPv6 network topology diagram.

9.1.1.3   Establishing a Network Baseline

Baseline Performance Level

The purpose of network monitoring is to watch network performance in comparison to a predetermined baseline. A baseline is used to establish normal network or system performance. Establishing a network performance baseline requires collecting performance data from the ports and devices that are essential to network operation. The figure shows several questions that a baseline is used to answer.

Measuring the initial performance and availability of critical network devices and links allows a network administrator to determine the difference between abnormal behavior and proper network performance as the network grows or traffic patterns change. The baseline also provides insight into whether the current network design can meet business requirements. Without a baseline, no standard exists to measure the optimum nature of network traffic and congestion levels.

Analysis after an initial baseline also tends to reveal hidden problems. The collected data shows the true nature of congestion or potential congestion in a network. It may also reveal areas in the network that are underutilized and quite often can lead to network redesign efforts, based on quality and capacity observations.

9.1.1.4   Establishing a Network Baseline, Cont.

Because the initial network performance baseline sets the stage for measuring the effects of network changes and subsequent troubleshooting efforts, it is important to plan for it carefully.

To plan the first baseline, perform the following steps:

Step 1.   Determine what types of data to collect. When conducting the initial baseline, start by selecting a few variables that represent the defined policies. If too many data points are selected, the amount of data can be overwhelming, making analysis of the collected data difficult. Start out simply and fine-tune along the way. Some good starting measures are interface utilization and CPU utilization. Figure 1 shows screenshots of CPU usage data, as displayed by the Cisco Wide Area Application Services (WAAS) software.

Step 2.   Identify devices and ports of interest.

Use the network topology to identify those devices and ports for which performance data should be measured. Devices and ports of interest include:

- Network device ports that connect to other network devices

- Servers

- Key users

- Anything else considered critical to operations

A logical network topology diagram can be useful in identifying key devices and ports to monitor. For example, in Figure 2 the network administrator has highlighted the devices and ports of interest to monitor during the baseline test. The devices of interest include PC1 (the Admin terminal), and SRV1 (the Web/TFTP server). The ports of interest include those ports on R1, R2, and R3 that connect to the other routers or to switches, and on R2, the port that connects to SRV1 (G0/0).

By shortening the list of ports that are polled, the results are concise, and the network management load is minimized. Remember that an interface on a router or switch can be a virtual interface, such as a switch virtual interface (SVI).

Step 3.   Determine the baseline duration.The length of time and the baseline information being gathered must be sufficient for establishing a typical picture of the network. It is important that daily trends of network traffic are monitored. It is also important to monitor for trends that occur over a longer period of time, such as weekly or monthly. For this reason, when capturing data for analysis, the period specified should be, at a minimum, seven days long.Figure 3 shows examples of several screenshots of CPU utilization trends captured over a daily, weekly, monthly, and yearly period. In this example, notice that the work week trends are too short to reveal the recurring utilization surge every weekend on Saturday evening, when a database backup operation consumes network bandwidth. This recurring pattern is revealed in the monthly trend. A yearly trend as shown in the example may be too long of a duration to provide meaningful baseline performance details. However, it may help identify long term patterns which should be analyzed further. Typically, a baseline needs to last no more than six weeks, unless specific long-term trends need to be measured. Generally, a two-to-four-week baseline is adequate.Baseline measurements should not be performed during times of unique traffic patterns, because the data would provide an inaccurate picture of normal network operations. Baseline analysis of the network should be conducted on a regular basis. Perform an annual analysis of the entire network or baseline different sections of the network on a rotating basis. Analysis must be conducted regularly to understand how the network is affected by growth and other changes.

Refer to
Online Course
for Illustration

9.1.1.5   Measuring Data

When documenting the network, it is often necessary to gather information directly from routers and switches. Obvious useful network documentation commands include `ping`, `traceroute`, and `telnet` as well as the following `show` commands:

- The `show ip interface brief` and `show ipv6 interface brief` commands are used to display the up or down status and IP address of all interfaces on a device.

- The `show ip route` and `show ipv6 route` commands are used to display the routing table in a router to learn the directly connected neighbors, more remote devices (through learned routes), and the routing protocols that have been configured.

- The `show cdp neighbor detail` command is used to obtain detailed information about directly connected Cisco neighbor devices.

Figure 1 lists some of the most common Cisco IOS commands used for data collection.

Manual data collection using `show` commands on individual network devices is extremely time consuming and is not a scalable solution. Manual collection of data should be reserved for smaller networks or limited to mission-critical network devices. For simpler network designs, baseline tasks typically use a combination of manual data collection and simple network protocol inspectors.

Sophisticated network management software is often used to baseline large and complex networks. For example, as shown in Figure 2, the Fluke Network SuperAgent module enables administrators to automatically create and review reports using its Intelligent Baselines feature. This feature compares current performance levels with historical observations and can automatically identify performance problems and applications that do not provide expected levels of service.

Establishing an initial baseline or conducting a performance-monitoring analysis may require many hours or days to accurately reflect network performance. Network management software or protocol inspectors and sniffers often run continuously over the course of the data collection process.

Refer to **Interactive Graphic** in online course.

9.1.1.6   Activity - Identify Benefits for Establishing a Network Baseline

Refer to **Interactive Graphic** in online course.

9.1.1.7   Activity - Identify Commands Used for Measuring Data

Refer to **Packet Tracer Activity** for this chapter

9.1.1.8   Packet Tracer - Troubleshooting Challenge - Documenting the Network

Background/Scenario

This activity covers the steps to take to discover a network using primarily the `telnet`, `show cdp neighbors detail`, and `show ip route` commands. This is Part I of a two-part activity. Part II is Packet Tracer - Troubleshooting Challenge - Using Documentation to Solve Issues, which comes later in the chapter.

The topology you see when you open the Packet Tracer activity does not reveal all of the details of the network. The details have been hidden using the cluster function of Packet Tracer. The network infrastructure has been collapsed, and the topology in the file shows only the end devices. Your task is to use your knowledge of networking and discovery commands to learn about the full network topology and document it.

Refer to **Online Course** for Illustration

9.1.2   Troubleshooting Process

9.1.2.1   General Troubleshooting Procedures

Troubleshooting takes a large portion of network administrators' and support personnel's time. Using efficient troubleshooting techniques shortens overall troubleshooting time when working in a production environment. There are three major stages to the troubleshooting process:

Stage 1. Gather symptoms - Troubleshooting begins with gathering and documenting symptoms from the network, end systems, and users. In addition, the network administrator determines which network components have been affected and how the functionality of the network has changed compared to the baseline. Symptoms may appear in many different forms, including alerts from the network management system, console messages, and user complaints. While gathering symptoms, it is important that the network administrator ask questions and investigate the issue in order to localize the problem to a smaller range of possibilities. For example, is the problem restricted to a single device, a group of devices, or an entire subnet or network of devices?

Stage 2. Isolate the problem - Isolating is the process of eliminating variables until a single problem, or a set of related problems has been identified as the cause. To do this, the network administrator examines the characteristics of the problems at the logical layers of the network so that the most likely cause can be selected. At this stage, the network administrator may gather and document more symptoms, depending on the characteristics that are identified.

Stage 3. Implement corrective action - Having identified the cause of the problem, the network administrator works to correct the problem by implementing, testing, and documenting possible solutions. After finding the problem and determining a solution, the network administrator may need to decide if the solution can be implemented immediately or if it must be postponed. This depends on the impact of the changes on the users and the network. The severity of the problem should be weighed against the impact of the solution. For example, if a critical server or router must be offline for a significant amount of time, it may be better to wait until the end of the workday to implement the fix. Sometimes, a workaround can be created until the actual problem is resolved. This is typically part of a network's change control procedures.

If the corrective action creates another problem or does not solve the problem, the attempted solution is documented, the changes are removed, and the network administrator returns to gathering symptoms and isolating the issue.

These stages are not mutually exclusive. At any point in the process, it may be necessary to return to previous stages. For instance, the network administrator may need to gather more symptoms while isolating a problem. Additionally, when attempting to correct a problem, another problem could be created. In this instance, remove changes and begin troubleshooting again.

A troubleshooting policy, including change control procedures, should be established for each stage. A policy provides a consistent manner in which to perform each stage. Part of the policy should include documenting every important piece of information.

Note   Communicate to the users and anyone involved in the troubleshooting process that the problem has been resolved. Other IT team members should be informed of the solution. Appropriate documentation of the cause and the fix will assist other support technicians in preventing and solving similar problems in the future.

Refer to
Online Course
for Illustration

9.1.2.2 Gathering Symptoms

When gathering symptoms, it is important that the administrator gather facts and evidence to progressively eliminate possible causes, and eventually identify the root cause of the issue. By analyzing the information, the network administrator formulates a hypothesis to propose possible causes and solutions, while eliminating others.

There are five steps to gathering information:

Step 1.   **Gather information** - Gather information from the trouble ticket, users, or end systems affected by the problem to form a definition of the problem.

Step 2.   **Determine ownership** - If the problem is within the control of the organization, move onto the next stage. If the problem is outside the boundary of the organization's control (for example, lost Internet connectivity outside of the autonomous system), contact an administrator for the external system before gathering additional network symptoms.

Step 3. **Narrow the scope** - Determine if the problem is at the core, distribution, or access layer of the network. At the identified layer, analyze the existing symptoms and use your knowledge of the network topology to determine which piece of equipment is the most likely cause.

Step 4. **Gather symptoms from suspect devices** - Using a layered troubleshooting approach, gather hardware and software symptoms from the suspect devices. Start with the most likely possibility and use knowledge and experience to determine if the problem is more likely a hardware or software configuration problem.

Step 5. **Document symptoms** - Sometimes the problem can be solved using the documented symptoms. If not, begin the isolating stage of the general troubleshooting process.

Use Cisco IOS commands and other tools to gather symptoms about the network, such as:

- `ping`, `traceroute`, and `telnet` commands
- `show` and `debug` commands
- packet captures
- device logs

The table in the figure describes the common Cisco IOS commands used to gather the symptoms of a network problem.

Note Although the `debug` command is an important tool for gathering symptoms, it generates a large amount of console message traffic and the performance of a network device can be noticeably affected. If the `debug` must be performed during normal working hours, warn network users that a troubleshooting effort is underway and that network performance may be affected. Remember to disable debugging when you are done.

Refer to
Online Course
for Illustration

9.1.2.3 Questioning End Users

In many cases the problem is reported by an end user. The information may often be vague or misleading, such as, "The network is down" or "I cannot access my email". In these cases, the problem must be better defined. This may require asking questions of the end users.

Use effective questioning techniques when asking the end users about a network problem they may be experiencing. This will help you to get the information required to document the symptoms of a problem. The table in the figure provides some guidelines and end-user example questions.

Refer to
Interactive Graphic
in online course.

9.1.2.4 Activity - Identify Commands for Gathering Symptoms

Refer to
Online Course
for Illustration

9.1.3   Isolating the Issue Using Layered Models

9.1.3.1   Using Layered Models for Troubleshooting

After all symptoms are gathered, if no solution is identified, the network administrator compares the characteristics of the problem to the logical layers of the network to isolate and solve the issue.

Logical networking models, such as the OSI and TCP/IP models, separate network functionality into modular layers. These layered models can be applied to the physical network to isolate network problems when troubleshooting. For example, if the symptoms suggest a physical connection problem, the network technician can focus on troubleshooting the circuit that operates at the physical layer. If that circuit functions as expected, the technician looks at areas within another layer that could be causing the problem.

OSI Reference Model

The OSI reference model provides a common language for network administrators and is commonly used in troubleshooting networks. Problems are typically described in terms of a given OSI model layer.

The OSI reference model describes how information from a software application in one computer moves through a network medium to a software application in another computer.

The upper layers (5 to 7) of the OSI model deal with application issues and generally are implemented only in software. The application layer is closest to the end user. Both users and application layer processes interact with software applications that contain a communications component.

The lower layers (1 to 4) of the OSI model handle data-transport issues. Layers 3 and 4 are generally implemented only in software. The physical layer (Layer 1) and data link layer (Layer 2) are implemented in hardware and software. The physical layer is closest to the physical network medium, such as the network cabling, and is responsible for actually placing information on the medium.

Figure 1 shows some common devices and the OSI layers that must be examined during the troubleshooting process for that device. Notice that routers and multilayer switches are shown at Layer 4, the transport layer. Although routers and multilayer switches usually make forwarding decisions at Layer 3, ACLs on these devices can be used to make filtering decisions using Layer 4 information.

TCP/IP Model

Similar to the OSI networking model, the TCP/IP networking model also divides networking architecture into modular layers. Figure 2 shows how the TCP/IP networking model maps to the layers of the OSI networking model. It is this close mapping that allows the TCP/IP suite of protocols to successfully communicate with so many networking technologies.

The application layer in the TCP/IP suite actually combines the functions of the three OSI model layers: session, presentation, and application. The application layer provides communication between applications, such as FTP, HTTP, and SMTP on separate hosts.

The transport layers of TCP/IP and OSI directly correspond in function. The transport layer is responsible for exchanging segments between devices on a TCP/IP network.

The TCP/IP Internet layer relates to the OSI network layer. The Internet layer is responsible for placing messages in a fixed format that allows devices to handle them.

The TCP/IP network access layer corresponds to the OSI physical and data link layers. The network access layer communicates directly with the network media and provides an interface between the architecture of the network and the Internet layer.

Refer to **Online Course** for Illustration

9.1.3.2   Troubleshooting Methods

Using the layered models, there are three primary methods for troubleshooting networks:

- Bottom-up
- Top-down
- Divide-and-conquer

Each approach has its advantages and disadvantages. This topic describes the three methods and provides guidelines for choosing the best method for a specific situation.

Bottom-Up Troubleshooting Method

In bottom-up troubleshooting, you start with the physical components of the network and move up through the layers of the OSI model until the cause of the problem is identified, as shown in Figure 1. Bottom-up troubleshooting is a good approach to use when the problem is suspected to be a physical one. Most networking problems reside at the lower levels, so implementing the bottom-up approach is often effective.

The disadvantage with the bottom-up troubleshooting approach is it requires that you check every device and interface on the network until the possible cause of the problem is found. Remember that each conclusion and possibility must be documented so there can be a lot of paper work associated with this approach. A further challenge is to determine which devices to start examining first.

Top-Down Troubleshooting Method

In Figure 2, top-down troubleshooting starts with the end-user applications and moves down through the layers of the OSI model until the cause of the problem has been identified. End-user applications of an end system are tested before tackling the more specific networking pieces. Use this approach for simpler problems, or when you think the problem is with a piece of software.

The disadvantage with the top-down approach is it requires checking every network application until the possible cause of the problem is found. Each conclusion and possibility must be documented. The challenge is to determine which application to start examining first.

Divide-and-Conquer Troubleshooting Method

Figure 3 shows the divide-and-conquer approach to troubleshooting a networking problem. The network administrator selects a layer and tests in both directions from that layer.

In divide-and-conquer troubleshooting, you start by collecting user experiences of the problem, document the symptoms and then, using that information, make an informed guess as to which OSI layer to start your investigation. When a layer is verified to be functioning properly, it can be assumed that the layers below it are functioning. The administrator can work up the OSI layers. If an OSI layer is not functioning properly, the administrator can work down OSI layer model.

For example, if users cannot access the web server, but they can ping the server, then the problem is above Layer 3. If pinging the server is unsuccessful, then the problem is likely at a lower OSI layer.

Refer to
Online Course
for Illustration

9.1.3.3   Troubleshooting Methods, Cont.

In addition to the systematic, layered approach to troubleshooting, there are also, less-structured troubleshooting approaches.

One troubleshooting approach is based on an educated guess by the network administrator, based on the symptoms of the problem. This method is more successfully implemented by seasoned network administrators, because seasoned network administrators rely on their extensive knowledge and experience to decisively isolate and solve network issues. With a less-experienced network administrator, this troubleshooting method may be more like random troubleshooting.

Another approach involves comparing a working and non-working situation, and spotting significant differences, including:

- Configurations
- Software versions
- Hardware and other device properties

Using this method may lead to a working solution, but without clearly revealing the cause of the problem. This method can be helpful when the network administrator is lacking an area of expertise, or when the problem needs to be resolved quickly. After the fix has been implemented, the network administrator can do further research on the actual cause of the problem.

Substitution is another quick troubleshooting methodology. It involves swapping the problematic device with a known, working one. If the problem is fixed, that the network administrator knows the problem is with the removed device. If the problem remains, then the cause may be elsewhere. In specific situations, this can be an ideal method for quick problem resolution, such as when a critical single point of failure, like a border router, goes down. It may be more beneficial to simply replace the device and restore service, rather than troubleshoot the issue.

Refer to
Online Course
for Illustration

9.1.3.4   Guidelines for Selecting a Troubleshooting Method

To quickly resolve network problems, take the time to select the most effective network troubleshooting method. The figure illustrates this process.

The following is an example of how to choose a troubleshooting method based on a specific problem:

Two IP routers are not exchanging routing information. The last time this type of problem occurred it was a protocol issue. Therefore, choose the divide-and-conquer troubleshooting method. Analysis reveals that there is connectivity between the routers. Start the troubleshooting process at the physical or data link layer. Confirm connectivity and begin testing the TCP/IP-related functions at next layer up in the OSI model, the network layer.

Refer to **Interactive Graphic** in online course.

9.1.3.5   Activity - Troubleshooting Methods

Refer to **Online Course** for Illustration

9.2   Network Troubleshooting

9.2.1   Troubleshooting Tools

9.2.1.1   Software Troubleshooting Tools

A wide variety of software and hardware tools are available to make troubleshooting easier. These tools may be used to gather and analyze symptoms of network problems. They often provide monitoring and reporting functions that can be used to establish the network baseline.

Common software troubleshooting tools include:

Network Management System Tools

Network management system (NMS) tools include device-level monitoring, configuration, and fault-management tools. Figure 1 shows an example display from the "WhatsUp Gold" NMS software. These tools can be used to investigate and correct network problems. Network monitoring software graphically displays a physical view of network devices, allowing network managers to monitor remote devices without actually physically checking them. Device management software provides dynamic status, statistics, and configuration information for switched products. Examples of other commonly used network management tools are CiscoView, HPBTO Software (formerly OpenView), and SolarWinds.

Knowledge Bases

On-line network device vendor knowledge bases have become indispensable sources of information. When vendor-based knowledge bases are combined with Internet search engines like Google, a network administrator has access to a vast pool of experience-based information.

Figure 2 shows the Cisco **Tools & Resources** page found at http://www.cisco.com. This is a free tool providing information on Cisco-related hardware and software. It contains troubleshooting procedures, implementation guides, and original white papers on most aspects of networking technology.

Baselining Tools

Many tools for automating the network documentation and baselining process are available. These tools are available for Windows, Linux, and AUX operating systems. Figure 3 shows a screen capture of the SolarWinds LANsurveyor and CyberGauge software. Baselining tools help with common documentation tasks. For example, they can draw network diagrams, help keep network software and hardware documentation up-to-date, and help to cost-effectively measure baseline network bandwidth use.

Refer to
Online Course
for Illustration

9.2.1.2   Software Troubleshooting Tools, Cont.

Host-Based Protocol Analyzers

A protocol analyzer decodes the various protocol layers in a recorded frame and presents this information in a relatively easy to use format. The figure shows a screen capture of the Wireshark protocol analyzer. The information displayed by a protocol analyzer includes the physical, data link, protocol, and descriptions for each frame. Most protocol analyzers can filter traffic that meets certain criteria so that, for example, all traffic to and from a particular device can be captured. Protocol analyzers such as Wireshark can help troubleshoot network performance problems. It is important to have both a good understanding of how to use the protocol analyzer and TCP/IP. To become more knowledgeable and skillful using Wireshark, an excellent resource is http://www.wiresharkbook.com.

Cisco IOS Embedded Packet Capture

The Cisco IOS Embedded Packet Capture (EPC) delivers a powerful troubleshooting and tracing tool. The feature allows for network administrators to capture IPv4 and IPv6 packets flowing through, to, and from, a Cisco router. The Cisco IOS EPC function is mainly used in troubleshooting scenarios where it is helpful to see the actual data being sent through, from, or to the network device.

For example, support desk personnel need to determine why a particular device cannot access the network or some application. It might be necessary to capture IP data packets and examine the data to discover the problem. Another example would be, determining an attack signature for a network threat or server system security breach. The Cisco IOS EPC can help capture packets flowing into the network at the origin or perimeter.

The Cisco IOS EPC is useful whenever a network protocol analyzer might be useful in debugging a problem, but when it is not practical to install such a device.

For more information on using and configuring Cisco EPC, consult the Embedded Packet Capture Configuration Guide.

Refer to
Online Course
for Illustration

9.2.1.3   Hardware Troubleshooting Tools

Common hardware troubleshooting tools include:

- **Network Analysis Module**- As shown in Figure 1, a network analysis module (NAM) can be installed in Cisco Catalyst 6500 series switches and Cisco 7600 series routers. NAMs provide a graphical representation of traffic from local and remote switches and routers. The NAM is an embedded browser-based interface that generates reports on the traffic that consumes critical network resources. In addition, the NAM can capture and decode packets and track response times to pinpoint an application problem to the network or the server.

- **Digital Multimeters**- Digital multimeters (DMMs), such as the Fluke 179 shown in Figure 2, are test instruments that are used to directly measure electrical values of voltage, current, and resistance. In network troubleshooting, most of the multimedia tests involve checking power-supply voltage levels and verifying that network devices are receiving power.

- **Cable Testers**- Cable testers are specialized, handheld devices designed for testing the various types of data communication cabling. Figure 3 shows two different Fluke cable testers. Cabling testers can be used to detect broken wires, crossed-over wiring, shorted connections, and improperly paired connections. These devices can be inexpensive continuity testers, moderately priced data cabling testers, or expensive time-domain reflectometers (TDRs). TDRs are used to pinpoint the distance to a break in a cable. These devices send signals along the cable and wait for them to be reflected. The time between sending the signal and receiving it back is converted into a distance measurement. The TDR function is normally packaged with data cabling testers. TDRs used to test fiber optic cables are known as optical time-domain reflectometers (OTDRs).

■ **Cable Analyzers**- Cable analyzers, such as the Fluke DTX Cable Analyzer in Figure 4, are multifunctional handheld devices that are used to test and certify copper and fiber cables for different services and standards. The more sophisticated tools include advanced troubleshooting diagnostics that measure distance to performance defect (NEXT, RL), identify corrective actions, and graphically display crosstalk and impedance behavior. Cable analyzers also typically include PC-based software. After field data is collected, the handheld device can upload its data to create up-to-date reports.

■ **Portable Network Analyzers**- Portable devices like the Fluke OptiView in Figure 5 are used for troubleshooting switched networks and VLANs. By plugging the network analyzer in anywhere on the network, a network engineer can see the switch port to which the device is connected, and the average and peak utilization. The analyzer can also be used to discover VLAN configuration, identify top network talkers, analyze network traffic, and view interface details. The device can typically output to a PC that has network monitoring software installed for further analysis and troubleshooting.

Refer to **Online Course** for Illustration

9.2.1.4   Using a Syslog Server for Troubleshooting

Syslog is a simple protocol used by an IP device known as a syslog client, to send text-based log messages to another IP device, the syslog server. Syslog is currently defined in RFC 5424.

Implementing a logging facility is an important part of network security and for network troubleshooting. Cisco devices can log information regarding configuration changes, ACL violations, interface status, and many other types of events. Cisco devices can send log messages to several different facilities. Event messages can be sent to one or more of the following:

■ **Console**- Console logging is on by default. Messages log to the console and can be viewed when modifying or testing the router or switch using terminal emulation software while connected to the console port of the router.

■ **Terminal lines**- Enabled EXEC sessions can be configured to receive log messages on any terminal lines. Similar to console logging, this type of logging is not stored by the router and, therefore, is only valuable to the user on that line.

■ **Buffered logging**- Buffered logging is a little more useful as a troubleshooting tool because log messages are stored in memory for a time. However, log messages are cleared when the device is rebooted.

■ **SNMP traps**- Certain thresholds can be preconfigured on routers and other devices. Router events, such as exceeding a threshold, can be processed by the router and forwarded as SNMP traps to an external SNMP server. SNMP traps are a viable security logging facility, but require the configuration and maintenance of an SNMP system.

■ **Syslog**- Cisco routers and switches can be configured to forward log messages to an external syslog service. This service can reside on any number of servers or workstations, including Microsoft Windows and Linux-based systems. Syslog is the most popular message logging facility, because it provides long-term log storage capabilities and a central location for all router messages.

Cisco IOS log messages fall into one of eight levels, shown in Figure 1. The lower the level number, the higher the severity level. By default, all messages from level 0 to 7 are logged to the console. While the ability to view logs on a central syslog server is helpful in troubleshooting, sifting through a large amount of data can be an overwhelming task. The `logging trap` level command limits messages logged to the syslog server based on severity. The level is the name or number of the severity level. Only messages equal to or numerically lower than the specified level are logged.

In the example in Figure 2, system messages from level 0 (emergencies) to 5 (notifications) are sent to the syslog server at 209.165.200.225.

Refer to **Interactive Graphic** in online course.

9.2.1.5 Activity - Identify Common Troubleshooting Tools

Refer to **Online Course** for Illustration

9.2.2 Symptoms and Causes of Network Troubleshooting

9.2.2.1 Physical Layer Troubleshooting

The physical layer transmits bits from one computer to another and regulates the transmission of a stream of bits over the physical medium. The physical layer is the only layer with physically tangible properties, such as wires, cards, and antennas.

Issues on a network often present as performance problems. Performance problems mean that there is a difference between the expected behavior and the observed behavior, and the system is not functioning as could be reasonably expected. Failures and suboptimal conditions at the physical layer not only inconvenience users but can impact the productivity of the entire company. Networks that experience these kinds of conditions usually shut down. Because the upper layers of the OSI model depend on the physical layer to function, a network administrator must have the ability to effectively isolate and correct problems at this layer.

Common symptoms of network problems at the physical layer include:

■ **Performance lower than baseline**- The most common reasons for slow or poor performance include overloaded or underpowered servers, unsuitable switch or router configurations, traffic congestion on a low-capacity link, and chronic frame loss.

■ **Loss of connectivity**- If a cable or device fails; the most obvious symptom is a loss of connectivity between the devices that communicate over that link or with the failed device or interface. This is indicated by a simple ping test. Intermittent loss of connectivity can indicate a loose or oxidized connection.

■ **Network bottlenecks or congestion**- If a router, interface, or cable fails, routing protocols may redirect traffic to other routes that are not designed to carry the extra capacity. This can result in congestion or bottlenecks in those parts of the network.

- **High CPU utilization rates**- High CPU utilization rates are a symptom that a device, such as a router, switch, or server, is operating at or exceeding its design limits. If not addressed quickly, CPU overloading can cause a device to shut down or fail.

- **Console error messages**- Error messages reported on the device console indicate a physical layer problem.

Issues that commonly cause network problems at the physical layer include:

- **Power-related**- Power-related issues are the most fundamental reason for network failure. Also, check the operation of the fans, and ensure that the chassis intake and exhaust vents are clear. If other nearby units have also powered down, suspect a power failure at the main power supply.

- **Hardware faults**- Faulty network interface cards (NICs) can be the cause of network transmission errors due to late collisions, short frames, and jabber. Jabber is often defined as the condition in which a network device continually transmits random, meaningless data onto the network. Other likely causes of jabber are faulty or corrupt NIC driver files, bad cabling, or grounding problems.

- **Cabling faults**- Many problems can be corrected by simply reseating cables that have become partially disconnected. When performing a physical inspection, look for damaged cables, improper cable types, and poorly crimped RJ-45s. Suspect cables should be tested or exchanged with a known functioning cable.

- **Attenuation**- Attenuation can be caused if a cable length exceeds the design limit for the media, or when there is a poor connection resulting from a loose cable or dirty or oxidized contacts. If attenuation is severe, the receiving device cannot always successfully distinguish the component bits of the stream from each other.

- **Noise**- Local electromagnetic interference (EMI) is commonly known as noise. Noise can be generated by many sources, such as FM radio stations, police radio, building security, and avionics for automated landing, crosstalk (noise induced by other cables in the same pathway or adjacent cables), nearby electric cables, devices with large electric motors, or anything that includes a transmitter more powerful than a cell phone.

- **Interface configuration errors**- Many things can be misconfigured on an interface to cause it to go down, such as incorrect clock rate, incorrect clock source, and interface not being turned on. This causes a loss of connectivity with attached network segments.

- **Exceeding design limits**- A component may be operating suboptimally at the physical layer because it is being utilized at a higher average rate than it is configured to operate. When troubleshooting this type of problem, it becomes evident that resources for the device are operating at or near the maximum capacity and there is an increase in the number of interface errors.

- **CPU overload**- Symptoms include processes with high CPU utilization percentages, input queue drops, slow performance, router services such as Telnet and ping are slow or fail to respond, or there are no routing updates. One of the causes of CPU overload in a router is high traffic. If some interfaces are regularly overloaded with traffic, consider redesigning the traffic flow in the network or upgrading the hardware.

Refer to
Online Course
for Illustration

9.2.2.2   Data Link Layer Troubleshooting

Troubleshooting Layer 2 problems can be a challenging process. The configuration and operation of these protocols are critical to creating a functional, well-tuned network. Layer 2 problems cause specific symptoms that, when recognized, will help identify the problem quickly.

Common symptoms of network problems at the data link layer include:

- **No functionality or connectivity at the network layer or above**- Some Layer 2 problems can stop the exchange of frames across a link, while others only cause network performance to degrade.

- **Network is operating below baseline performance levels**- There are two distinct types of suboptimal Layer 2 operation that can occur in a network. First, the frames take a suboptimal path to their destination but do arrive. In this case, the network might experience high-bandwidth usage on links that should not have that level of traffic. Second, some frames are dropped. These problems can be identified through error counter statistics and console error messages that appear on the switch or router. In an Ethernet environment, an extended or continuous ping also reveals if frames are being dropped.

- **Excessive broadcasts**- Operating systems use broadcasts and multicasts extensively to discover network services and other hosts. Generally, excessive broadcasts result from one of the following situations: poorly programmed or configured applications, large Layer 2 broadcast domains, or underlying network problems, such as STP loops or route flapping.

- **Console messages**- In some instances, a router recognizes that a Layer 2 problem has occurred and sends alert messages to the console. Typically, a router does this when it detects a problem with interpreting incoming frames (encapsulation or framing problems) or when keepalives are expected but do not arrive. The most common console message that indicates a Layer 2 problem is a line protocol down message.

Issues at the data link layer that commonly result in network connectivity or performance problems include:

- **Encapsulation errors**- An encapsulation error occurs because the bits placed in a particular field by the sender are not what the receiver expects to see. This condition occurs when the encapsulation at one end of a WAN link is configured differently from the encapsulation used at the other end.

- **Address mapping errors**- In topologies, such as point-to-multipoint, Frame Relay, or broadcast Ethernet, it is essential that an appropriate Layer 2 destination address be given to the frame. This ensures its arrival at the correct destination. To achieve this, the network device must match a destination Layer 3 address with the correct Layer 2 address using either static or dynamic maps. In a dynamic environment, the mapping of Layer 2 and Layer 3 information can fail because devices may have been specifically configured not to respond to ARP or Inverse-ARP requests, the Layer 2 or Layer 3 information that is cached may have physically changed, or invalid ARP replies are received because of a misconfiguration or a security attack.

- **Framing errors**- Frames usually work in groups of 8-bit bytes. A framing error occurs when a frame does not end on an 8-bit byte boundary. When this happens, the receiver may have problems determining where one frame ends and another frame starts. Too many invalid frames may prevent valid keepalives from being exchanged. Framing errors can be caused by a noisy serial line, an improperly designed cable (too long or not properly shielded), or an incorrectly configured channel service unit (CSU) line clock.

- **STP failures or loops**- The purpose of the Spanning Tree Protocol (STP) is to resolve a redundant physical topology into a tree-like topology by blocking redundant ports. Most STP problems are related to forwarding loops that occur when no ports in a redundant topology are blocked and traffic is forwarded in circles indefinitely, excessive flooding because of a high rate of STP topology changes. A topology change should be a rare event in a well-configured network. When a link between two switches goes up or down, there is eventually a topology change when the STP state of the port is changing to or from forwarding. However, when a port is flapping (oscillating between up and down states), this causes repetitive topology changes and flooding, or slow STP convergence or re-convergence. This can be caused by a mismatch between the real and documented topology, a configuration error, such as an inconsistent configuration of STP timers, an overloaded switch CPU during convergence, or a software defect.

Refer to
Online Course
for Illustration

9.2.2.3   Network Layer Troubleshooting

Network layer problems include any problem that involves a Layer 3 protocol, both routed protocols (such as IPv4 or IPv6) and routing protocols (such as EIGRP, OSPF, etc.).

Common symptoms of network problems at the network layer include:

- **Network failure**- Network failure is when the network is nearly or completely non-functional, affecting all users and applications on the network. These failures are usually noticed quickly by users and network administrators, and are obviously critical to the productivity of a company.

- **Suboptimal performance**- Network optimization problems usually involve a subset of users, applications, destinations, or a particular type of traffic. Optimization issues can be difficult to detect and even harder to isolate and diagnose. This is because they usually involve multiple layers, or even the host computer itself. Determining that the problem is a network layer problem can take time.

In most networks, static routes are used in combination with dynamic routing protocols. Improper configuration of static routes can lead to less than optimal routing. In some cases, improperly configured static routes can create routing loops which make parts of the network unreachable.

Troubleshooting dynamic routing protocols requires a thorough understanding of how the specific routing protocol functions. Some problems are common to all routing protocols, while other problems are particular to the individual routing protocol.

There is no single template for solving Layer 3 problems. Routing problems are solved with a methodical process, using a series of commands to isolate and diagnose the problem.

Here are some areas to explore when diagnosing a possible problem involving routing protocols:

- **General network issues**- Often a change in the topology, such as a down link, may have effects on other areas of the network that might not be obvious at the time. This may include the installation of new routes, static or dynamic, or removal of other routes. Determine whether anything in the network has recently changed, and if there is anyone currently working on the network infrastructure.

- **Connectivity issues**- Check for any equipment and connectivity problems, including power problems such as outages and environmental problems (for example, overheating). Also check for Layer 1 problems, such as cabling problems, bad ports, and ISP problems.

- **Neighbor issues**- If the routing protocol establishes an adjacency with a neighbor, check to see if there are any problems with the routers forming neighbor adjacencies.

- **Topology database**- If the routing protocol uses a topology table or database, check the table for anything unexpected, such as missing entries or unexpected entries.

- **Routing table**- Check the routing table for anything unexpected, such as missing routes or unexpected routes. Use `debug` commands to view routing updates and routing table maintenance.

Refer to **Online Course** for Illustration

9.2.2.4   Transport Layer Troubleshooting - ACLs

Network problems can arise from transport layer problems on the router, particularly at the edge of the network where traffic is examined and modified. Two of the most commonly implemented transport layer technologies are access control lists (ACLs) and Network Address Translation (NAT), as shown in Figure 1.

The most common issues with ACLs are caused by improper configuration, as shown in Figure 2. Problems with ACLs may cause otherwise working systems to fail. There are several areas where misconfigurations commonly occur:

- **Selection of traffic flow**- The most common router misconfiguration is applying the ACL to incorrect traffic. Traffic is defined by both the router interface through which the traffic is traveling and the direction in which this traffic is traveling. An ACL must be applied to the correct interface, and the correct traffic direction must be selected to function properly.

- **Order of access control entries**- The entries in an ACL should be from specific to general. Although an ACL may have an entry to specifically permit a particular traffic flow, packets never match that entry if they are being denied by another entry earlier in the list. If the router is running both ACLs and NAT, the order in which each of these technologies is applied to a traffic flow is important. Inbound traffic is processed by the inbound ACL before being processed by outside-to-inside NAT. Outbound traffic is processed by the outbound ACL after being processed by inside-to-outside NAT.

- **Implicit deny all**- When high security is not required on the ACL, this implicit access control element can be the cause of an ACL misconfiguration.

- **Addresses and IPv4 wildcard masks**- Complex IPv4 wildcard masks provide significant improvements in efficiency, but are more subject to configuration errors. An example of a complex wildcard mask is using the IPv4 address 10.0.32.0 and wildcard mask 0.0.32.15 to select the first 15 host addresses in either the 10.0.0.0 network or the 10.0.32.0 network.

- **Selection of transport layer protocol**- When configuring ACLs, it is important that only the correct transport layer protocols be specified. Many network administrators, when unsure whether a particular traffic flow uses a TCP port or a UDP port, configure both. Specifying both opens a hole through the firewall, possibly giving intruders an avenue into the network. It also introduces an extra element into the ACL, so the ACL takes longer to process, introducing more latency into network communications.

- **Source and destination ports**- Properly controlling the traffic between two hosts requires symmetric access control elements for inbound and outbound ACLs. Address and port information for traffic generated by a replying host is the mirror image of address and port information for traffic generated by the initiating host.

- **Use of the `established` keyword** - The `established` keyword increases the security provided by an ACL. However, if the keyword is applied incorrectly, unexpected results may occur.

- **Uncommon protocols**- Misconfigured ACLs often cause problems for protocols other than TCP and UDP. Uncommon protocols that are gaining popularity are VPN and encryption protocols.

The `log` keyword is a useful command for viewing ACL operation on ACL entries. This keyword instructs the router to place an entry in the system log whenever that entry condition is matched. The logged event includes details of the packet that matched the ACL element. The `log` keyword is especially useful for troubleshooting and also provides information on intrusion attempts being blocked by the ACL.

Refer to
Online Course
for Illustration

9.2.2.5 Transport Layer Troubleshooting – NAT for IPv4

There are a number of problems with NAT such as not interacting with services like DHCP and tunneling. These can include misconfigured NAT inside, NAT outside, or ACL. Other issues include interoperability with other network technologies, especially those that contain or derive information from host network addressing in the packet. Some of these technologies include:

- **BOOTP and DHCP**- Both protocols manage the automatic assignment of IPv4 addresses to clients. Recall that the first packet that a new client sends is a DHCP-Request broadcast IPv4 packet. The DHCP-Request packet has a source IPv4 address of 0.0.0.0. Because NAT requires both a valid destination and source IPv4 address, BOOTP and DHCP can have difficulty operating over a router running either static or dynamic NAT. Configuring the IPv4 helper feature can help solve this problem.

- **DNS and WINS**- Because a router running dynamic NAT is changing the relationship between inside and outside addresses regularly as table entries expire and are recreated, a DNS or WINS server outside the NAT router does not have an accurate representation of the network inside the router. Configuring the IPv4 helper feature can help solve this problem.

- **SNMP**- Similar to DNS packets, NAT is unable to alter the addressing information stored in the data payload of the packet. Because of this, an SNMP management station on one side of a NAT router may not be able to contact SNMP agents on the other side of the NAT router. Configuring the IPv4 helper feature can help solve this problem.

- **Tunneling and encryption protocols**- Encryption and tunneling protocols often require that traffic be sourced from a specific UDP or TCP port, or use a protocol at the transport layer that cannot be processed by NAT. For example, IPsec tunneling protocols and generic routing encapsulation protocols used by VPN implementations cannot be processed by NAT.

Note   DHCPv6 from an IPv6 client can be forwarded by the router using the `ipv6 dhcp relay` command.

Refer to
Online Course
for Illustration

9.2.2.6   Application Layer Troubleshooting

Most of the application layer protocols provide user services. Application layer protocols are typically used for network management, file transfer, distributed file services, terminal emulation, and email. New user services are often added, such as VPNs and VoIP.

The figure shows the most widely known and implemented TCP/IP application layer protocols include:

- **SSH/Telnet**- Enables users to establish terminal session connections with remote hosts.

- **HTTP**- Supports the exchanging of text, graphic images, sound, video, and other multimedia files on the web.

- **FTP**- Performs interactive file transfers between hosts.

- **TFTP**- Performs basic interactive file transfers typically between hosts and networking devices.

- **SMTP**- Supports basic message delivery services.

- **POP**- Connects to mail servers and downloads email.

- **Simple Network Management Protocol (SNMP)**- Collects management information from network devices.

- **DNS**- Maps IP addresses to the names assigned to network devices.

- **Network File System (NFS)**- Enables computers to mount drives on remote hosts and operate them as if they were local drives. Originally developed by Sun Microsystems, it combines with two other application layer protocols, external data representation (XDR) and remote-procedure call (RPC), to allow transparent access to remote network resources.

The types of symptoms and causes depend upon the actual application itself.

Application layer problems prevent services from being provided to application programs. A problem at the application layer can result in unreachable or unusable resources when the physical, data link, network, and transport layers are functional. It is possible to have full network connectivity, but the application simply cannot provide data.

Another type of problem at the application layer occurs when the physical, data link, network, and transport layers are functional, but the data transfer and requests for network services from a single network service or application do not meet the normal expectations of a user.

A problem at the application layer may cause users to complain that the network or the particular application that they are working with is sluggish or slower than usual when transferring data or requesting network services.

Refer to
Interactive Graphic
in online course.

9.2.2.7   Activity - Identify the OSI Layer Associated with a Network Issue

Refer to
Online Course
for Illustration

9.2.3   Troubleshooting IP Connectivity

9.2.3.1   Components of Troubleshooting End-to-End Connectivity

Diagnosing and solving problems is an essential skill for network administrators. There is no single recipe for troubleshooting, and a particular problem can be diagnosed in many different ways. However, by employing a structured approach to the troubleshooting process, an administrator can reduce the time it takes to diagnose and solve a problem.

Throughout this topic, the following scenario is used. The client host PC1 is unable to access applications on Server SRV1 or Server SRV2. The figure shows the topology of this network. PC1 uses SLAAC with EUI-64 to create its IPv6 global unicast address. EUI-64 creates the Interface ID using the Ethernet MAC address, inserting FFFE in the middle, and flipping the seventh bit.

When there is no end-to-end connectivity, and the administrator chooses to troubleshoot with a bottom-up approach, these are common steps the administrator can take:

Step 1.   Check physical connectivity at the point where network communication stops. This includes cables and hardware. The problem might be with a faulty cable or interface, or involve misconfigured or faulty hardware.

Step 2.   Check for duplex mismatches.

Step 3.   Check data link and network layer addressing on the local network. This includes IPv4 ARP tables, IPv6 neighbor tables, MAC address tables, and VLAN assignments.

Step 4.   Verify that the default gateway is correct.

Step 5.   Ensure that devices are determining the correct path from the source to the destination. Manipulate the routing information if necessary.

Step 6.   Verify the transport layer is functioning properly. Telnet can also be used to test transport layer connections from the command line.

Step 7.   Verify that there are no ACLs blocking traffic.

Step 8.   Ensure that DNS settings are correct. There should be a DNS server that is accessible.

The outcome of this process is operational, end-to-end connectivity. If all of the steps have been performed without any resolution, the network administrator may either want to repeat the previous steps or escalate the problem to a senior administrator.

Refer to
Online Course
for Illustration

9.2.3.2   End-to-End Connectivity Problem Initiates Troubleshooting

Usually what initiates a troubleshooting effort is the discovery that there is a problem with end-to-end connectivity. Two of the most common utilities used to verify a problem with end-to-end connectivity are `ping` and `traceroute`, as shown in Figure 1.

Ping is probably the most widely-known connectivity-testing utility in networking and has always been part of Cisco IOS Software. It sends out requests for responses from a specified host address. The `ping` command uses a Layer 3 protocol that is a part of the TCP/IP suite called ICMP. Ping uses the ICMP echo request and ICMP echo reply packets. If the host at the specified address receives the ICMP echo request, it responds with an ICMP echo reply packet. Ping can be used to verify end-to-end connectivity for both IPv4 and IPv6. Figure 2 shows a successful ping from PC1 to SRV1, at address 172.16.1.100.

The `traceroute` command in Figure 3 illustrates the path the IPv4 packets take to reach their destination. Similar to the `ping` command, the Cisco IOS `traceroute` command can be used for both IPv4 and IPv6. The `tracert` command is used with Windows operating system. The trace generates a list of hops, router IP addresses and the final destination IP address that are successfully reached along the path. This list provides important verification and troubleshooting information. If the data reaches the destination, the trace lists the interface on every router in the path. If the data fails at some hop along the way, the address of the last router that responded to the trace is known. This address is an indication of where the problem or security restrictions reside.

As stated, the ping and traceroute utilities can be used to test and diagnose end-to-end IPv6 connectivity by providing the IPv6 address as the destination address. When using these utilities, the Cisco IOS utility recognizes whether the address is an IPv4 or IPv6 address and uses the appropriate protocol to test connectivity. Figure 4 shows the `ping` and `traceroute` commands on router R1 used to test IPv6 connectivity.

Refer to
Online Course
for Illustration

9.2.3.3   Step 1 - Verify the Physical Layer

All network devices are specialized computer systems. At a minimum, these devices consist of a CPU, RAM, and storage space, allowing the device to boot and run the operating system and interfaces. This allows for the reception and transmission of network traffic. When a network administrator determines that a problem exists on a given device, and that problem might be hardware-related, it is worthwhile to verify the operation of these generic components. The most commonly used Cisco IOS commands for this purpose are `show processes cpu`, `show memory`, and `show interfaces`. This topic discusses the `show interfaces` command.

When troubleshooting performance-related issues and hardware is suspected to be at fault, the `show interfaces` command can be used to verify the interfaces through which the traffic passes.

The output of the `show interfaces` command in the figure lists a number of important statistics that can be checked:

- **Input queue drops** - Input queue drops (and the related ignored and throttle counters) signify that at some point, more traffic was delivered to the router than it could process. This does not necessarily indicate a problem. That could be normal during traffic peaks. However, it could be an indication that the CPU cannot process packets in time, so if this number is consistently high, it is worth trying to spot at which moments these counters are increasing and how this relates to CPU usage.

- **Output queue drops** - Output queue drops indicate that packets were dropped due to congestion on the interface. Seeing output drops is normal for any point where the aggregate input traffic is higher than the output traffic. During traffic peaks, packets are dropped if traffic is delivered to the interface faster than it can be sent out. However, even if this is considered normal behavior, it leads to packet drops and queuing delays, so applications that are sensitive to those, such as VoIP, might suffer from performance issues. Consistently seeing output drops can be an indicator that you need to implement an advanced queuing mechanism to provide good QoS to each application.

- **Input errors** - Input errors indicate errors that are experienced during the reception of the frame, such as CRC errors. High numbers of CRC errors could indicate cabling problems, interface hardware problems, or, in an Ethernet-based network, duplex mismatches.

- **Output errors** - Output errors indicate errors, such as collisions, during the transmission of a frame. In most Ethernet-based networks today, full-duplex transmission is the norm, and half-duplex transmission is the exception. In full-duplex transmission, operation collisions cannot occur; therefore, collisions and especially late collisions often indicate duplex mismatches.

Refer to **Online Course** for Illustration

9.2.3.4 Step 2 - Check for Duplex Mismatches

Another common cause for interface errors is a mismatched duplex mode between two ends of an Ethernet link. In many Ethernet-based networks, point-to-point connections are now the norm, and the use of hubs and the associated half-duplex operation is becoming less common. This means that most Ethernet links today operate in full-duplex mode, and while collisions were seen as normal for an Ethernet link, collisions today often indicate that duplex negotiation has failed, and the link is not operating in the correct duplex mode.

The IEEE 802.3ab Gigabit Ethernet standard mandates the use of autonegotiation for speed and duplex. In addition, although it is not strictly mandatory, practically all Fast Ethernet NICs also use autonegotiation by default. The use of autonegotiation for speed and duplex is the current recommended practice. Duplex configuration guidelines are listed in Figure 1.

However, if duplex negotiation fails for some reason, it might be necessary to set the speed and duplex manually on both ends. Typically, this would mean setting the duplex mode to full-duplex on both ends of the connection. However, if this does not work, running half-duplex on both ends is preferred over a duplex mismatch.

Troubleshooting Example

In the previous scenario, the network administrator needed to add additional users to the network. To incorporate these new users, the network administrator installed a second switch and connected it to the first. Soon after S2 was added to the network, users on both switches began experiencing significant performance problems connecting with devices on the other switch, as shown in Figure 2.

The network administrator notices a console message on switch S2:

```
*Mar  1 00:45:08.756: %CDP-4-DUPLEX_MISMATCH: duplex mismatch discovered on
FastEthernet0/20 (not half duplex), with Switch FastEthernet0/20 (half duplex).
```

Using the **show interfaces fa 0/20** command, the network administrator examines the interface on S1 used to connect to S2 and notices it is set to full-duplex, as shown in Figure 3. The network administrator now examines the other side of the connection, the port on S2. Figure 4 shows that this side of the connection has been configured for half-duplex. The network administrator corrects the setting to **duplex auto** to automatically negotiate the duplex. Because the port on S1 is set to full-duplex, S2 also uses full-duplex.

The users report that there are no longer any performance problems.

Refer to **Online Course** for Illustration

9.2.3.5   Step 3 - Verify Layer 2 and Layer 3 Addressing on the Local Network

When troubleshooting end-to-end connectivity, it is useful to verify mappings between destination IP addresses and Layer 2 Ethernet addresses on individual segments. In IPv4, this functionality is provided by ARP. In IPv6, the ARP functionality is replaced by the neighbor discovery process and ICMPv6. The neighbor table caches IPv6 addresses and their resolved Ethernet physical (MAC) addresses.

IPv4 ARP Table

The **arp** Windows command displays and modifies entries in the ARP cache that are used to store IPv4 addresses and their resolved Ethernet physical (MAC) addresses. As shown in Figure 1, the **arp** Windows command lists all devices that are currently in the ARP cache. The information that is displayed for each device includes the IPv4 address, physical (MAC) address, and the type of addressing (static or dynamic).

The cache can be cleared by using the **arp -d** Windows command if the network administrator wants to repopulate the cache with updated information.

Note   The **arp** commands in Linux and MAC OS X have a similar syntax.

IPv6 Neighbor Table

As shown in Figure 2, the **netsh interface ipv6 show neighbor** Windows command lists all devices that are currently in the neighbor table. The information that is displayed for each device includes the IPv6 address, physical (MAC) address, and the type of addressing. By examining the neighbor table, the network administrator can verify that destination IPv6 addresses map to correct Ethernet addresses. The IPv6 link-local addresses on all of R1's interfaces have been manually configured to FE80::1. Similarly, R2 has been configured with the link-local address of FE80::2 on its interfaces and R3 has been configured with the link-local address of FE80::3 on its interfaces. Remember, link-local addresses only have to be unique on the link or network.

Note The neighbor table for Linux and MAC OS X can be displayed using `ip neigh show` command.

Figure 3 shows an example of the neighbor table on the Cisco IOS router, using the `show ipv6 neighbors` command.

Note The neighbor states for IPv6 are more complex than the ARP table states in IPv4. Additional information is contained in RFC 4861.

Switch MAC Address Table

A switch forwards a frame only to the port where the destination is connected. To do this, the switch consults its MAC address table. The MAC address table lists the MAC address connected to each port. Use the `show mac address-table` command to display the MAC address table on the switch. An example of PC1's local switch is shown in Figure 4. Remember, a switch's MAC address table only contains Layer 2 information, including the Ethernet MAC address and the port number. IP address information is not included.

VLAN Assignment

Another issue to consider when troubleshooting end-to-end connectivity is VLAN assignment. In the switched network, each port in a switch belongs to a VLAN. Each VLAN is considered a separate logical network, and packets destined for stations that do not belong to the VLAN must be forwarded through a device that supports routing. If a host in one VLAN sends a broadcast Ethernet frame, such as an arp request, all hosts in the same VLAN receive the frame; hosts in other VLANs do not. Even if two hosts are in the same IP network, they will not be able to communicate if they are connected to ports assigned to two separate VLANs. Additionally, if the VLAN to which the port belongs is deleted, the port becomes inactive. All hosts attached to ports belonging to the VLAN that was deleted are unable to communicate with the rest of the network. Commands such as `show vlan` can be used to validate vlan assignments on a switch.

Troubleshooting Example

Refer to the topology in Figure 5. To improve the wire management in the wiring closet, the cables connecting to S1 were reorganized. Almost immediately afterward, users started calling the support desk stating that they could no longer reach devices outside their own network. An examination of PC1's ARP table using the `arp` Windows command shows that the ARP table no longer contains an entry for the default gateway 10.1.10.1, as shown in Figure 6. There were no configuration changes on the router, so S1 is the focus of the troubleshooting.

The MAC address table for S1, as shown in Figure 7, shows that the MAC address for R1 is on a different VLAN than the rest of the 10.1.10.0/24 devices including PC1. During the re-cabling, R1's patch cable was moved from Fa 0/4 on VLAN 10 to Fa 0/1 on VLAN 1. After the network administrator configured S1's Fa 0/1 port to be on VLAN 10, as shown in Figure 8, the problem was resolved. As shown in Figure 9, the MAC address table now shows VLAN 10 for the MAC address of R1 on port Fa 0/1.

Refer to **Online Course** for Illustration

9.2.3.6 Step 4 - Verify Default Gateway

If there is no detailed route on the router or if the host is configured with the wrong default gateway, then communication between two endpoints in different networks does not work. Figure 1 illustrates that PC1 uses R1 as its default gateway. Similarly, R1 uses R2 as its default gateway or gateway of last resort.

If a host needs access to resources beyond the local network, the default gateway must be configured. The default gateway is the first router on the path to destinations beyond the local network.

Troubleshooting Example 1

Figure 2 shows the `show ip route` Cisco IOS command and the `route print` Windows command to verify the presence of the IPv4 default gateway.

In this example, the R1 router has the correct default gateway, which is the IPv4 address of the R2 router. However, PC1 has the wrong default gateway. PC1 should have the default gateway of R1 router 10.1.10.1. This must be configured manually if the IPv4 addressing information was manually configured on PC1. If the IPv4 addressing information was obtained automatically from a DHCPv4 server, then the configuring on the DHCP server must be examined. A configuration problem on a DHCP server is usually seen by multiple clients.

Troubleshooting Example 2

In IPv6, the default gateway can be configured manually or by using stateless autoconfiguration (SLAAC), or DHCPv6. With SLAAC, the default gateway is advertised by the router to hosts using ICMPv6 Router Advertisement (RA) messages. The default gateway in the RA message is the link-local IPv6 address of a router interface. If the default gateway is configured manually on the host, which is very unlikely, the default gateway can be set either to the global IPv6 address or to the link-local IPv6 address.

As shown in Figure 3, the `show ipv6 route` Cisco IOS command displays the IPv6 default route on R1 and the `ipconfig` Windows command is used to verify the presence of the IPv6 default gateway.

R1 has a default route via router R2, but notice the `ipconfig` command reveals the absence of an IPv6 global unicast address and an IPv6 default gateway. PC1 is enabled for IPv6 because it has an IPv6 link-local address. The link-local address is automatically created by the device. Checking the network documentation, the network administrator confirms that hosts on this LAN should be receiving their IPv6 address information from the router using SLAAC.

Note   In this example, other devices on the same LAN using SLAAC would also experience the same problem receiving IPv6 address information.

Using the `show ipv6 interface GigabitEthernet 0/0` command in Figure 4, it can be seen that although the interface has an IPv6 address, it is not a member of the All-IPv6-Routers multicast group FF02::2. This means the router is not sending out ICMPv6 RAs on this interface. In Figure 5, R1 is enabled as an IPv6 router using the `ipv6 unicast-routing` command. The `show ipv6 interface GigabitEthernet 0/0` command now reveals that R1 is a member of FF02::2, the All-IPv6-Routers multicast group.

To verify that PC1 has the default gateway set, use the `ipconfig` command on the Microsoft Windows PC or the `ifconfig` command on Linux and Mac OS X. In Figure 6, PC1 has an IPv6 global unicast address and an IPv6 default gateway. The default-gateway is set to the link-local address of router R1, FE80::1.

9.2.3.7   Step 5 - Verify Correct Path

Troubleshooting the Network Layer

When troubleshooting, it is often necessary to verify the path to the destination network. Figure 1 shows the reference topology indicating the intended path for packets from PC1 to SRV1.

In Figure 2, the `show ip route` command is used to examine the IPv4 routing table.

The IPv4 and IPv6 routing tables can be populated by the following methods:

- Directly connected networks
- Local host or local routes
- Static routes
- Dynamic routes
- Default routes

The process of forwarding IPv4 and IPv6 packets is based on the longest bit match or longest prefix match. The routing table process will attempt to forward the packet using an entry in the routing table with the greatest number of far left matching bits. The number of matching bits is indicated by the route's prefix length.

Figure 3 shows a similar scenario with IPv6. To verify that the current IPv6 path matches the desired path to reach destinations, use the `show ipv6 route` command on a router to examine the routing table. After examining the IPv6 routing table, R1 does have a path to 2001:DB8:ACAD:4::/64 via R2 at FE80::2.

The following list, along with Figure 4, describes the process for both the IPv4 and IPv6 routing tables. If the destination address in a packet:

- Does not match an entry in the routing table, then the default route is used. If there is not a default route that is configured, the packet is discarded.
- Matches a single entry in the routing table, then the packet is forwarded through the interface that is defined in this route.
- Matches more than one entry in the routing table and the routing entries have the same prefix length, then the packets for this destination can be distributed among the routes that are defined in the routing table.
- Matches more than one entry in the routing table and the routing entries have different prefix lengths, then the packets for this destination are forwarded out of the interface that is associated with the route that has the longer prefix match.

Troubleshooting Example

Devices are unable to connect to the server SRV1 at 172.16.1.100. Using the `show ip route` command, the administrator should check to see if a routing entry exists to network 172.16.1.0/24. If the routing table does not have a specific route to SRV1's network, the network administrator must then check for the existence of a default or summary route entry in the direction of the 172.16.1.0/24 network. If none exists, then the problem may be with routing and the administrator must verify that the network is included within the dynamic routing protocol configuration, or add a static route.

Refer to
Online Course
for Illustration

9.2.3.8   Step 6 - Verify the Transport Layer

Troubleshooting the Transport Layer

If the network layer appears to be functioning as expected, but users are still unable to access resources, then the network administrator must begin troubleshooting the upper layers. Two of the most common issues that affect transport layer connectivity include ACL configurations and NAT configurations. A common tool for testing transport layer functionality is the Telnet utility.

Caution   While Telnet can be used to test the transport layer, for security reasons, SSH should be used to remotely manage and configure devices.

A network administrator is troubleshooting a problem where someone cannot send email through a particular SMTP server. The administrator pings the server, and it responds. This means that the network layer, and all layers below the network layer, between the user and the server is operational. The administrator knows the issue is with Layer 4 or up and must start troubleshooting those layers.

Although the telnet server application runs on its own well-known port number 23 and Telnet clients connect to this port by default, a different port number can be specified on the client to connect to any TCP port that must be tested. This indicates whether the connection is accepted (as indicated by the word "Open" in the output), refused, or times out. From any of those responses, further conclusions can be made concerning the connectivity. Certain applications, if they use an ASCII-based session protocol, might even display an application banner, it may be possible to trigger some responses from the server by typing in certain keywords, such as with SMTP, FTP, and HTTP.

Given the previous scenario, the administrator Telnets from PC1 to the server HQ, using IPv6, and the Telnet session is successful, as shown in Figure 1. In Figure 2 the administrator attempts to Telnet to the same server, using port 80. The output verifies that the transport layer is connecting successfully from PC1 to HQ. However, the server is not accepting connections on port 80.

The example in Figure 3 shows a successful Telnet connection from R1 to R3, over IPv6. Figure 4 is a similar Telnet attempt using port 80. Again, the output verifies a success transport layer connection, but R3 is refusing the connection using port 80.

Refer to
Online Course
for Illustration

9.2.3.9   Step 7 - Verify ACLs

On routers, there may be ACLs configured that prohibit protocols from passing through the interface in the inbound or outbound direction.

Use the `show ip access-lists` command to display the contents of all IPv4 ACLs and the `show ipv6 access-list` command to show the contents of all IPv6 ACLs configured on a router. The specific ACL can be displayed by entering the ACL name or number as an option for this command; you can display a specific ACL. The `show ip interfaces` and `show ipv6 interfaces` commands display IPv4 and IPv6 interface information that indicates whether any IP ACLs are set on the interface.

Troubleshooting Example

To prevent spoofing attacks, the network administrator decided to implement an ACL preventing devices with a source network address of 172.16.1.0/24 from entering the inbound S0/0/1 interface on R3, as shown in Figure 1. All other IP traffic should be allowed.

However, shortly after implementing the ACL, users on the 10.1.10.0/24 network were unable to connect to devices on the 172.16.1.0/24 network, including SRV1. The `show ip access-lists` command shows that the ACL is configured correctly, as shown in Figure 2. However, the `show ip interfaces serial 0/0/1` command reveals that the ACL was never applied to the inbound interface on s0/0/1. Further investigation reveals that the ACL was accidentally applied to the G0/0 interface, blocking all outbound traffic from the 172.16.1.0/24 network.

After correctly placing the IPv4 ACL on the s0/0/1 inbound interface, as shown in Figure 3, devices are able to successfully connect to the server.

Refer to
Online Course
for Illustration

9.2.3.10   Step 8 - Verify DNS

The DNS protocol controls the DNS, a distributed database with which you can map hostnames to IP addresses. When you configure DNS on the device, you can substitute the hostname for the IP address with all IP commands, such as `ping` or `telnet`.

To display the DNS configuration information on the switch or router, use the `show running-config` command. When there is no DNS server installed, it is possible to enter names to IP mappings directly into the switch or router configuration. Use the `ip host` command to enter name to IPv4 mapping to the switch or router. The `ipv6 host` command is used for the same mappings using IPv6. These commands are demonstrated in Figure 1. Because IPv6 network numbers are long and difficult to remember, DNS is even more important for IPv6 than for IPv4.

To display the name-to-IP-address mapping information on the Windows-based PC, use the `nslookup` command.

Troubleshooting Example

The output in Figure 2 indicates that either the client was unable to reach the DNS server or the DNS service on the 10.1.1.1 was not running. At this point, the troubleshooting needs to focus on communications with the DNS server, or to verify the DNS server is running properly.

To display the DNS configuration information on a Microsoft Windows PC, use the `nslookup` command. There should be DNS configured for IPv4, IPv6, or both. DNS can provide IPv4 and IPv6 addresses at the same time, regardless of the protocol that is used to access the DNS server.

Because domain names and DNS are a vital component of accessing servers on the network, many times the user thinks the "network is down" when the problem is actually with the DNS server.

Refer to
Interactive Graphic
in online course.

Refer to **Packet
Tracer Activity**
for this chapter

9.2.3.11   Activity - Identify Commands to Troubleshoot a Network Issue

9.2.3.12   Packet Tracer - Troubleshooting Enterprise Networks 1

Background/Scenario

This activity uses a variety of technologies you have encountered during your CCNA studies including VLANs, STP, routing, inter-VLAN routing, DHCP, NAT, PPP, and Frame Relay. Your task is to review the requirements, isolate and resolve any issues, and then document the steps you took to verify the requirements.

Refer to **Packet
Tracer Activity**
for this chapter

9.2.3.13   Packet Tracer - Troubleshooting Enterprise Networks 2

Background/Scenario

This activity uses IPv6 configurations including DHCPv6, EIGRPv6, and IPv6 default routing. Your task is to review the requirements, isolate and resolve any issues, and then document the steps you took to verify the requirements.

Refer to **Packet
Tracer Activity**
for this chapter

9.2.3.14   Packet Tracer - Troubleshooting Enterprise Networks 3

Background/Scenario

This activity uses a variety of technologies you have encountered during your CCNA studies including routing, port security, EtherChannel, DHCP, NAT, PPP, and Frame Relay. Your task is to review the requirements, isolate and resolve any issues, and then document the steps you took to verify the requirements.

Refer to **Packet
Tracer Activity**
for this chapter

9.2.3.15   Packet Tracer - Troubleshooting Challenge - Using Documentation to Solve Issues

Background/Scenario

This is Part II of a two-part activity. Part I is Packet Tracer - Troubleshooting Challenge - Documenting the Network, which you should have completed earlier in the chapter. In Part II, you will use your troubleshooting skills and documentation from Part I to solve connectivity issues between PCs.

Refer to
Online Course
for Illustration

Refer to
Lab Activity
for this chapter

9.3   Summary

9.3.1.1   Class Activity - Documentation Development

Documentation Development

As the network administrator for a small business, you want to implement a documentation system to use with troubleshooting network-based problems.

After much thought, you decide to compile simple network documentation information into a file to be used when network problems arise. You also know that if the company gets larger in the future, this file can be used to export the information to a computerized, network software system.

To start the network documentation process, you include:

- A physical diagram of your small business network.

- A logical diagram of your small business network.

- Network configuration information for major devices, including routers and switches.

Refer to
Online Course
for Illustration

9.3.1.2   Summary

For network administrators to be able to monitor and troubleshoot a network, they must have a complete set of accurate and current network documentation, including configuration files, physical and logical topology diagrams, and a baseline performance level.

The three major stages to troubleshooting problems are gather symptoms, isolate the problem, then correct the problem. It is sometimes necessary to temporarily implement a workaround to the problem. If the intended corrective action does not fix the problem, the change should be removed. In all process steps, the network administrator should document the process. A troubleshooting policy, including change control procedures, should be established for each stage. After the problem is resolved, it is important to communicate this to the users, anyone involved in the troubleshooting process, and to other IT team members.

The OSI model or the TCP/IP model can be applied to a network problem. A network administrator can use the bottom-up method, the top-down method, or the divide-and-conquer method. Less structured methods include shoot-from-the-hip, spot-the-differences, and move-the-problem.

Common software tools that can help with troubleshooting include network management system tools, knowledge bases, baselining tools, host-based protocol analyzers, and Cisco IOS EPC. Hardware troubleshooting tools include a NAM, digital multimeters, cable testers, cable analyzers, and portable network analyzers. Cisco IOS log information can also be used to identify potential problems.

There are characteristic physical layer, data link layer, network layer, transport layer, and application layer symptoms and problems of which the network administrator should be aware. The administrator may need to pay particular attention to physical connectivity, default gateways, MAC address tables, NAT, and routing information.

Go to the online course to take the quiz and exam.

Chapter 9 Quiz

This quiz is designed to provide an additional opportunity to practice the skills and knowledge presented in the chapter and to prepare for the chapter exam. You will be allowed multiple attempts and the grade does not appear in the gradebook.

Chapter 9 Exam

The chapter exam assesses your knowledge of the chapter content.

Your Chapter Notes

Notes

Notes

Notes

Notes

Notes